June 1978.

A Theory of
Communication
and Use of
Language

Per Saugstad

A Theory of Communication and Use of Language

Foundations for the Study of Psychology

Universitetsforlaget

Oslo - Bergen - Tromsö

Cover design by Per Syversen

ISBN 82-00-01631-5

Distribution offices:

NORWAY
Universitetsforlaget
Postbox 6589-Rodeløkka
Oslo 5

UNITED KINGDOM
Global Book Resources Ltd.
37, Queen Street
Henley on Thames
Oxon RG9 1AJ

UNITED STATES and CANADA
Columbia University Press
136 South Broadway
Irvington-on-Hudson
New York 10533

To David Krech

Printed in Norway by
Tangen-Trykk, Drammen

Contents

PART 2
THE THEORY

Chapter 12
INTRODUCTION

Preface

After one hundred years of intensive empirical research psychologists still disagree on the question of what constitutes the subject matter of their field of science. As will be known, some psychologists base their research on conceptions of behaviour and some on conceptions of consciousness of various sorts. This disagreement reflects the fact that psychologists have not made clear what constitutes sound scientific thinking in their field. Apparently subject matter and method have not yet been brought into a fruitful relationship with each other.

A closer examination of current conceptions of psychology reveals that research workers have difficulties in communicating about their subject matter. As a result of inadequate communication a wide gap has arisen between, on the one hand, the theoretical statements and, on the other hand, the data collected. There is no sign in modern psychology that this gap is decreasing as more data are collected through empirical research. Clearly psychology lacks a reference system which will allow research workers to determine the events which may constitute the subject matter of a scientific study of psychology. The present book represents an attempt to provide such a reference system.

The difficulties met with in communicating about the subject matter of psychology suggest that the reference system must be a theory of communication. In my opinion it is not possible to treat fundamental problems in communication without carefully considering use of language. Use of language in turn is closely related to perceiving, remembering, imagining, thinking and a variety of other psychological activities. In other words questions to be asked in attempts to develop a reference system are closely related to questions asked in the empirical study of psychology. Unless the two types of question are kept apart confusion may easily arise. In addition to the two types of question mentioned, the theorist in psychology has to consider questions in the philosophy of science. Thus, there are questions to be dealt with in empirical psychology, in the philosophy of language, and in the philosophy of science. All these types of question are closely related to each other. The only way of avoiding a confused treatment appears to be to develop a coherent and consistent argument, in other words to develop a philosophical position. New conceptions of psychology require new positions on philosophical issues.

Since the beginning of the twentieth century problems of meaning, communication and use of language have been discussed by a large number of thinkers. The psychologist attempting to develop a theory of communication can learn from many of these thinkers. Nevertheless, substantial help can be obtained only from thinkers who have attemped to deal *systematically* with the problems met with. I have only found serious attempts at systematic treatment in four thinkers, namely in Charles Sanders Peirce, Ferdinand de Saussure, Ludwig Wittgenstein and Lev Semenovich Vygotsky. In particular Wittgenstein, especially in his later period, when he examined the idea of a private language and further argued that language should be conceived of as a way of life, has represented a main source of inspiration, and also a main challenge, because he pointed out difficulties met with in attempts at making general statements about use of language. While I agree with Wittgenstein that it is difficult to conceive of communication and meaning as having separate existences independent of use of language, I think his position was too extreme and in certain respects inadequate or even erroneous. In agreement with Peirce, I believe that communication and meaning ought to be regarded in terms of biological adjustment and in certain respects as being logically prior to use of language. The latter belief has received expression in the title of my book, in which I have inserted the word 'communication', so that it reads: 'A Theory of Communication and Use of Language' and not simply: 'A Theory of Use of Language'. My agreement with Peirce with regard to the necessity of considering communication and thinking from the point of view of biological adjustment, does not of course imply that I accept Peirce's ideas of consciousness.

Saussure emphasized the fact that the signs used in language, as well as all other signs used for communication, were arbitrary. This emphasis is important. It draws attention to an aspect of communication and use of language which must be reconciled with a Wittgensteinian approach.

I agree with Vygotsky that a fruitful theory of thinking must allow one to account for the development of meaning; to use his words it must explain how word meaning evolves. In my opinion this point is essential. My agreement with Vygotsky on this point does not of course imply that I accept his ideas concerning the phylogenetic and ontogenetic development of thinking. However inspiring they may be, these ideas seem to be based on inadequate conceptions of development.

The present book sprang from an attempt to construct a theory of thinking, learning and intelligence. Since this work can thus be said to have grown out of my interest in problems of thinking, learning and intelligence, I have dedicated it to David Krech, now professor emeritus at the University of California, Berkeley, who aroused my interest in these problems when he lectured at the University of Oslo during the academic year 1949-50.

Acknowledgements

During the many years I have been working on the problems dealt with in this book I have been fortunate in receiving help and encouragement from a number of teachers, friends and colleagues. I should like to repeat the thanks directed to my teachers at the University of Chicago and to my Scandinavian colleagues in my previous book: *An Inquiry into the Foundations of Psychology,* which appeared in 1965.

During the last 10 years I have received much help from my close friend Kaare Meidell Sundal, who has repeatedly gone over my main positions with me. In so doing he has given me a more appropriate understanding of what can be meant by a reference system in science. Members of the staff of the Philosophical Institute of the University of Oslo have assisted me on innumerable occasions. Particular thanks are due to Viggo Rossvær, who has helped me to reach a better understanding not only of the philosophies of Kant and Wittgenstein — with which he is so familiar — but also of a variety of problems concerning use of language and thinking. If this book, as I hope, proves to be useful, much of the credit belongs to Sundal and Rossvær, who have on so many occasions — and so kindly and patiently — set my thinking straight. I am also indebted to my colleague Lars Smith, who has helped me to achieve a better understanding of biological psychology and thus of the nature of learning. In addition I am indebted to Trygve Haavelmo of the Institute of Economics, who has elucidated various problems in the philosophy of science for me. My collaborators in my present research project on the ontogenetic development of thinking and use of language, Harald Martinsen and Ernst Ottem, have gone through the manuscript and have criticized important points. I am also grateful to Martinsen for the fact that he has pointed out to me various difficulties attaching to the use of the term 'development' in the study of the child. Mona Duckert and Jan Lanesskog have helped me understand that my ideas might be worked out so as to represent a general theory of psychology, and I should like to take this opportunity to thank them for this aid. Thanks are also due to my colleague Ragnar Rommetveit and to Lars Hellan, now at the Institute of Linguistics of the University of Trondheim, for seminar discussions.

I am grateful to the secretarial staff of the Psychological Institute for their patient help in the typing and retyping of the manuscript. Particular thanks are due to Erna Haanes, who in addition to doing much typing has also given advice on editorial questions. In the day-to-day-problems which have arisen in connection with the writing of this book, the help and advice of Arnold Havelin have proved invaluable.

I should also like to thank William Mulholland, who has corrected the English and who, by eliminating various inconsistencies, ambiguities and other obscurities, has also made the presentation appreciably clearer.

During the years in which I struggled to formulate my ideas clearly, I was constantly encouraged by the fact that Professor Oliver L. Zangwill had promised to read the manuscript upon its completion. I should like to thank him for this encouragement and for the trouble he has taken both in reading the manuscript and in recommending its publication.

Oslo, January 1977 *Per Saugstad*

Introduction

CHAPTER 1

On the nature of science

Those who have philosophized on science have drawn attention to a number of important aspects of scientific thinking. Still it is not yet clear what the fundamental questions to be asked by the individual wanting to develop a scientific theory in some relatively unstructured field are.

The problem of method

When a comparison is made between the procedures followed in the diverse fields of science, such as physics, chemistry, biology, medicine, linguistics, law, sociology and psychology, it is not easy to see what they have in common. Some science philosophers, particularly those of a positivist orientation, have been eager to argue that the procedures of all fields of science are essentially the same, or at least that they could be made the same, though when the basis for arguments of this sort is examined, it is found to depend upon dubious beliefs.

Thus, for example, when the methods used in the diverse fields of science are compared, it is difficult to see what they have in common. This point was emphasized by Caws (1967, p. 339) in a critical article on the nature of method:

> The term 'scientific method', if applied to scientific investigation in general or to something allegedly embodied in the practice of every branch of science, can only refer to the lowest common denominator of a range of methods devised to cope with problems as diverse as classifying stars and curing diseases. If such a lowest common denominator exists — that is, if some recognizable characteristics are shared by the extremes of the continuum of methods plausibly called 'scientific' — it can amount to little more than fidelity to empirical evidence and simplicity of logical formulation, fidelity to the evidence taking precedence in cases of conflict. However, these two overriding requirements for scientific activity do not constitute a specification of steps to be taken by scientists, and even the primary requirement (fidelity to empirical evidence) must be given up if mathematics is to be regarded as a science.

Against the conclusion arrived at by Caws one might object that it is difficult to conceive of method isolated from subject matter, and that for this reason it is not very meaningful to compare the methods used in the diverse fields of science. However, since it is difficult to see how the diverse fields of science could be compared at the same time with regard to both method and subject matter, this objection seems to amount to saying that we are not capable of stating what more precisely is meant by method. If this is admitted it is not very informative to say that thinking in the diverse fields of science has in common that scientific method is used.

The problem of explanation

Instead of comparing the fields of science with regard to method one might believe that one might compare them with regard to the aim at which the thinking of scientists is directed. However, a comparison of this sort also meets with difficulties. While it may be accepted as more or less meaningful to say that the physical sciences aim at description and explanation, it can be, and has been, contested that fields of science such as history, sociology, and psychology do not aim at explanation. It has been argued that thinking in the latter fields is better characterized as aiming at an understanding. (For a review of this issue, see Wright, 1971.) The positivist view that explanation follows the same pattern in all fields of science is thus contested. (For a review of the positivist conception of explanation, see Kim, 1967.)

Actually, when the term 'explanation' is examined it is not very easy to see what it means. One difficulty is met when explanations are to be distinguished from scientific laws. Hesse (1967) argued that in the advanced systems of science, such as the physical sciences, scientific laws and theories are not clearly distinguishable. In general I would say that description and explanation are hardly ever clearly distinguishable. This is revealed when the positivist conception of explanation is more carefully examined. This conception, originating with Stuart Mill, is referred to by Kim (ibid, p. 159) as 'the covering-law theory of explanation'. According to this theory an analysis of explanation takes the following form:

> The fundamental idea in the covering-law analysis of explanation is the view that the occurrence of an event is explained when it is subsumed under or covered by a law of nature, i.e., when it is shown to have occurred in accordance with some general regularity of nature.

An analysis of explanation according to this view seems to be relatively simple until one asks what is meant by an event. Apparently as long as an event is regarded as some sort of fact the analysis according to the theory seems fairly simple. However, if one asks what is meant by a fact and thus also by an event, difficulties arise.

Is it possible to conceive of something as a certain type of event without at the same time also conceiving of some regularity of nature? If this question must be answered in the negative, it will be seen that we have already presupposed some regularity of nature when we have identified something as an event, and if this regularity of nature is also involved in the law of nature, we are engaged in circular reasoning. As admitted by Kim (ibid) in the article quoted, it is not easy to characterize precisely the logical relationship between what is to be explained and the premises in terms of which the explanation is offered. Therefore, the positivist theory of explanation may possibly only amount to a statement to the effect that the scientist aims at the formulation of empirical laws of general validity.

It must be admitted that it is difficult to understand what the thinking carried out in the diverse fields of science has in common, and a comparison of thinking in the diverse fields, such as that undertaken by Nagel (1961), may be of limited usefulness.

A different approach to the problem of explanation may possibly be achieved by placing the point of departure in Hegelian dialectics. (For a review of Hegel's philosophy, see Acton, 1967, c.) According to Hegel, contradiction inhered in any incomplete abstract view. By elaborating on the nature of these contradictions less incomplete, abstract views could be produced. The following quote from Acton (ibid, p. 436) will make this clearer:

> It is the business of the philosopher, he held, to bring out the contradictions latent in partial or abstract views and to emphasize and elaborate them in such a way that less partial and less abstract views can be constructed that nevertheless retain in themselves what there was of truth in the original views. The same method is to be brought to bear on the less partial and less abstract views in their turn and to be pressed as thoroughly as it can be. This method of pressing and accentuating contradictions is not to be used merely to discard error but also to preserve truth.

There can be no doubt that in order to better understand the relationships involved in a particular situation, it is often useful to bring out what seem to be contradictions. This is a way in which problems can be formulated within a wider context. However, in order to represent a general method, the dialectical principle would have to be based on general rules specifying how one must go about finding what must be regarded as contradictions. These rules in turn would have to be established by the development of a reference system. This reference system is lacking in the Hegelian system, and it has been overlooked by Hegel and his followers that such a system would be required to support the claim that the dialectical principle could be regarded as a general methodological principle.

There are two main reasons for the neglect of the point made above by Hegelian-inspired thinkers. In the first place, it is overlooked that the Hegelian system can only be regarded as coherent as long as one accepts the Cartesian idea of consciousness. When this idea, on which the Hegelian system rests, is rejected, it is difficult to see what can be meant by contradictions. Secondly, as is evidenced by a study of the use made of the dialectical principle by Hegelian-inspired thinkers (on this point, see Acton, 1967, b), contradictions are easily mistaken for contradictions in a logical sense. It would, of course, be meaningless to conceive of contradictions in the dialectical principle as involving logical contradictions. However, by inadvertently conceiving of contradictions in this sense, one has come to believe that no reference system is needed to establish that two conditions are opposed to each other. When this point is accepted, it will be understood that it is difficult to regard the dialectical principle as a general method.

In opposition to the positivist ideas about scientific thinking, Dilthey (for a review of his philosophy, see Rickman, 1967) argued that the procedures which had proved useful in the physical sciences were not valid in the study of man, the social sciences and the humanities. Only in the physical sciences could explanations formulated as general principles be worked out. The study of man had to be based on what Dilthey designated as understanding. Dilthey's ideas concerning a distinction between the physical sciences and the sciences about man have had a strong influence and by way of the so-called humanistic psychology they are now influencing modern psychological thinking.

Dilthey's distinctions appear to be of limited usefulness, for two reasons. In the first place, as I underlined above, it is far from clear what is meant by an explanation in the physical sciences. Secondly, Dilthey's idea of understanding as forming the basis for a study of man is extremely obscure. Dilthey conceived of understanding in terms of highly speculative ideas of consciousness and an inner man. The criticism in Part 1 of this book aimed against the idea of consciousness and an inner man will, I hope, make this clear. Thus, since we have only inadequate understanding both of what is meant by an explanation in the physical sciences and of what is meant by understanding in the study of man, it is premature to attempt to establish a line of division between the two types of study. On this point, the argument presented by Nagel (ibid) referred to above is relevant.

In connection with the problem of distinguishing between the physical sciences and the study of man, it is of interest to note that it is not reasonable to regard mathematics as a physical science. It developed prior to the modern physical sciences and served as a paradigm for the development of these sciences.

There are no a priori reasons why the study of man could not be advanced by general formulations in the form of rigorous definitions and explicit statements of postulates. There can be no doubt that reasoning along the lines adopted in mathematics can be extremely powerful, and thus that studies in a field into which this way of reasoning can be introduced will be decisively advanced. As has been made clear, this way of reasoning does not involve an imitation of the physical sciences.

Before leaving Dilthey, mention should be made of his elaboration of the so-called hermeneutic method taken over from Schleiermacher. (For a review of this method, see Palmer, 1969.) Dilthey emphasized the fact that an expression, a text, a piece of art, an individual or an historical period had to be understood within some context or whole. In attempts at arriving at understanding one had to consider what one could imagine as some whole in terms of what one could imagine as some sort of parts, and vice versa, one had to consider what one could imagine as some sort of parts in terms of what one could imagine as some sort of whole. The parts and the whole could not be clearly separated from each other and consequently could not be conceived of as being independent of each other. They were said to represent a closed circle, the hermeneutic circle. Rickman (ibid, p. 406), referring to the whole and the parts by the term 'system', characterized Dilthey's thinking about the hermeneutic method in this way:

> First, we are theoretically involved in a circle. To understand a word we must understand the language, yet to understand a language we must have come to understand the words that constitute it. In practice we solve this problem by a kind of shuttlecock movement. From approximate knowledge of individual words an understanding of the language grows; this, in turn, makes our understanding of individual words more precise; and so on. This procedure is characteristic of the human studies.

Actually, Dilthey's thinking about the hermeneutic circle may be just as applicable to the physical and biological sciences as to the study of man. Probably it represents a far more realistic picture of the thinking of science carried out by the theorist than the picture given by positivists from Mach to the present day. Dilthey's ideas may help to counteract the tendency in the theorist to proceed in a mechanistic fashion. After all, neither the goal to be achieved by the theorist nor the parts to which he makes reference can be clearly conceived of. When the goal and the parts are treated as isolated components, the system in some way becomes devoid of power. On the other hand, it is easy to see that speculations about the hermeneutic circle may become obscure and useless.

Instead of attempting to find out what characterizes scientific thinking by comparing the procedures of the diverse fields to each other, one might take the more pragmatic attitude and concentrate study on the fields of science which have been most decisively advanced. This attitude has frequently been taken by science philosophers and, as there can be little doubt that the physical sciences have been decisively advanced, study has been concentrated on them, in particular on the science of mechanics. To develop a useful procedure one has regarded the procedures in these sciences as an ideal and has suggested how this ideal might be adhered to. By regarding the physical sciences as an ideal one has come to stress the use of techniques for measurement, the use of experiments, the application of mathematical systems and a more formal logical treatment of theoretical statements. It is difficult to argue for or against the suggestion that the theorist in other fields of science ought to emphasize these aspects of scientific procedures. There can be no denial that the procedures mentioned have proved extremely useful in a variety of fields of science, and, if applied appropriately, such procedures would most likely be of great usefulness in a field such as psychology. The difficulty is that it is not easy to see what can be meant by an appropriate way until some theorist has demonstrated that he has devised one. Apparently it is difficult to understand in more detail how one might proceed in order to introduce measurements and mathematics in an appropriate way. Also there can be little doubt that it is difficult to state how a research worker ought to design experiments of help in the clarification of significant theoretical relationships. Apparently a statement to the effect that a given field of science is fruitfully advanced by the performance of experiments is of highly restricted usefulness. In a discussion of the introduction of techniques such as those mentioned, it must be noted that in the initial phase of development of modern evolutionary theory neither advanced techniques for measurement nor mathematical systems were introduced, and, what may be even more noteworthy, Darwin advanced his thinking without designing new experiments. It should also be noted that, even if Newton based his theory of gravitation on experiments and measurements performed by other research workers, he did not himself attempt to devise experiments in support of the theory. The instances mentioned may lead one to suspect that in the last analysis it is not techniques for measurement or the application of mathematical systems or the performance of experiments which represent the most decisive aspects of scientific thinking. By stressing the aspects mentioned here, science philosophers, particularly the positivists, have tended to stress what after all may perhaps be the more superficial aspects of scientific thinking and have thus tended to introduce an attitude which might more appropriately be termed scientistic than scientific.

Since positivist thinking has dominated empirical psychology from the latter half of the nineteenth century to the present, I shall consider in more detail the positivist conception of science.

Positivist thinking about science

It should be noted that positivism represents a cluster of beliefs, and that thinkers inspired by this intellectual movement have placed more or less emphasis on the various beliefs. Nevertheless, the listing of the following points for characterizing the movement set up by Abbagnano (1967, p. 414) is probably fairly representative of the beliefs supported by leading positivist thinkers:

> The characteristic theses of positivism are that science is the only valid knowledge and facts the only possible objects of knowledge; that philosophy does not possess a method different from science; and that the task of philosophy is to find the general principles common to all the sciences and to use these principles as guides to human conduct and as the basis of social organization. Positivism, consequently, denies the existence or intelligibility of forces or substances that go beyond facts and the laws ascertained by science. It opposes any kind of metaphysics and, in general, any procedure of investigation that is not reducible to scientific method.

As Abbagnano here pointed out, positivists have tended to regard facts as the only objects of knowledge. This point is central in positivism, and, as we shall see in a later chapter, it reflects the positivists' conceptions of use of language. The early positivist thinkers, Comte and Mill, did not specify what they believed to constitute the facts. (For a review of the thinking of Comte and Mill, see the articles by Mazlish, 1967; Schneewind, 1967.) However, later positivists, such as Mach and the logical positivists inspired by him, tended to conceive of facts in terms of sensations. (For review articles of Mach and the logical positivists, see the articles by Alexander, 1967, a; Passmore, 1967, a.) Under the influence of Mill and Mach positivism fused with the empiricism of Hume. The positivists, therefore, tended to take an idealist or, more adequately expressed, an immaterialist position on the question of reality. Mach, who exerted a fundamental influence on the philosophy of science, regarded empirical concepts as arrangements of sensations and reduced the task of theory construction to that of providing economical descriptions of the relationship between the facts. The logical positivist added to these ideas that theory construction might be fruitfully advanced by giving a consistent logical interpretation of models taken from mathematics or logic. Harré (1967, p. 291) summed up the positivist conception of science in this way:

> By the beginning of the twentieth century the reductionist views of Mach, Pearson, and Duhem had been clearly and strongly formulated, and during the following thirty years they profoundly influenced the development of European philosophy. The logical positivism of the Vienna circle was entirely in the spirit of Mach, whose sensationalism gave authority both to the famous dictum that the meaning of a statement is its method of verification and to the metaphysics of phenomenalism, with which logical positivism quickly became linked. The net effect of this movement was a steady denigration of the power of theory in favor of logically ordered structures of empirical concepts. The marriage of Mach's views on science with Russellian logic initiated the era of hypothetico-deductivism, when a theory was thought to be an axiomatic structure, like formal logic or geometry. The fact that axiomatic structures can never lead into the new and hitherto unknown, that they are, precisely because of their logical coherence, quite unfruitful, does not seem to have bothered the advocates of the hypothetico-deductive view. The logicians of this era were apparently not interested in the question of theory origin or theory growth, but only in the question of the best mode of formalizing theories that were already known. The power and beauty of the Russellian logic in mathematics seems to have exerted a restricting effect upon the analytical methods of logicians interested in science.

The positivist conception of fact was opposed to central beliefs in Hegelianism and Marxism. In the latter half of the nineteenth century Peirce gave a criticism of important points in empiricism. (For an account of this point in Peirce, see the chapter by Thayer, 1964.) At the turn of the century Lenin [1909] criticized the inadequate conception of reality in the positivists, and Husserl pointed out that the sensation represented an abstraction from some whole. (For a review of Husserl, see the article by Schmitt, 1967, a.) Later in the twentieth century Wittgenstein questioned the belief that sensations could be regarded as existing outside a linguistic context. He also subjected to a critical examination the Cartesian belief that sensations could be regarded as private experience, a belief that had been transmitted to the positivists via British empiricism. (For a review of these points in Wittgenstein's thinking, see Malcolm, 1967.) Finally, mention should be made of the criticism more recently made of the position taken on reality and the treatment of explanation in the positivist philosophy of science. (For a review of these issues, see the articles by Harré, ibid; Taylor, 1967.)

Evidently the positivist conception of fact meets with serious difficulties. When this conception is abandoned, positivist philosophy of science seems to reduce to an emphasis on certain general points concerning scientific procedure. However, it should be noted that this emphasis is important. For example, by emphasizing the fact that the empirical concepts of science have a basis in concrete observations and operations, the positivists pointed to ways of purging scientific theories of useless speculative elements. Particularly in a field such as psychology, where it is so easy to present seemingly fruitful speculation, the advice to examine empirical concepts in terms of concrete empirical procedures is important. As Franck (1950) remarked in his book on the development of logical positivism, scientific theorizing from time to time needs to be purged of excessive speculative elements; Mach represented such a purge. Moreover, even if too extreme, the positivist thesis of explanation, emphasizing the intimate relationship between description and explanation, may also be of help in the effort to eliminate useless speculation.

In retrospect it is easy to see how the positivist emphasis on facts led to simplified conceptions of scientific thinking. The concentration on the sensation as an isolated fact led thinkers to overlook the context and thus the fact that scientific systems represented complicated reference systems. Instead of emphasizing the need for developing reference systems in the new fields of science, the positivists encouraged theorists to proceed either by testing separate hypotheses or by introducing models taken from already developed fields of science. The first type of encouragement led research workers to proceed in a piecemeal fashion and the latter type led them to proceed in a mechanistic fashion.

In addition the positivist belief that methods of a general applicability had been developed in the physical sciences had the unfortunate effect that theorists tended to conceive of method and subject matter as existing independently of each other. In scientific thinking the nature of the methods chosen must determine what is to be considered the subject matter. Science has no subject matter independent of method. Conversely the choice of method is determined by the nature of the subject matter. Method and subject matter interact closely at all phases of the development of theory. This interaction has the result that in an advanced field of science it is not possible to speak of subject matter or method without referring to the total theory developed.

What makes theorizing in science so strenuous is the very fact that as theories are developed conceptions of subject matter change. The central terms are successively being redefined as theories are developed, and it is impossible to keep track of these redefinitions if they are not carefully stated in an explicit formal manner. The theorist must be careful to keep track of these changes. This is the reason why creative theorists in science are so extremely careful with the definitions of central terms.

The point made here concerning the close interaction between method and subject matter must not, of course, lead one to overlook the fact that at an initial phase in the development of a theory method and subject matter must be indicated independently of each other. Otherwise scientific work cannot get started. Moreover the fact that changes in definitions must be carefully kept track of by explicit formal definitions, must not lead one to overlook the fact that definitions must be formulated in such a way that they allow of innovations. The creative theorist must understand what is known in his field and also to a certain extent what can be known. If he is concentrating too closely on what is already known, he will be in no position to visualize the future.

A further unfortunate outcome of positivist thinking about science which should be mentioned was that the concentration on the sensation or the observational report as the ultimate basis of scientific theories led theorists to believe that theoretical terms could be defined solely by reference to observations and procedures. The operationalism of Bridgman (1927) strengthened this belief. Obviously, as emphasized by Schlesinger (1967, p. 544), it is not possible to define a theoretical term in science solely in an operational manner.

> Bridgman soon had to retreat from his first extreme statement of operationalism. He had maintained that every scientifically meaningful concept must be capable of full definition in terms of performable physical operations and that a scientific concept is nothing more than the set of operations entering into its definition. The untenability of this view was quickly noticed — for example, by L. J. Russell, who in 1928 pointed out that in science one often speaks of certain operations as being better than others and that one cannot do so except in relation to something existing over and above them. Moreover, useful physical concepts do not as a rule lend themselves to an exhaustive definition. Any connection they have with instrumental operations may be loose and indirect: statements in which the concepts appear may, in the context of a set of other statements (but not on their own), entail statements describing physical operations. Consequently, in his later writings Bridgman freely permitted 'paper and pencil operations', by which he meant mathematical and logical maneuverings with the aid of which no more is required of a concept than that it should be 'indirectly making connection with instrumental operations'.

As a result of the dominance of the empiricist thinking adopted by the positivists this belief — which must be considered a prejudice — became widespread. In psychology, where it is so difficult to make clear how terms are used, this belief had a most unfortunate effect.

In spite of the emphasis on measurement, use of mathematics and a formal characterization of the scientific system, positivism had the effect of wiping out the distinction between, on the one hand, the scientific system, and on the other hand, use of language and general cultural knowledge. It will be understood that, when subject matter is determined by specific methods, central theoretical terms in a scientific theory are introduced in a manner which makes clear how the use of the terms differs from the use of words and expressions used in ordinary language. It is reasonable to regard the introduction of subject matter by reference to specific methods as a fundamental characteristic of science. In this connection it should be emphasized that if the theorist is not in possession of methods for making distinctions between words or expressions used in ordinary language, theoretical terms should not be based on these distinctions. When terms are introduced, as is widely done by empirical psychologists, by reference solely to procedures, it is easily overlooked that distinctions made in the ordinary use of language may not be adequate for the development of a scientific theory. The point being stressed here is the difference between the scientific system and the ordinary use of language. It should not be taken to imply that scientific systems are not ultimately based on ordinary use of language and on existent cultural knowledge.

In general one may say that the positivist emphasis on the sensation led to the neglect of questions pertaining to the nature of the reality studied. This neglect made theorists overlook the fact that the various fields of science each had their own characteristics and thus that the reference systems developed for the various fields of science would naturally have to differ in essential respects.

It may be regarded as a characteristic of positivist thinking that the question of objectivity was reduced to a question of inter-subjective agreement in the observational reports given by the scientist. It was not realized that whether or not it was reasonable to speak of objectivity must be determined by an examination of the reference systems. In reference systems which have been developed in such a way that they have a certain coherence and consistency, events can be determined in a manner which may reasonably be designated as objective. An argument to the effect that coherence and consistency are always a matter of degree, cannot be regarded as an argument against the belief in objectivity. As Hamlyn (1967, b) emphasized, we speak of knowledge even if we are not capable of stating with absolute certainty what our basis for this knowledge is.

In the social sciences, where the relationships studied are so complex, it is easy to overlook the fact that these sciences must also deal with a reality of some sort. It should be noted that if the theorists in these fields cannot in some way conceive of the reality to be studied, they will not be in a position to state what their theories are about.

25

Scientific theories are, of course, constructed with a view to their usefulness in dealing with specific types of events. The fact that they are frequently applied to fields other than those for which they were originally constructed, must not lead one to overlook this point.

To sum up the discussion in this chapter, I would say that so far the philosophy of science has only arrived at a highly fragmentary understanding of the nature of scientific thinking. Thus, only in a tentative manner is it possible to say what is meant by method and explanation. The positivist thinking concerning the nature of science is at best only partially correct, and adherence to this thinking can obviously have unfortunate consequences for the development of a field of science. In the next chapter I shall briefly indicate some of the less fortunate consequences which this type of thinking has had for empirical psychology. However, before I conclude the present chapter I should like to outline a way of approaching theory construction in a new field of science which may be sounder than that expressed in positivist thinking.

A view on the nature of theory construction

It follows from the discussion of the problems in the philosophy of science undertaken above, that at present it is hardly possible to present a coherent and consistent argument for a procedure to be followed by the thinker wanting to construct a scientific theory. He therefore more or less has to make guesses with regard to how to proceed in order to accomplish his task in the best manner. I would state as my belief that theory construction in science is essentially concerned with the question of how to develop reference systems which allow research workers to deal with various types of events.

As I have emphasized in the previous section, psychologists have had little success in developing good reference systems for dealing with the events studied. In my opinion there are two main reasons for this lack of success. In the first place the positivist belief that certain types of events can be regarded as facts independent of a reference system, has had the effect that theorists have tended to overlook the need for such systems. As was emphasized, positivist thinking about facts seems to have dominated psychology from the days of Wundt to the present. Secondly psychologists have tended to believe that language as ordinarily used may constitute a reference system in terms of which they might fruitfully deal with the events to be studied.

While I shall reject the positivist belief that something may be regarded as some sort of fact independent of a reference system, I shall also reject what appears to be a Hegelian belief — that the nature of the various types of events can be specified in terms solely of relations within the system. This type of coherence, as I shall argue in Chapter 10 of Part 1, is hardly conceivable. I shall say that the aim of the theorist is to construct a reference system which, from the point of view of the events to be studied, contains the presuppositions made when something is regarded as some type of event, and which from the point of view of the reference system can be regarded as the specification of a domain which is of such a nature that certain types of events can be identified. In the construction of the reference system the theorist must have in mind what may possibly constitute types of events which may be fruitfully studied as well as what may possibly represent the domain in which types of events to be studied are contained. In an attempt to contrast my procedure with that of the positivist thinker I shall not begin simply by postulating as the subject matter of my study certain types of events. I shall begin by considering concurrently what may possibly be certain types of events which may be studied and the domain which possibly may contain these events. Characterizing the domain will make it clearer what the types of events to be studied are, and specifying the events will make it clearer what the domain studied is. (Cp. what was said above about the hermeneutic method.)

As will be remembered, in his critical article on scientific method Caws (ibid) concluded that a common denominator for scientific methods could hardly amount to more than fidelity to empirical evidence and simplicity of logical formulation. In the discussion of the positivist thesis of explanation in science I mentioned that this thesis might possibly amount to a mere statement to the effect that the scientist aims at the formulation of empirical laws of general validity. In whatever way one conceives of procedure in science, it is essential that the theorist attempts to adhere to the ideal of fidelity to empirical evidence by aiming at the formulation of empirical laws of general validity and to the ideal of simplicity of logical formulation. Therefore, in considering what is to be regarded as the types of events and the domain to be studied, adherence to the two ideals should be strictly observed.

It will be understood that if the domain is so chosen that what may count as important empirical evidence is excluded, the ideal of fidelity to empirical evidence is not adhered to. Moreover a choice of a too restricted domain will have the effect that the theorist must take into account questions which have been formulated outside his reference system. This will have the effect that he does not adhere to the ideal of simplicity of logical formulation. It is therefore essential that the theorist takes care to conceive of the domain in a way that is sufficiently comprehensive. To put it somewhat differently I would say that at the initial stage he must attempt to formulate empirical laws of a very general nature.

In order to choose a domain which is sufficiently comprehensive, the theorist must take care to examine the questions he wants to ask about the events so that he can decide upon the order in which to ask the questions. The most appropriate order would be one in which the first question asked would not depend upon the answers given to questions to be asked later. To give an example, if the question 'what is meant by behaviour?' cannot be answered unless reference is made to use of language, it is not appropriate to place the point of departure in events designated as behaviour. Similarly, if the question 'what is meant by consciousness?' cannot be answered unless reference is made to use of language, it is not appropriate to place the point of departure in events designated as consciousness. To achieve maximal adherence to the ideal of both fidelity to empirical evidence and simplicity of logical formulation, it is essential that the theorist carefully considers the order in which he ought to ask his questions. When psychological literature is examined, it will be found that theorists have devoted little attention to the problem of the order in which the questions are to be asked.

In connection with the problem of the choice of domain attention should also be called to the fact that the theorist must take care not to seek explanations of the events investigated by referring to types of events outside the domain. This will result in empty explanations of the sort given in the mythology of the ancient Greeks when they answered the question of what held the earth in position in space by saying that Atlas supported the earth on his shoulders.

Such empty explanations are probably obtained in psychology when, for example, use of language is explained by reference to a capacity for thinking, for remembering, for perceiving, or by reference to mental or physiological processes. Explanations must be provided by reference to the way the types of events dealt with have been specified. Therefore, in the good reference system no clear distinction can be drawn between empirical laws and theoretical statements. This seems to be in line with the point made by Hesse (ibid) referred to above. In addition to this point I should like to emphasize the fact that the reference system also provides epistemological rules because it specifies what is to count as knowledge. A scientific theory which does not make clear what is to count as knowledge is a poor theory. In the attempt at specifying the types of events to be dealt with it is essential that the theorist does not base his specifications on distinctions which are dubious in the sense that they are difficult to maintain or in the sense that they lead to paradoxical statements concerning the types of events to be studied.

It will be understood that when theoretical statements involve terms which are based on dubious distinctions, adherence to the ideal of fidelity to empirical evidence is made difficult. Consequently it is essential that in specifying the nature of the events to be studied the theorist does not base this specification on dubious distinctions. As emphasized in the preceding section, a characteristic of scientific procedure is that subject matter is defined in terms of specific methods. This means that theoretical terms must be introduced by reference to specific methods. As I shall make clear in later chapters, we do not know the basis for the use of words and expressions in everyday language. This implies that we are in a fundamental sense ignorant about the basis for the distinctions made between the various words and expressions used in everyday language. Therefore, if the theorist introduces his terms without specifically making reference to method, he will have to rely on arbitrary distinctions.

As has already been mentioned, a main reason why positivist thinking about science must be considered as defective is found in the fact that it rests upon an inadequate conception of use of language. According to positivist thinking sensations or other types of postulated facts are regarded as being independent of use of language. The relationship between the events studied and use of language was believed to be arbitrary or contingent, and the distinctions made between different words, expressions or even theoretical terms was believed to rest on some sort of ability to discriminate. With Wittgenstein (1953) I shall insist that both the use of words and expressions and the use of theoretical terms are based on rules which are not statable simply in terms of discriminations of some sort. In a scientific system distinctions between terms must be made by reference to rules for communication. If these rules are missing, communication breaks down.

As pointed out by Poincaré [1902], the introduction of theoretical terms in empirical science involves a certain arbitrariness; however, as he has emphasized, this arbitrariness does not imply that the use of the terms does *not* reflect some sort of reality. (On this important point in the philosophy of science, see Harré, 1967; Alexander, 1967, a.) If the theorist introduces his distinctions without reference to specified methods, he may easily lose contact with the reality to be studied. Apparently it is important that the theorist takes advantage of the freedom he has to define his terms in an arbitrary manner. However, if he does not understand the restrictions imposed upon him by the nature of the reality studied, he will most probably engage in empty speculation. Positivist thinking about science gives the theorist too much freedom to define his terms. As I shall make clear in the following chapters, this has had fatal consequences for the development of scientific psychology.

In line with what has been said here about the making of distinctions between terms, I should like to stress the fact that when the theorist is unable to make clear the basis for the making of some important distinction, he is confronted with a difficulty which must be avoided if he is to adhere to the ideal of fidelity to empirical evidence. This means that a theory must be evaluated in terms of the difficulties which are avoided by using it. A theory is reasonable only as long as it avoids difficulties which at some stage appear as fundamental. Of course, a theory must also prove fruitful for research. Whether it is fruitful or not is by and large a question to be decided as empirical research progresses, but it is reasonable to believe that theories which have not been constructed with careful consideration of the nature of the reality to be studied will prove to be unfruitful. The lax attitude in positivist thinkers towards the problem of definitions of theoretical terms has led psychologists to overestimate the significance of predictions and to underestimate the fact that in order to be useful, scientific theories must have a high degree of reasonableness in the sense that they avoid difficulties.

CHAPTER 2

An historical sketch of approaches to psychology

Empirical psychology as it originated in the latter half of the nine-teenth century was profoundly influenced by positivist thinking about science. As a result of this influence empirical psychologists — from the days of Wundt to the present — have tended to believe that some ready-made subject matter exists waiting to be explored by the scientific psychologist. Wundt and the early generation of empiri-cal psychologists believed that this subject matter was to be found in consciousness as constituted by mental elements. The next generation of Continental psychologists as well as present-day psychologists inspired by phenomenology and existentialism also believed the sub-ject matter was to be found in consciousness; not, however, in a consciousness constituted by mental elements, but in one made up of wholes, internal structures, intentions, and meanings. At the beginning of the twentieth century American psychologists rejected the idea that consciousness of some sort constituted the subject matter and instead insisted that it was an entity they labelled behaviour. In all three schools of psychology subject matter tended to be conceived of as being independent of a reference system in terms of which various types of events could be dealt with.

The belief that various types of events represent some sort of facts without dependence upon some definite reference system has re-sulted in the neglect of questions pertaining to the subject matter of psychology. It has not been realized that what are regarded as facts, or as various types of events, cannot be so regarded unless the presuppositions which make one believe that the facts or types of events exist are stated. If these presuppositions cannot be stated in terms of existent knowledge, it is not possible to say in what sense the types of events postulated may be said to exist. Empirical psychologists have tended to believe that their theoretical terms could be introduced either by reference to metaphysical entities such as consciousness or behaviour or by reference to operational definitions alone. The former way of introducing the terms has led to various types of scholasticism of which psychoanalysis is a representative example, and the latter way to the collection of an enormous un-structured mass of empirical data.

Apparently what has turned empirical psychology into such a dis-concerted enterprise is the fact that one is so easily led to believe that language as ordinarily used constitutes a reference system in terms of which the types of events postulated can be said to exist. Difficulties met with when ordinary use of language is taken as the reference system for psychology have been laid bare in the philosophy developed by Moore, Wittgenstein and philosophers inspired by them. (For a review of Moore's philosophy, see Nelson, 1967; for a review of Wittgenstein's philosophy, see Malcolm, 1967; and for a review of the later development of British philosophy, see Quinton, 1964; Warnock, 1966.) Thinkers such as Hamlyn (1971) and Malcolm (1971) have argued convincingly that many of the types of events postulated by empirical psychologists do not exist. Apparently theorists in psychology must pay much more attention to problems in the philosophy of language. In connection with this point it should be emphasized that problems in the philosophy of science must also be treated as problems in the philosophy of language. As was mentioned in the previous section the philosophy of science of the positivists may be regarded as deficient mainly for the reason that it represents a defective philosophy of language.

Psychology and metaphysical systems

The lack of concern in empirical psychologists for the nature of their subject matter is clearly manifested in the way they have adopted beliefs from the metaphysical systems predominant in their intellectual environment. Thus Wundt and the early psychologists took over from British empiricism the belief that elements of consciousness constituted the subject matter of psychology. (For a review of this early psychology, see Boring, 1950; Pongratz, 1967.) The next generation of Continental psychologists rejected the belief in the mental elements, but instead adopted the belief developed in the phenomenology of Husserl and other thinkers that mental structures, wholes, or Gestalts represented the subject matter. (For a review of phenomenology, see Schmitt, 1967, b; Chisholm, 1960; and of Husserl's philosophy in particular, see Schmitt, 1967, a; on the ideas of the Gestalt psychologists, see Koffka, 1935; Boring, ibid; Woodworth and Shean, 1964.) The behaviourists rejected the idea that consciousness — whether in the form of mental elements or structures — could be said to constitute the subject matter of psychology, but — like the early psychologists — they retained fundamental beliefs contained in British empiricism and also came to base their views on fundamental

32

beliefs found in the analytic philosophy of Russell and the logical positivists. (For a review of behaviourism, see Boring, ibid; Woodworth and Shean, ibid; and for a review of analytic philosophy, see Weitz, 1967.)

Of course, it cannot be raised as a general point of criticism that scientists take their ideas on empirical research from some philosophical system. The thinking of the philosopher cannot be regarded as fundamentally different from that of the scientist, and philosophers such as Descartes, Kant, Hegel, Marx, Husserl, to mention only some, are rightly credited with the power of developing an argument which allows one to see reality, or some aspect of it, in a unitary manner. As emphasized by Walsh (1963), metaphysical systems are of help in attempts to understand which questions are related and thus of help in achieving a better understanding of various types of relationships. However, what must be clearly realized is that the empirical research worker cannot adopt beliefs from some philosophical system without carefully examining the nature of the argument in terms of which the beliefs are presented. This examination must be held as essential for three reasons. In the first place the point of departure used by the philosopher may have been different from the one used by the empirical research worker. Obviously when the point of departure is different the belief cannot be the same. Secondly the argument of the philosopher may not be coherent and consistent. Thirdly the thinking of the philosopher may not be in agreement with empirical evidence. It will be understood that if the thinking of the philosopher was developed at a moment prior in time to that at which the scientist is to do his research this agreement may not be present.

It will be seen that the taking over of beliefs from some previously developed philosophy can hardly be done in a fruitful manner unless the scientist takes a highly independent attitude to that philosophy so that he carefully examines the argument in terms of existent knowledge and also takes care to consider seriously arguments presented by philosophers in opposition to that philosophy. It seems fair to state that empirical psychologists have rarely taken this independent attitude to philosophy. On this point a marked difference in attitude is found between empirical psychologists and pioneer physicists such as Galileo and Newton, who took a highly independent attitude to the philosophies of their time. (On this point, see Caws, ibid.) Below I shall illustrate the lack of independence in empirical psychologists as regards predominant metaphysical systems by considering the beliefs concerning the nature of the subject matter expressed by psychologists of the three schools mentioned above.

Before I proceed to discuss the adoption by empirical psychologists of beliefs from metaphysical systems I should like to emphasize that so far no metaphysical system has been created which is so coherent and consistent that it follows from the system that some definite belief is necessarily tenable. In summing up some main points in the discussion between Bradley and Russell on the issue over the nature of relations, Walsh (1964, p. 436) emphasized this point.

> Metaphysics is an attempt to give conceptual expression to a certain way of looking at the world, and no metaphysics will convince unless it can claim intellectual coherence. But mere intellectual coherence is not enough here, nor in judging whether it is present can we entirely abstract from the point of view with which it is bound up. What seems coherent to a Russell will not seem coherent to a Bradley.

The point made by Walsh is important because by adopting some metaphysical system one may easily come to think that its coherence implies tnat certain beliefs follow by logical necessity and that tney cannot be considered outside of the system. On the one hand, one must obviously not lose sight of the advantage involved in attempts to conceive of the world or some aspect of it in a unitary way. On the other hand, it must be clear that beliefs from one system may be combined with beliefs from other systems. If a combination of beliefs from various systems were not possible, it would be difficult to see how progress could ever be achieved in thinking. For the development of theory in scientific psychology this combination of beliefs is probably essential. However, in considering a given belief contained in a given system the theorist should keep in mind that the creators of the various philosophies have developed their systems precisely with a view to presenting a coherent argument, and that care must therefore be taken to examine the presuppositions which form the basis for the belief.

Wundt (1874, 1896) claimed that elements of consciousness constituted the subject matter of psychology. In order to support this claim he would have had to examine the Cartesian system in whose terms Locke and Hume had postulated the mental element as existing. He might then have discovered that it is difficult, if not impossible, to state the presuppositions we make when we conceive of something as an event in consciousness. If these presuppositions cannot be stated in terms of existent knowledge, it is not possible to make an empirical study of consciousness in the Wundtian sense. The difficulty of stating these presuppositions was first pointed out in the philosophy of language developed by Moore and Wittgenstein (the philosophy referred to above).

In retrospect it is difficult to understand how Wundt and his contemporaries could take such an uncritical attitude to the philosophy of the British empiricists. In effect the early psychologists may have been led astray by an erroneous conception of the nature of the study of perceiving begun a few years before Wundt presented his ideas about psychology. About the middle of the nineteenth century physicists and physiologists such as Helmholtz, Fechner, Mach, and Hering had begun making a fruitful study of perceiving. In this study the sensation was regarded as an element of consciousness. Wundt and his contemporaries may have been led to believe that this study might be further extended by empirical investigations into what might represent other characteristics of the mental element. What they did not realize — and what has probably become clear only as a result of Wittgenstein's (1953) examination of the concept of the sensation — is that in the study of perceiving the sensation forms part of the structure of use of language. As I (Saugstad, 1965) have previously emphasized, in the study of perceiving the sensation is introduced by a verbal instruction or by some procedure developed on analogy to this instruction. There is thus no need in this study to conceive of the sensation as an element of consciousness. (That there is no need to do so was not made clear in my earlier work.)

The next generation of Continental psychologists — like the previous one — stayed within the Cartesian tradition, conceiving of their subject matter in terms of consciousness, and as a consequence their use of the term 'internal structure', or, as they frequently called it, the 'Gestalt' or 'whole', meets the same fundamental difficulty as the use of the term 'mental element'. This, of course, is also true of the use of terms such as 'intentions' and 'meanings' in the phenomenological psychology developed later in the twentieth century. It is difficult to see what reference system is available for the use of terms such as those mentioned. What are the presuppositions in terms of which one can postulate the existence of internal structures, meanings, or intentions?

It follows from what has been said above about the use of the term 'sensation' in the study of perceiving, that the contributions of Gestalt psychologists to this study do not justify their introduction of the term 'structure' as an entity of consciousness. Their contributions — which must be accepted as substantial to this study — may be seen simply as demonstrations that the presuppositions made by earlier research workers in this area of research are not always warranted.

In a later chapter on consciousness and behaviour I shall discuss difficulties met with in attempts at drawing distinctions between reference to consciousness and use of language. At this point I shall just call attention to the fact that the thinking of Freud — as well as that of later psychoanalyst psychologists — is based on the Cartesian

35

framework. This point is eaily overlooked because the psychoanalytic school of psychology rejected the belief that consciousness plays the dominant role in man's thinking and actions, but this does not mean that the theoretical terms of psychoanalysis have not been introduced by reference to the Cartesian conception of consciousness. In order to develop a scientific reference system, Freud and his students — like Wundt and his students — would have had to examine the Cartesian framework. Since they failed to realize this point their theoretical terms — the unconscious, the ego, the id, the super-ego, primary processes, secondary processes, identification, resistance, etc. — could only be given a vague and diffuse reference to existent knowledge. This is so whether existent knowledge is conceived of in terms of events occurring within the so-called therapeutic situation or whether it is more broadly conceived of in terms of existent cultural knowledge. Future generations of psychologists may come to look in vain for what may be regarded as a creative aspect in the thinking of Freud and later psychoanalytists.

Before leaving the problem of conceiving of the subject matter of psychology in terms of consciousness, it ought to be pointed out that when Cartesianism was revived in the 1950's by Bruner and coworkers (1956), Chomsky (1957, 1966) and Miller and coworkers (1960) in the modern study designated 'cognition' no attempt was made to state the presuppositions underlying the belief that use of language is based on consciousness or mind of some sort.

To turn to behaviourism it should be noted that the behaviourists — like the earlier psychologists — never discarded the Cartesian framework; they merely discarded it as providing the subject matter of psychology, and behaviourists from the days of Watson to the present have remained confused regarding the role to be attributed to consciousness. For example, Tolman (1932) found that he had to introduce the idea of purpose taken from a Cartesian framework to make his behaviourism work. Spence (1948) accepted consciousness as forming the basis for the observations made, but did not make clear what the relationship between consciousness and behaviour might be. Skinner (1964) — 26 years after the publication of his first book based on the postulates of behaviourism — admitted that in some way behaviourist psychologists were concerned with events of an internal nature, but — like Spence and Tolman — he did not make clear what this admission meant to his thinking. As I shall emphasize in a later chapter on consciousness and behaviour, the concessions of behaviourists to Cartesianism reveal that they make an illegitimate use of the term observation, and, as I (Saugstad, 1965) have previously pointed out, this leaves their thinking in a fundamental state of confusion.

When behaviourist psychologists have tended to believe that it is not necessary to examine the relationship between consciousness and behaviour, as mentioned above, the reason has probably been that they have taken over beliefs uncritically from analytic philosophers of the twentieth century. Their stimulus—response paradigm for analysing psychological events is formed on analogy to the idea in analytic philosophy that complex beliefs might be analysed into statements of a simple perceptual nature. Since the presuppositions made in applying this paradigm were never stated, the use of the terms 'stimulus' and 'response', as I shall have the opportunity to show in a later chapter, could only be introduced by an arbitrary and diffuse reference to use of language.

Psychology and operational definitions

As was pointed out in the previous section on problems in the philosophy of science, positivist thinking in Mill, Mach and the logical positivists became closely allied with British empiricism. This alliance led positivist science philosophers to overestimate the use that can be made of ostensive definitions and the use of reference to steps in the empirical procedure in attempts to clarify the meaning of the theoretical terms (called operational definitions). I shall return to this essential point later in this book. Here reference will merely be given to the article by Hamlyn (1967, a) on empiricism and by Schlesinger (1967) on operational definitions.

As a consequence of the heavy emphasis of the positivist thinkers on ostensive and operational definitions, psychologists came to adhere to the practice of introducing their theoretical terms by reference only to a single type of situation or to a single type of situation and procedural steps undertaken by the research worker in this situation. It must be clear that this kind of procedure leaves theoretical terms vaguely and diffusely defined. Therefore, when the psychologist places his point of departure in data collected according to this procedure, he can only conjecture loosely about the nature of the type of events postulated. Since the reference system is lacking there is no way in which by collecting more data the theorist can arrive at a more rigorous — and thus more fruitful — definition of his terms. As might be expected, the central terms in empirical psychology, such as 'perceiving', 'remembering', 'thinking', 'learning', 'intelligence', 'motivation', 'personality', etc., are scarcely used more consistently today than at the beginning of the twentieth century.

The tendency of psychologists to introduce theoretical terms without due regard for existent cultural knowledge was strengthened by the positivist belief that scientific methods of a general applicability had been developed in the physical sciences. By using these methods it was believed that unfortunate or wrong presuppositions would be corrected. As pointed out in the previous section, the belief in scientific methods of a general applicability seems to rest on dubious foundations. For this reason the procedures used in psychology may be of little usefulness in correcting inadequate or wrong presuppositions. In fact when the history of empirical psychology is examined, one is struck by the length of the period of time psychologists have continued their empirical work on the basis of what today appear as wrong or inadequate presuppositions. For example, as I shall argue below, both the study of learning in the Thorndikian tradition and the study of intelligence have persisted for more than 70 years in spite of the fact that little progress seems to have been made. Similarly the continued efforts over about the same period of time to improve upon psychoanalytic conceptions of personality and psychotherapy may be regarded as an illustration of the difficulty of correcting inadequate or wrong presuppositions by the empirical procedures used in psychology.

Representative of the tendency to introduce the theoretical terms in an ostensive and operational manner is the study of learning in the tradition of Thorndike. Thorndike [1898] proceeded by constructing a box (referred to as a puzzle box) in such a way that in order to escape from it a cat, when placed in it, would have to manipulate some string or other device. Thorndike registered the repeated trials of the cat to escape from the box. On the basis of this description he concluded that learning of some definite type had taken place. He referred to this learning by the term 'trial-and-error'. Obviously — unless it is possible to define a given type of event by means of an ostensive definition — it is not possible to state what is meant by learning by trial-and-error according to this procedure. Thorndike's followers, of which there have been a large number, failed to see this point. Some of them, such as Skinner (1938) and Guthrie and Horton (1946), modified the box so that registration of the animal's activities could be made more accurately and conveniently while others, such as Estes (1950), proceeded to treat mathematically what were regarded as the reactions of the animal in this type of situation. In neither case, of course, did it become clearer what was meant by learning in the organism studied. Pavlov, who began his investigations of the conditioned reflex about 1900, was also inspired by Thorndike, but he realized that he would have to introduce his fundamental theoretical terms by means of some reference system. This reference system he believed he would be able to develop by elaborating the idea of the biological reflex. This insight in Pavlov represents a considerable improvement on the procedure of Thorndike, but as it has turned out, the reflex represents a far more complicated reaction than Pavlov thought it would be. Moreover Pavlov came to introduce his second term, the conditional or conditioned stimulus, according to the empiricist belief that ostensive definitions could be regarded as fundamental. Consequently this term has been left hanging in the air. (I shall return to this point in the Pavlovian procedure in a later chapter.) While the possibility cannot be excluded that the Pavlovian procedure might be elaborated so as to be more meaningful, and while it must be admitted that the development of the law of effect undertaken by Skinner (1938, 1969, 1974), i.e. that the activity of an organism is modified by the consequences of this activity, must be said to have revealed mechanisms of some fundamental sort, it seems fair to state that the study of learning from Thorndike to the present has proved by and large to be a sterile affair. (For reviews of the numerous theories of learning and the innumerable experiments performed, the reader is referred to Hilgard and Bower, 1966.)

Galton (1883), a contemporary of Wundt in Great Britain, proceeded to introduce his terms in an operational manner somewhat different from that of Thorndike and earlier and later experimental psychologists. He constructed various types of tests and introduced his central term 'human faculty' (later referred to by the term 'intelligence'), by reference to the performance of individuals on these tests. Research workers following Galton, such as Binet, Spearman, Thurstone and Guilford, improved on his procedure by introducing more appropriate tests and better statistical and mathematical techniques for dealing with the performances of the individuals on the various tests. (For a review of this work, see Anastasi, 1958; Cronbach, 1960; and Guilford, 1967.) Without denying that information of some usefulness has been obtained it seems fair to state that few, if any, principles of theoretical significance have been formulated on the basis of testing procedure. Apparently the construction of tests as well as the performance of the individuals on tests is heavily influenced by culture and thus by man's use of language. In order to construct an adequate theory based on this procedure it is essential that the psychologist is capable of handling the various types of cultural influences present in different tests and in the performances of different individuals. This clearly creates great difficulties. The study of human intelligence by the testing procedure places in focus the difficulties met with in psychology. It is evident that in an extremely complicated manner the various activities of the human individual are influenced by culture. Culture is again intimately related to use of language. This means that in order to handle psychological problems in a fruitful manner it is necessary in some way to handle existent cultural knowledge and to structure man's use of language. When this is accepted, it will be understood that the establishment of a scientific psychology raises a variety of intricate questions.

In the twentieth century there has been an ever-increasing interest in the study of meaning, use of language and symbols. From the beginning of the century philosophers such as Frege, Russell, Wittgenstein and Carnap were preoccupied with attempts to find relationships between logic and use of language, and Moore sought to understand the philosopher's expressions by relating them to the ordinary use of language. Cassirer hoped to reveal aspects of man's nature by accounting for his use of symbols. This interest in meaning, use of language and symbols was later, around the middle of the century, increased by the development of information theory in telephone engineering, by the possibility of analysing use of language and simulating thinking by means of computers, and by the development of what seemed to be a new type of grammar by Chomsky and followers.

In the 1950's the study of use of language and communication became central in psychology. About this time behaviourist psychologists shifted their attention from the study of learning in animals to the study of learning and remembering of verbal material in human individuals. (For a review of this work, see Dixon and Horton, 1968.) Headed by theorists such as Osgood (1953), Skinner (1957) and Mowrer (1960) psychologists renewed the study of the acquisition of use of language in children. The behaviourist approach was based on the presupposition that behaviour could be regarded as having logical priority over use of language. Use of language was simply regarded as a subvariety of behaviour and was termed 'verbal behaviour'. The difficulties involved in taking this position were left unnoticed, and so far, the relationship between use of language and behaviour does not seem to have been examined by modern behaviourists.

Another group of research workers applied the concept of information or uncertainty to psychological research. While the introduction of information theory to psychology may be said to have had the salutary effect of drawing attention to the fact that human activities must be understood in terms of the receiving and utilization of information, the term 'information' was never systematically examined. In line with empiricist conceptions of meaning, the theorists adopting this orientation limited themselves to introducing the term by reference to operational procedures. This made the whole endeavour a sterile one. (For reviews of this work, see Neisser, 1967; Norman, 1969.) The unfortunate practice of defining information merely in terms of operational procedures was continued in the further development of this approach into what is generally termed 'information processing'. (For reviews of this work, see Neisser, ibid; Norman, ibid, 1970; Newell and Simon, 1972.)

The approach in terms of information processing was followed or paralleled by a return to conceptions of psychology in terms of consciousness. Under the designation of 'cognition' a renewed interest in problems of perceiving, remembering, imagining and thinking took place. (For an introduction to this work, see Bruner et al. 1956; Bruner et al., 1966; Miller et al., ibid; Neisser, ibid; Paivio, 1971.) In the approach developed the term 'process' replaced the previous terms 'mental element' and 'mental structure'. It was left unnoticed that the fundamental difficulties met with in the early *Denk-Psychologie* from the beginning of the century remained in what was now believed to constitute a new approach. As had happened in the case of the term 'information', the relationship between the term 'process' and use of language was left unexamined.

A parallel trend to that of information processing was introduced in psychology through the development of communication theory. This type of theory was applied to abnormal functioning and emphasized the effects of various types of interaction between human individuals (Watzlawick et al., 1967). Once again the central term, in this case 'communication', was not examined in relation to use of language. The presupposition was made more or less implicitly that principles of communication could be developed without consideration of use of language. This approach was apparently decisively influenced by Russellian ideas about the nature of use of language.

Finally, so as not to miss out the most recent outgrowth of the new orientation, mention should be made of the interest in the study of use of language based on the new grammar developed by Chomsky (1957, 1965, 1972). In this approach, designated as 'psycholinguistics', attempts have been made to study perceiving, remembering, imagining and thinking in terms of grammar and (vice versa) grammar in terms of perceiving, remembering, imagining and thinking. Unfortunately the relationship between the activities mentioned and use of language was not made clear. The fundamental question of whether one could conceive of a psyche independent of use of language was never examined. It is difficult to see what is to be studied in this approach. Explanation and description seem to be confused. As was the case for the study designated as 'cognition', the approach represents a revival of Cartesianism.

Reductionism and ideas about development
As has been emphasized, the tendency in empirical psychologists

41

to introduce their theoretical terms without due regard for existent cultural knowledge and the nature of man's use of language has been upheld by the empiricist belief in ostensive and operational definitions. It should be noted that the tendency has also been upheld by other types of beliefs. For example, it has been widely believed that various activities in man could be studied by analogy with activities of a simpler nature found in individuals of other species. Thus learning, remembering, thinking, emotions and motivation in man were conceived of in terms of principles found in the study of individuals of other species.

While there can be no doubt that comparative studies of activities in individuals of different species are essential for the advancement of psychology, it must be understood that it is difficult to compare specific activities in one species with specific activities in another species. The various activities in a definite species form part of a total adjustment. This means that unless the total adjustments of the species to be compared are taken into account, it may not be meaningful to compare specific activities in different species. In this connection it should be noted that from an evolutionary point of view the primate species are just as old as the other mammalian species. Specific activities in the human species cannot, therefore, be regarded simply as more complicated versions of activities found in other species. If — as seems to be the case in many instances — comparisons can be made in a meaningful manner only when the adjustment of the species as a totality is taken into account, man's adjustment as a totality must be taken into account. This seems to lead us back to the problem of evaluating the effect on man's activities of cultural knowledge and use of language. The procedure of studying simple activities in simpler organisms to clarify human activities thus meets with serious difficulties. (For accounts of the evolutionary origins of man, see Clark, 1959; Simpson, 1949; and for attempts to bring comparative psychology more in line with modern conceptions of biology, see Hinde, 1974. The Scandinavian reader is also referred to Smith and Bjerke, 1974.)

Related to the belief discussed above is the belief that psychological activities are explainable in terms of physiological processes, so-called physiological reductionism. As I shall point out in the two chapters on consciousness, the belief in physiological reductionism seems to be a result of the Cartesian idea of the inner man. When it is realized that psychological activities must be conceived of in terms of interaction between an organism and its environment, it will also be realized that it does not make sense to attempt to explain psychological activities in terms of physiological processes, and, therefore, that the theorist in psychology cannot circumvent the difficulties arising in attempts to structure existent cultural knowledge and use of language by basing psychology on speculation about physiological processes.

Another type of belief which has strengthened the tendency in empirical psychologists to introduce their theoretical terms without due regard for existent cultural knowledge and man's use of language, is the belief that activities at later ontogenetic stages may be conceived of as the development of activities at earlier stages and thus be studied in terms of ontogenetic development. Thus by studying activities in the infant and child one may avoid — so one has thought — the difficulties arising in connection with the study of complex activities in the adult. This approach in terms of the ontogenetic development rests on the presupposition that it is possible to state what is meant by ontogenetic development. When the use of the term 'development' in psychology is examined, it becomes clear that this use has an inadequate basis. While the term 'development' can be given a precise meaning in embryology and biology this is hardly possible in psychology. Theorists in developmental psychology tend to use the term in a global, diffuse manner.

To illustrate the difficulties met with in using the term 'development', I shall begin by considering an example where such difficulties have already been recognized. Much research and discussion has been devoted to the problem of the constancy of intelligence. (For a review of this problem, see Anastasi, 1958.) When the term 'intelligence' is taken in the global sense of an intelligence quotient, low correlations are found between IQ's at early and later stages. There are a number of reasons for this result. One obvious reason is that the contents of the tests used at the different stages are different. Thus, for instance, at the age of about 6 months the test items are of a sensory-motor type. In contrast, at a later stage, say, at 6 years, the items contain questions which require understanding of words and mastering of abstract reasoning. Clearly the contents of the tests used at the different stages are different. Apparently, in order to speak of development in a more precise manner, the theorist must provide criteria which enable one to identify at an earlier stage an activity found at a later stage. This requirement is not easily met, and theorists in developmental psychology have underestimated the difficulties involved. The example discussed below will illustrate the point made here.

I shall consider development of use of language. The question of what is developing where use of language is concerned is a most puzzling one. If, for example, we choose as the activity to be investigated the use of the one-word utterance in the child, we will have great difficulty in finding the type of activity at earlier stages which can be identified as corresponding to the activity to be investigated. We might, as has been done by thinkers such as Osgood (1953), Skinner (1957) and Quine (1960), concentrate on the fact that the one-word utterance involves a vocalization. This would lead us to consider speaking as a development of babbling in the child. While it is not unreasonable to believe that babbling in some way is connected to speaking, speaking has characteristics which make it different from babbling. Speaking is a way of communicating. This may or may not be the case for babbling. Communicating, on the other hand, may be regarded as connected to a number of activities which do not involve vocalization. Prior to the occurrence of the one-word utterance in the child, the child has been engaged in activities such as crying, smiling, gesturing, imitating other individuals and making movements in relation to them which involve social interaction. (Werner and Kaplan, 1967, have emphasized the role most probably played by these activities in the development of speaking in the child.) Whatever the role played by these activities, it is reasonable to expect that they affect speaking as a way of communicating. It will also be noted that speaking in contrast to babbling involves an arrangement of sounds in a definite sequence. This is clearly not the case for babbling at all stages. This arrangement of sounds in speaking depends upon a mastery of the production of phonemes in articulated speaking. This mastery depends most probably upon a variety of activities which do not involve vocalization. This example shows how difficult it is to state how the one-word utterance of the child develops. To say, as Skinner (1957) and Quine (1960) did that speaking can be understood as a shaping of the child's babbling, clearly involves a simplification. Lenneberg (1967) has provided good evidence that the development of use of language is not so closely related to vocalization or on the whole to the giving of responses as has been presupposed by behaviourists.

As demonstrated by Brown (1973), it is possible to study the development of grammar by taking as one's point of departure the one-word utterance without considering the prior activities in the child leading to this performance. But it must be clear, as noted by Brown, that the neglect of the prior activities seriously limits the fruitfulness of the study of the development of grammar. One important limitation is the fact that we do not know how to conceive grammatically of the one-word utterance. Does the one-word utterance represent a sentence or simply one word? Evidently grammar depends upon the conception of what constitutes a sentence. Therefore, if it cannot be made clear what is meant by a sentence, it is not possible to conceive of the study of the development of grammar in a clear way. As I shall have ample opportunity to show later in this book, it is difficult to throw light on man's use of language by appealing to developmental studies in the child. The reason is, as will be understood from what has been said above, that it is difficult to get a clear picture of what is meant by development in this case.

Theorists dealing with the ontogenetic development of man have devoted scant attention to the difficulties involved in stating that some definite activity has developed from other activities occurring at earlier stages. It should be noted that in order to speak meaningfully about the ontogenetic development of the child, it is necessary to have a complicated reference system. This reference system is lacking in the work of the theorists. Below I shall consider two influential theorists, Piaget and Vygotsky.

Piaget (1950; 1971; 1972; see also Furth, 1969) adopted three essential terms, 'assimilation', 'accommodation', and 'equilibration', from biology. While the terms can be used in biology in reference to an interaction between a given describable organism and its environment, Piaget introduced his terms by presupposing a Cartesian framework of consciousness. None of the terms were related to man's use of language or to existent cultural knowledge, and it is difficult to see what their basis is. Malcolm (1971) may rightly have characterized the reference to internal structures in Piaget as the postulation of myths. Furthermore Piaget conceived of intelligence in terms of logical operations. This conception makes it difficult to see what can be meant by development. In the first place Piaget failed to relate his term 'logical operation' to use of language. An attempt to do so would have involved him in difficulties of a fundamental nature, which was overlooked by philosophers contemporary to Piaget. (For a review of some of these difficulties, see the critical articles by Gale, 1967, on the proposition, and by Linsky, 1967, a, on the problem of referring.) As long as the term 'logical operation' has not been related to use of language it is difficult to see how it can be used in an account of the acquisition of use of language in the child and also how one might properly investigate the development of logical thinking in the child. Secondly Piaget (1950) conceived of the logical operations as a priori in nature. If they are a priori in nature it is difficult to see what can be meant by saying that a logical operation is not present in a child at a certain stage of the ontogenetic development. The only statement that can be made with regard to a child unable to perform any one of these operations is that it functions as a defective adult human being. As will be realized, this is hardly a fruitful conception of the ontogenetic development. After having examined Piaget's use of the term 'concept', Hamlyn (1971) seems to have arrived at the same conclusion with regard to the underlying conception of development, namely that it implies an idea of the child as a defective adult human being.

In this chapter I have pointed out that the leading theorists in psychology have based their approaches on beliefs adopted from some philosophical tradition predominant in their intellectual environment. Thus Wundt and the early structuralist psychologists based their approach on British empiricism and positivism. Similarly the behaviourists, although conceiving differently of the subject matter, based their approach on these two philosophical traditions, and Gestalt psychologists adopted fundamental beliefs from the phenomenology of Husserl. One may ask what was the philosophy in fashion on which Piaget based his approach? Apparently Piaget can hardly have been decisively influenced by empiricism, positivism, or phenomenology. His ideas were derived from ideas regarding the nature of logic which dominated much of the philosophy around 1900. As was made clear by Ryle (1957), philosophers such as Frege, Meinong, Husserl and Russell investigated logical relationships as if these made up a realm of Platonic events. In his *Philosophical Investigations* Wittgenstein (1953) directed heavy criticism against the idea of logic as providing some sort of substrate for man's use of language. Obviously a number of difficulties attach to the ideas about logic predominant at the beginning of the twentieth century. However, it is on these ideas of logic that Piaget based his approach. Above I made reference to articles which make clear some of the fundamental difficulties met with by Piaget. Here I shall only mention that he (Piaget, 1950, 1972) conceived of classes in a manner similar to that of Russell. This conception of class in Piaget is central. Obviously the term 'class' represents an abstraction. How can we conceive of a class as an abstraction independent of use of language? In a later chapter I shall discuss the idea of class in Russell's work. The difficulties inherent in Russell's idea are also present in the idea of class as used by Piaget. It is thus highly obscure how he can relate his concept of class to the procedures required by empirical research.

In general I would say that Piaget's terms referring to logic are not introduced in such a way that one can understand how they may be communicated about. This means that the end result of the ontogenetic development to which Piaget has to anchor his term 'development', can only be hinted at in a diffuse manner. The earlier stages, the phases representing the various stages in the child's development, are only introduced in terms of speculation about mental structures and mechanisms in the child. As a consequence of the diffuse reference to the end result of development and to the initial stages, Piaget could only make a diffuse reference to the development of what he termed 'symbolic processes'. (On the term 'symbolic process' in Piaget, see Furth, 1969.)

I shall illustrate the way Piaget determines the initial stages of development, by his introduction of the term 'schema'. This schema is central. (Operations are also conceived of as types of schema. (An account of the use of the term schema in Piaget's work is given by Furth, 1969.)) The introduction of this term illustrates a confusion which has permeated Piaget's thinking, namely that between statements in the first and third persons. As was made clear by Malcolm (1964), it is essential that this distinction is maintained in psychology. While in a fundamental sense statements in the first person are incorrigible, statements in the third person must be verified. In introducing terms to explain how thinking could arise from action Piaget (1972, p. 48) wrote:

> However, in maintaining that the origin of the various forms of knowledge never results from perception alone and arises from the whole of action, whose schematism engulfs perception but also overtakes it, one will doubtless come up against the following objection: action itself is only known to us through a certain variety of perceptions known as proprioceptive (whereas the external results of action are registered through exteroceptive pathways). For example, if I classify or order objects with actual manipulation, I will sense my movements through the interplay of proprioceptive perceptions and will find out their physical effects through the habitual visual or tactual pathways.
>
> However, the relevance of this as far as knowledge is concerned is not the sequence of such actions considered in isolation: it is the 'schema' of these actions, that is to say that which is general in them and can be transposed from one situation to another (for example a schema of order or a schema of collection, etc.). The schema is not drawn from perception, proprioceptive or otherwise. It is the direct result of the generalization of actions themselves, and not of the perception of them, and it is not in the least perceptible as such.

Clearly, reference to activity in the child represents statements in the third person and must be verified. The question arises: How can we ascertain that a child possesses some sort of schema? We can describe the perceptions and actions of the child, but how can we describe the schema? In order to describe the schema we would in some way have to communicate with the child. It is difficult to see how one can communicate about a schema in the child. Moreover, as will be seen, it is difficult to see how one can communicate about a schema in an adult. It will be noticed that in the quote given from Piaget he uses statements in the first person saying: 'For example, if I classify or order objects with actual manipulation, I will sense my movements . . .' From this position Piaget might possibly in a meaningful way introduce a notion like a schema, but this way of introducing the term, as I have mentioned, would not be meaningful as far as the child is concerned. The point to be emphasized is that the term 'development' can only be given a more precise meaning in psychology when a system for communicating has been constructed.

In contrast to contemporary and later theorists in psychology in the West, Vygotsky (1962) carefully considered a number of questions pertaining to an empirical study of thinking. Thus as early as the 1920's he realized that in the adult human individual it is difficult to distinguish between thinking and use of language, and that development would therefore have to be conceived of in terms of word meaning. However, as I shall show in a later chapter, his attempt to separate thinking from speaking in terms of ontogenesis and phylogenesis in man meets with difficulties. Furthermore Vygotsky elaborated the old idea of thinking as internal speech. (For a review of the history of this idea, see Aune, 1967.) However, in so doing he came to introduce three different terms for thinking: (1) pure thinking, (2) verbal thinking, and (3) thinking in terms of internal speech. Obviously it is extremely difficult to delimit the meaning of these three terms, and consequently also to relate the three terms to each other in a developmental theory.

Positivist conceptions of science have not unanimously been accepted by empirical psychologists. Phenomenologically oriented psychologists, for example, have insisted that the situations in which the various reactions are studied must be explored before the research worker proceeds to develop a theory of a more extensive nature. (On this point, see for example Rubin, 1927; Macleod, 1964.) However, the criticism which psychologists of the phenomenological orientation have made can hardly be said to have been elaborated to represent an alternative to the positivist conception of science. Mention should also be made of the fact that the Marxian emphasis on practice, where it is held that thinking and action cannot be separated and that advancement of science is closely related to practical improvement, leads to a point of departure for the development of psychological theories different from that taken by the positivists. (For a review of the development of the Marxian thesis of practice in Soviet psychology, see Vygotsky, 1962; Rubinstejn, 1963; Leont'ev, 1971, a, b.)

In this brief sketch of the history of empirical psychology from the days of Wundt and Galton to the present I have emphasized the necessity of a reference system for the introduction of theoretical terms. I have pointed out that an uncritical attitude to existing metaphysical systems, a belief in operational definitions, and simplified ideas about physiology, learning, and development have prevented psychologists from undertaking a serious examination of their conceptions of subject matter and methods. Until this examination is undertaken, no answers can be given to the central questions raised by attempts to establish a scientific psychology. I am not denying that in the course of the history of psychology a number of problems have been clarified. Nor am I denying that empirical research has provided information which has increased our understanding of a number of psychological activities. But I do insist that no decisive progress can be made unless research can be carried out in terms of a reference system which allows the research worker to see how the results of the empirical research are to be integrated and to decide on whether or not some theoretical formulation is of significance.

It is apparent that a number of the questions raised by attempts at establishing a scientific psychology are of such a nature that an answer to them is required in order that the research worker shall understand which presuppositions are involved when he adopts various types of procedures. They must therefore be examined prior to the beginning of empirical research. In the next section I shall indicate a number of questions relevant to the establishment of a scientific psychology which need reexamination.

Some central problems in scientific psychology

In my sketch of the history of empirical psychology I have emphasized the fact that method and subject matter have not yet been brought into a fruitful relationship with one another. To achieve this it is essential to reconsider some problems met with in attempts to conceive of a subject matter for psychology. Broadly speaking, psychology may be conceived of as the study of the interaction between the human organism and its environment. As was made clear in the historical sketch presented above, this conception of psychology seems to have come into focus in the more recent discussions of what is meant by a scientific psychology. The definition offered here will be more fruitful when it is extended also to include species other than man. This extension raises problems of a fundamental nature, but at the present moment I shall leave them aside. In a later chapter I shall have occasion to return to them.

In order to make the definition presented above useful, it is necessary to specify what is meant by the term 'organism' and what is meant by the term 'environment'. It must be clear that it is not meaningful to speak of interaction unless a specification is made of properties in the organism which are related to specific aspects of the environment. Because it is not easy to distinguish between the organism and its environment, this specification meets with fundamental difficulties. I shall briefly discuss some of these here.

In the adult human individual, interaction is determined by complicated cultural relationships. Evidently it is difficult to state with any degree of preciseness what the specific properties in the organism which interact with specific aspects of man's environnent are. As scientific psychology has been advanced, it has become increasingly clear that it is of little help to specify man's interactions with his environment by reference to intrapsychic entities or mechanisms. This type of reference informs us neither about the properties of the organism nor about the aspects of the environment which are involved in the interaction. Futhermore conceptions of interaction in terms of behaviour, stimuli and responses are highly defective. As should be abundantly clear by now, the use of the term 'behaviour' is closely dependent upon presuppositions concerning properties in the organism. The same is also true for the use of the terms 'stimulus' and 'response'. Neither of them can be defined without reference to properties of the organism. As long as this reference is lacking, the behaviourist is unable to specify in a more precise manner how the organism interacts with its environment.

To avoid dealing with interaction between the organism and its environment on the complex level of the adult human individual, empirical psychologists have believed that they might be able to begin the study of interaction at less complex levels represented by earlier stages of the ontogenetic development. At earlier ontogenetic stages culture has not affected the organism so strongly as at later stages. For this reason interaction between the child and its environment is of a less complex nature. However, as was pointed out in the historical sketch, it is difficult to conceive of development and learning in a clear manner. The psychologists may be said to be in the following dilemma: The interaction of the adult human individual with its environment is so complicated that it is difficult to study it fruitfully. On the other hand, the interaction of the child with its environment, which one may assume is of a simpler nature, can be speculated upon only in a manner which makes it resistant to fruitful empirical research.

For reasons which will be discussed in Part 1 of this book, I shall reject conceptions of psychology both in terms of consciousness and behaviour. Instead I shall speak of reactions or activities of the organism. As indicated in the historical sketch, communication about the subject matter of psychology conceived of in terms of consciousness and behaviour becomes highly deficient. Empirical psychologists seem to be entangled in fundamental problems concerning use of language. As a result of this entanglement definitions of terms in psychology are scarcely more precise than the use of words and expressions in ordinary use of language. As indicated in the sections above, in all areas of psychological research the central terms

50

have remained inadequately defined. The following list of terms may be regarded as more or less representative: Perception, memory, image, thought, speech, learning, development, concept, problem, process, information, symbol, system, behaviour, verbal behaviour, stimulus, response, association, element, structure, Gestalt, motive, emotion, intelligence, ability, factor, personality, ego, self, set, attitude.

As I stressed in the discussion of problems in the philosophy of science, the development of a scientific system presupposes that subject matter is related to method in such a way that it can be defined successively as empirical research progresses. Evidently, such methods are lacking in psychology, and, as has been made clear, they must be methods involving rules of communication. Therefore, in order to arrive at a fruitful discussion of subject matter, it is essential that it is made clear what is meant by communication.

In Chapter 1 I mentioned that at present we are not in possession of knowledge of rules which allows us to state how we communicate when language is used. As Wittgenstein (1953) has argued, we are not capable of stating the rules followed when we use language. Now, if we are not in possession of knowledge of the rules followed when language is used, it will be seen that we are not in a position to state what is meant by defining subject matter in terms of method. This is so because at the initial stage subject matter must be described by using words and expressions taken from the ordinary use of language.

In connection with the point made above, it should be made clear that definitions of terms for a scientific psychology cannot be conceived of as the making of more and more subtle distinctions. The making of more subtle distinctions is essential for improving mastery of use of language in ordinary life situations, and in psychology it is, of course, important that distinctions between words and expressions relevant to the subject matter are not overlooked. However, development of a scientific system requires explicitly stated rules which make clear that the terms are to be used in accordance with some specific method or methods. I shall therefore, in accordance with this line of reasoning, take issue with the idea expressed by Koch (1964, pp. 25-26) that the definition of psychological terms may be regarded as at bottom a perceptual training process:

> If we look at the problem of definition *psychologically*, we immediately see that a definition, if apprehended by a recipient, must result in a process of perceptual learning and that what is learned is the discrimination of the properties, relations, or system thereof that the definer wishes to designate by the term. This clearly means that definition, at bottom, is a *perceptual training process* and that everything that we know about the *conditions* of perceptual training and learning must apply to the analysis of definition.

Obviously the activity of using language cannot be conceived of simply as depending upon an ability to discriminate. The use of words, expressions and scientific terms depends on complicated rules which are not understood in terms of an analogy with perceptual discrimination. This simplified idea was explicitly introduced into psychology by Stevens (1935) in a period dominated by analytic philosophy. In order to state in an adequate manner what can be meant by definition of a theoretical term in psychology, it is necessary to consider carefully what can be meant by 'use of language'. In Part 1, difficulties attaching to conceptions of use of language in analytic philosophers will be discussed. At this point I shall merely repeat what was said in Chapter 1, that if distinctions between theoretical terms are not based on explicit rules, it is difficult to achieve rigour in reasoning about scientific problems.

To return to the definition of psychology as the study of the interaction between the human organism and its environment, it should be clear that this interaction is not understandable unless it is made clear how the organism perceives the material objects in the external world and individuals in his environment. This perceiving is in turn closely related to remembering, imagining and thinking. For this reason it is of prime importance to clarify the use of terms referring to the activities of perceiving, remembering, imagining and thinking. This will lead us to a consideration of a variety of problems, some of which are age-old in philosophy. In the first four chapters of Part 1 (Chapters 3, 4, 5 and 6) I shall consider some of these problems.

Of course, the interaction between man and his environment cannot solely be conceived of in terms of the activities mentioned above. Man's biological adjustment involves motivational and emotional aspects as well. In this book I am primarily concerned with problems of communication. For this reason it is natural to concentrate on the activities mentioned. Communication about the aspects of motivation and emotion will also be dependent upon conceptions of the activities mentioned, and as I shall argue, the same fundamental rules which must be followed in communicating about material objects in the external world must also be followed in communicating about human individuals, and motivational and emotional aspects.

An examination of problems related to the activities of perceiving, remembering, imagining and thinking leads into problems concerning use of language. In two chapters (Chapters 5 and 6) I shall discuss problems concerning the relationship between the four activities and use of language. An examination of the relationship between, on the one hand, the activities of perceiving, remembering, imagining and thinking, and, on the other hand, use of language, will make clear why it is an unfortunate practice to conceive of the subject matter of psychology in terms both of consciousness and behaviour. In three specific chapters (Chapters 7, 8 and 9) I shall deal more explicitly with difficulties inherent in these conceptions. Conceptions of the use of language are closely related to ideas about meaning. Problems of meaning have been hotly discussed by philosophers in the nineteenth and twentieth centuries, and no systematic treatment of problems concerning use of language can be undertaken unless this discussion is considered. I shall show that this discussion is highly relevant to the problems in psychology, and that the belief — so widespread among psychologists — that the adoption of specific empirical procedures may exempt the research worker from entering into this discussion is incorrect. In Chapters 10 and 11 I shall discuss some central problems found in attempts to account for how meaning arises.

In Part 1 I have pointed to a variety of difficulties attaching to a definition of the subject matter of a scientific psychology. In Part 2 I shall proceed to suggest a method for defining such a subject matter. Then I shall show how one might develop a theory of communication and use of language which will allow the research worker to determine types of events which may be studied in accordance with the method suggested.

Part 1

Problems of theory construction in scientific psychology

CHAPTER 3

On the nature of perceiving, remembering, imagining and thinking

Perceiving, remembering, imagining and thinking conceived of as capacities

One way of conceiving of perceiving, remembering, imagining and thinking is to say that these activities represent capacities. One might assume, as is frequently done by modern research workers in psychology, that man (and other species) is in possession of the following three capacities: 1. A capacity for receiving information from the outside world and from within the body which allows the organism to orient itself in relation to its environment, 2. a capacity for storing this information and 3. a capacity for utilizing this information in new ways. These capacities may be designated respectively as a capacity for perception, a capacity for memory, and a capacity for thinking.

One may further argue that the capacity for perception includes a variety of capacities, capacities which may be designated by the nouns 'vision', 'audition', 'gustation' 'olfaction', etc.; similarly that the capacity for memory includes another variety of capacities, capacities which may be designated by the nouns 'recognition', 'recollection', 'recall' etc.; and finally that the capacity for thinking includes a third variety of capacities, capacities which may be designated by simple and compound nouns such as 'planning', 'problem-solving', 'reasoning' and 'concept formation'.

In the study of psychology approaches in terms of capacities or faculties have played a fundamental role. Thus, the study of perceiving which began to flower in the middle of the nineteenth century was mainly approached as a study of man's discriminatory powers or capacities. Research workers were interested in answering questions such as the following: What is the smallest angle an object can subtend to the eye and still be visible? What is the range of wavelengths that can be visually detected? What is the amplitude of the weakest sound that can be detected? etc. The study of perceiving was made fruitful because progress in the physical sciences made possible control of experimental variables as well as accurate descriptions of the discriminatory capacities. By means of the development of the so-called psychophysical methods, absolute and differential limens or thresholds were determined for a variety of sensory attributes. In addition the ranges over which the sensory systems could function were investigated; for example the range of wavelengths to which the visual system could respond, or the range of frequencies to which the auditory system could respond, were determined. The capacities specified by reference to physical measurements were further correlated to descriptions of anatomical structures and physiological processes. In this way a fruitful branch of science, which has progressed steadily to the present, came into being. It is correct that the early theorists in the study of perceiving were profoundly influenced by British empiricism, and that as a result of this influence they tended to conceive of perceiving in terms of sensations and mental elements, but this should not overshadow the fact that in this study conceptions of sensory capacities played a fundamental role.

Moreover, in the study of remembering and thinking the idea of capacities played an important role. Thus, when Ebbinghaus [1885] performed the first experiments on remembering, he conceived of remembering as a capacity. In his approach to the study of thinking Köhler (1917) also stressed that the higher animals, just like the human individual, possessed a capacity for reacting to relationships which they utilized in their attempts at solving problems. In connection with the remarks made here on the role played by the idea of capacity in the study of perceiving, remembering and thinking, mention should be made of the fact that the investigation of intelligence initiated by Galton (1883) was undertaken in terms of conceptions of a faculty or capacity. The conceptions of the study of psychology in terms of capacities which can be traced back to older ideas in British as well as other philosophies (on this point, see Boring, 1950) have continued to play a fundamental role. For example, in modern communication and information theory, as well as in the study at present frequently referred to as neuro-psychology, the approach is frequently made in terms of conceptions of a capacity for receiving, a capacity for storing, and a capacity for utilizing information.

While there can be little doubt that the conception of capacities has been and still is a useful one in the study of psychology, it must be clear that its usefulness has definite limitations. In order to be fruitfully studied the capacities must be identified by use of language. While this has proved to be possible in the study of perceiving, it is clearly not so easy in a study of remembering and thinking. As I shall point out later, the conception of remembering and thinking as capacities meets with serious difficulties. The same is true of the conception of capacity in the study of intelligence. Empirical psychologists have tended to overlook such difficulties, the reason probably being that the early research workers tended to conceive of their study in terms of consciousness and thus came to overlook the role played by the verbal instructions. When in the later history of psychology the study of psychology was extended to species other than man, the fact that this was possible was interpreted by behaviourists as evidence of the fact that the study could be undertaken in terms of the stimulus-response paradigm. It was not taken into account that the animal studies had been undertaken on analogy to the studies on human individuals, and that as I (Saugstad, 1965) have previously pointed out, training procedures had taken the place of verbal instructions. Thus the animal studies clearly cannot be cited as evidence of the fact that it is possible to approach the study of psychology fruitfully in terms of conceptions of behaviour.

Instead of placing the point of departure in the conception of capacity some modern research workers conceive of perceiving, remembering, imagining and thinking in terms of activities. This conception is more fruitful because it underlines the fact that the organism interacts with its environment. In addition it may help to draw attention to the developmental — the phylogenetic as well as the ontogenetic — aspect. By emphasizing the interaction one may more easily avoid the pitfall of resorting to empty speculation. In accordance with this line of reasoning I shall speak of perceiving, remembering, imagining and thinking as activities.

Bartlett (1932) was one of the first theorists to emphasize the fact that the organism is active in remembering, remembering representing a construction. This point has later been elaborated by a group of research workers concentrating on what they call the study of cognition. Influenced by information theory they have extended Bartlett's idea of a construction also into the study of perceiving, imagining, and thinking. (For a review of this work, see Neisser, 1967; Paivio, 1971; Kaufmann, 1975.) This reorientation in the study of psychology is important, and it is worth while reflecting on the following quote from Neisser (1972, pp. 236-237), in which today's approach is contrasted with the former:

> Most of the history of psychology has been dominated by what may be called the 'storehouse' conception of mental life. The mind has long been thought to be a kind of vessel or a place in which various entities such as ideas, feelings, sensations, and images were to be found. These entities had a discrete existence, they could disappear and reappear again and be recognized (in 1967 I called this the 'Reappearance Hypothesis'). The task of psychology was to identify, define, or explain them. This was the

working assumption of the introspective psychologists who founded experimental psychology around the 1870's and dominated it until the 1920's. They not only believed that the mind was rather like a storehouse, but that its contents could be discovered, classified, and analyzed by systematic introspection. In fact, they could not think of any other way to psychologize at all: for them, it was introspection or nothing. How could a good observer be wrong about the contents of his own mind? How indeed, unless the mind is not a storehouse to begin with?

The founders of psychology were not the only ones who held the storehouse conception. Indeed, it has been so pervasive that psychologists who differ on every other point have adopted it without question. Freud, for example, took it for granted. Although he made the radical suggestion that some of the entities in the storehouse were 'unconscious' (in the cellar, more or less) and could not be examined, his cognitive theory was comfortably based on 'association' between continuously existing and potentially conscious 'ideas'. The believers in psychical phenomena and their successors who try to study extrasensory perception are another example: their only heresy was the belief that the contents of one person's storehouse could occasionally wander over into another's. Even the behaviorists did not avoid the trap; they still believed that the mind was full of mental objects, but insisted that no one discuss these objects during working hours.

While there can be no doubt that the emphasis on the activity of the organism is an important step in the right direction, it should be noted that the use of the term 'process' by the psychologists of this new orientation has led to an entanglement in the Cartesian problem of consciousness. As I shall make clear in a later chapter, the term 'process' is simply a substitute for earlier terms such as 'mental element' and 'mental structure'.

In connection with the emphasis on the activity of the organism mention should also be made of the fact that the behaviourist approach in terms of learning also represented a healthy reaction to the conception of psychology in terms of capacities. However, as I shall make clear in the next chapter, the term 'learning' as used by behaviourist psychologists is a highly diffuse one.

While an approach in terms of activities is preferable to one in terms of capacities because it gives a better biological orientation, it should be noted that serious difficulties also attach to the former approach.

In the first place the activities of perceiving, remembering, imagining and thinking are closely related to each other. Secondly it is not possible to conceive of these activities as independent of other activities and as independent of use of language. Therefore, descriptions and explanations in terms of perceiving, remembering, imagining and thinking as activities are of little usefulness.

The fact that the four activities mentioned above are so closely interrelated might indicate that they have important characteristics in common. However, the drawing of this conclusion meets with the difficulty that it is not easy to see more exactly what they have in common. Consider for example the following list of verbs and verbal expressions which are more or less representative of the activities of perceiving, remembering, imagining and thinking: To see, to hear, to smell, to taste, to feel, to identify, to recognize, to recollect, to recall, to reflect, to expect, to foresee, to anticipate, to imagine, to believe, to plan, to decide, to judge, to mean, to understand, to reason, to abstract, to form concepts, to solve problems. Apparently it is not easy to say more precisely what the activities indicated have in common. Furthermore the drawing of the conclusion meets with the difficulty that, as I have mentioned, the activities of perceiving, remembering, imagining and thinking have characteristics in common with other activities. Consider, for example, the following list of verbs which may be taken to indicate activities of various sorts having a motor aspect: To grasp, to reach, to walk, to run, to climb, to jump, to dance, to play, to fish, to hunt, to collect, to row, to work, to operate. Apparently the verbs in the two lists have characteristics in common. Moreover verbs and expressions in a list indicating emotional and motivational states would seem to have characteristics in common with the verbs in the two lists above: To love, to hate, to caress, to fight, to fly, to rage, to be glad, to be satisfied, to be anxious, to feel sorrow, to be depressed, to be happy, to be excited, to be eager, to be thirsty, to be hungry. One could also list verbs indicating various activities which seem to combine properties of the verbs in the first and third lists: to fear, to wish, to hope, to hesitate, to dream.

In accordance with the placing of emphasis on the activity of the organism I shall speak of use of language and not simply of language. By adopting the expression 'use of language' one can emphasize the fact that language is always used in some definite context and consequently must be understood in this context. The concentration on grammaticality in linguists has led them to neglect the role played by the context. Moreover, by using the expression 'use of language' one may counteract the tendency to conceive of meaning as some sort of Platonized entity whose existence is independent of use of language. This is in line with Wittgenstein's slogan: 'Do not look for the meaning, look for use'. It is also in line with Skinner's (1957, 1974) emphasis on the fact that language has a function.

Although I shall adopt the term 'use of language' I should like to draw attention to the fact that the use of the term is unfortunate because it may lead one to concentrate one-sidedly on the individual expressing himself and thereby come to neglect the individual who is affected by what is expressed. For this reason I should like to emphasize that the term 'use of language' here is meant to cover both the fact that an individual is expressing something as well as the fact that an individual is understanding something which is being expressed.

It is important that the term 'use of language' is extended also to cover the understanding of language. Otherwise the close relationship between language and culture is left out of focus. Language and culture are woven into each other in such a way that — in our present state of knowledge — they are rarely, if ever, distinguishable. This means that as a human individual grows up he is probably profoundly influenced by language through the culture in which he lives. Therefore, prior to an ontogenetic stage at which the child starts speaking — or is capable of understanding speaking — he is affected by use of language. The expression 'use of language' — and thus the emphasis on the specific activity when language is used — may lead one to overlook the indirect effect of language on man through his culture. In Chapter 5 I shall point out that psychologists tend to confuse speech and use of language.

In connection with the points made on terminology here, I should also like to call attention to the fact that as a result of my rejection of conceptions of psychology both in terms of consciousness and behaviour, I shall have to speak of psychological activities, reactions or functioning.

The relationship between the activities of perceiving, remembering, imagining and thinking

In English as well as in many other languages we distinguish between the verbs 'to perceive', 'to remember' and 'to think'. The normal adult speaker thus distinguishes between the following types of expressions: 'I see some definite stone', 'I remember some definite stone' and 'I think of some definite stone'. The speaker is capable of using the verbs mentioned in these sentences in a consistent manner and also a number of other verbs listed above as indicating activities of perceiving, remembering, imagining and thinking. Therefore, there must be some basis for the distinctions made and, as would seem reasonable, philosophers and psychologists have attempted to develop their arguments concerning the nature of knowledge by emphasizing the distinctions between the activities mentioned. This emphasis has frequently led thinkers to regard the distinctions as fundamental, i.e. one type of activity was believed to take place without being dependent upon the other types. Upon a more careful examination it is found to be difficult to make clear what the bases for the distinctions are. If this is so, obviously it is a questionable practice to base a scientific system on this distinction. (The problem of making distinctions between theoretical terms in scientific systems was discussed in Chapter 1.) Empirical research in psychology has also shown that it is difficult to distinguish clearly between the activities. Apparently the philosophers and psychologists who have regarded the distinctions as fundamental have overlooked the fact that the distinctions are based on use of language by the normal adult speaker in situations in everyday life and consequently that the distinctions may not be meaningful when applied to human individuals at early stages of ontogenetic development, to individuals of other species or to human individuals in situations which are not of the type ordinarily met with. At present the difficulties attaching to the distinctions appear to be so great that it can hardly be regarded as advisable to attempt to base an argument on them. I shall consider some of the difficulties met with in attempts to draw distinctions between perceiving, remembering, imagining and thinking.

Perceiving and remembering

The verbs 'to perceive' and 'to remember' are both used in such a way that they involve what may be regarded as events of definite types. For example, we see definite rocks, stones, trees, bushes, houses, cars, landscapes, or definite bodies moving; we hear definite noises, tones, melodies, voices, etc. Also we remember definite rocks, stones, trees, bushes, houses, etc. Evidently the use of any linguistic expression must in some way presuppose remembering. Therefore, unless one could in some way specify or define the activity of perceiving without having to use the verb 'perceive' or some other verb indicating some mode of perceiving, such as 'to see', 'to hear', 'to feel', 'to taste', etc., or any derivative of these words, it is difficult to understand how one might communicate about perceiving without presupposing the activity of remembering. In a later chapter I shall argue that this use of the verb 'to perceive' or any other sensory verb must be made, and consequently I shall reject the distinction between the activity of perceiving and that of remembering as a fundamental one. Moreover the activity of perceiving must be involved in some way in the activity of remembering because it is difficult to see what could be meant by the activity of remembering unless the presupposition is made that that which is remembered has at some previous point in time been perceived. Consequently the activities of perceiving and remembering would seem to be closely interrelated.

One might perhaps think that at some point in the ontogenetic development of the various mammalian species the activity of perceiving might take place without the activity of remembering. On reflection it is seen that it is difficult to understand what can be meant by such a statement. Even if we grant that mammalian species, including man at early stages, tend to react to certain types of stimulation in ways that indicate preferences for certain types of stimulation (for example, as the new-born infant turns his eyes in the direction of a sound, or smiles at sounds of specific types, and tends to fixate visually presented patterns in preference to homogeneously coloured surfaces), this does not mean that the activity of remembering is not involved. (For a review of the activity of perceiving at early ontogenetic stages in man, see Hinde, 1974; Cohen and Salapatek, 1975; Zaporožec and Zinčenko, 1971.)

When this argument appears as valid the reason is probably that it has not been taken into account that the activity of perceiving, just like the activity of remembering, involves some specifiable event. In order for the argument to be valid we would have to be capable of stating what the event perceived in these instances was. For example, can we say that the infant sees patterned figures of definite types or that it sees a patterned surface? Both statements meet with difficulties because it is not reasonable to believe that the infant — as the adult individual does — contrasts various types of patterned figures with other types of patterned figures or that it contrasts visual surfaces with parts of the visual field which are not regarded as surfaces. Clearly it is difficult to say more precisely what the event perceived by the infant is and consequently it is difficult to say that this event was not dependent upon some activity of remembering. The point made here does not imply that the findings referred to are not important in attempts to account for the development of man and other mammalian species. What it implies is that it is difficult to apply words taken from the language of the normal adult to describe reactions at early ontogenetic stages. The point made here illustrates the difficulties met with in the study of ontogenetic development to which reference was made in the previous chapter.

Perceiving and imagining

While it seems safe to state that imagining presupposes that something has previously been perceived, it is more difficult to understand what can be meant by the converse statement that perceiving presupposes something imagined. I shall make no attempt to elucidate the latter distinction. Instead I shall discuss along more general lines the interrelationship between the activities of perceiving and imagining.

As has been mentioned, in English as well as in many other languages a distinction is made between 'to perceive' and 'to imagine'. One distinguishes, for example, between the expressions, 'I see a particular stone' and 'I imagine a particular stone', and between the expressions 'I hear someone speaking' and 'I imagine someone speaking'. There can be no doubt that this distinction is vitally important. Human individuals would hardly have been able to survive as hunters and collectors if the capacity for the making of this distinction had not been developed. Characteristically it is taken as a symptom of abnormality when an individual in certain situations confuses the activity of imagining and the activity of perceiving.

In the 1940's and 1950's there was a tendency among psychologists to overemphasize the effect of motivational, emotional and social factors on the activity of perceiving. This tendency became less pronounced as research workers realized that central theoretical terms in this approach were not easy to define. Moreover when the experimental evidence was more carefully examined, strong or clear effects of these factors were not found to be present. As might be expected when the role of the activity of perceiving is viewed in terms of biological evolution, the experimental literature points clearly in the direction of the conclusion that perceiving in the sense of seeing, hearing, smelling, tasting and feeling represents an activity which is governed in a highly stable manner by sensory stimulation. In contrast the experimental literature of the period reveals clear effects of motivational, emotional and social factors on the activity of imagining. This may explain why the so-called projective tests constructed by Rorschach (1942), Murray (1938) and others appear to be of so little usefulness. (For a critical review of these issues, see Saugstad, 1966.)

Still, there is evidence that the distinction is not a fundamental one. In the first place there exist some individuals, the so-called eidetics, who are capable of giving reports based upon the activity of imagining which can only be distinguished by means of refined research techniques from reports given on the basis of the activity of perceiving. (For a review of this literature, reference is made to Neisser, 1967; Paivio, 1971.) Further support for this view may be found in the fact that some individuals have so-called hallucinations, i.e., on certain occasions they confuse the two activities, believing that the information received is the result of the activity of perceiving while it is the result of the activity of imagining. Reactions produced by hypnotic procedures also indicate that perceiving is not so closely governed by sensory stimulation as is found to be the case in what may be the more usual types of stimulation. Furthermore mention should be made of the results of an early experiment by Perky (1910), which have been duplicated more recently by Segal (1972). Perky found that when given instructions to imagine some object, an individual may, as is evidenced by his report, react to sensory stimulation and still believe that his report has been made on the basis only of the activity of imagining.

In conclusion I shall say that while the distinction between perceiving and imagining is of great importance in many respects it is hardly a fundamental one in the sense that any one of the activities can be defined in such a way that it can be regarded as uninfluenced by or independent of the other. As has been mentioned above, the difficulty of defining the two activities and the other activities involved makes research in this area problematic.

Perceiving and thinking

In attempts to account for the origin and nature of knowledge Western philosophers have attributed fundamental importance to the distinction between the activities of perceiving and thinking, and in the various approaches to the empirical study of psychology this distinction plays a central role. The distinction is based on the fact that in perceiving, the organism seems to make a contact with the external world which is not mediated by any activity on the part of the organism. Thus in seeing, hearing, smelling, etc. the individual seems to be passively receiving information from the external world. When the sensory organs are stimulated a sensory content seems to be impressed upon the organism. Thus when our eyes are open we receive impressions of definite scenes, and when we are located at definite distances from sources of sound we receive impressions of noises or tones, etc. Within certain limits we can change the impressions received by concentrating on various aspects of what is perceived, but by and large the impressions seem to be received without the necessity for any effort on the part of our organism. In contrast, in the activity of thinking the individual would seem to be manipulating information of various sorts. His reactions to the external world are mediated by this manipulation and would seem to involve his making an effort.

It would be unreasonable to deny that important differences exist between the activities of perceiving and of thinking. On the other hand, one might well ask whether the differences are of such a nature that the distinction should be regarded as fundamental in the sense that one of the activities can take place without the other also taking place. When it is taken into account that little is known about the phylogenetic or the ontogenetic development of the activities of perceiving and of thinking, one can understand that the thinkers of the past may easily have come to attach too great an importance to this distinction.

That the distinction is not so clear-cut as one might at first believe is indicated by the fact that we use expressions for the activity of perceiving in situations which apparently involve abstraction, as is the case when more than one object is involved. Thus we can say, for example, 'I see 10 nuts'. Clearly the counting of the nuts involves abstraction or thinking on the part of the organism. How many objects must be present in order that we shall perceive them immediately? Do we immediately perceive three nuts, while on the other hand we have to count when as many as 10 nuts are present? Perhaps the seeing of one nut also represents an abstraction? Apparently the level of ontogenetic development, at least to some extent, determines the capacity for what may be regarded as perceiving a definite number of objects. Thus an adult individual may instantly report that he sees seven nuts while the five-year-old child, even if familiar with counting, may have to point successively to each nut while counting before he can ascertain that seven nuts are present.

The drawing of a distinction between the activity of perceiving and the activity of thinking is further complicated when man's relationship to material objects and other persons is considered. We say that we see a stone, a tree, a house, a person, etc., but our expressing ourselves in this way does not preclude the possibility that this seeing involves thinking.

Since the days of Descartes epistemological theorists have met difficulties in treating the material object. Descartes [1641] noted that in spite of the fact that the perceptual attributes of the material object underwent changes, the impression that a definite object was present did not change. To him this suggested that the conception of the material object was intuited, that it represented an innate idea. The Lockian [1690] conception of knowledge as being composed of sensations led Berkeley [1710] and Hume [1739] to conceive of the material object as being composed of complexes of perceptual impressions and as being immaterial in nature. (For critical reviews of the philosophies of Berkeley and Hume, see Acton, 1967, a, and MacNabb, 1967.)

The Berkeleian-Humian idea was transmitted to Mill [1843] and Mach [1886]. Husserl [1913] objected to the belief that sensations were primary and insisted that the material object represented a whole.

In the study of sensory perceiving the material object was made central in the approaches of phenomenologically oriented research workers, such as Katz (1930), and the Berliner Gestaltists (see Koffka, 1935). They concentrated on the fact that the sensory attributes of the object, its colour, size and shape, appeared to be more or less invariant in spite of the fact that retinal stimulation varied widely. (For a review of these research problems, see Fieandt and Moustgaard, 1977; Lian, in press.)

I shall make no attempt here to develop a theory to account for how man perceives the material object. In a later chapter I shall deal with difficulties arising in attempts to state what the relationship between use of language and the material object(s) is. At this juncture I shall merely point out that however we conceive of the material object it seems most reasonable to state that the indentification of it represents some sort of abstraction and thus that this identification involves the activity of thinking.

For example, if it is presupposed that the perceptual field of which the material object forms a part is the result of an interaction between various sensory modalities, for example, an interaction between the vestibular, the tactile and the kinesthetic senses, vision and hearing, then the identification of the object by any one sense, say, vision or touch, will represent an abstraction. If we take the position that the material object can be perceived by one sense alone, say, vision, we meet with the difficulty of conceiving of the object as being isolated from the perceptual field as a totality. We are here faced with a fundamental problem in attempts to account for the perceiving of space: On the one hand, it is difficult to conceive of this perceiving as developing independently of and without regard to the perceiving of material objects; on the other hand, it is difficult to conceive of the perceiving of material objects as being independent of characteristics of the perceptual field, such as direction and distance relative to the perceiver. This suggests that the identification of material objects in visual perceiving represents an abstraction.

Further mention should be made of the fact that the identification of the material object may develop as a result of the fact that the object has specific functions such as giving support to the human body (e.g., when leaned on or sat on), giving shelter, or being used as an instrument. In these cases the identification of the material object clearly represents an abstraction.

Objections to the above arguments to the effect that the material object is given as a whole in immediate experience and thus does not represent an abstraction are based on presuppositions of a dubious nature. As will be made clear below, it is difficult to see what is meant by the statement that something is given in the sense of being independent of a particular context. Furthermore the problem of privacy is involved by the use of the term 'immediate experience', and still further the use of the term 'experience' raises the question of what is meant by consciousness, a question which, it should be emphasized, was never treated by Husserl and other phenomenologists. It makes no sense to speak of a whole unless it is made clear what the parts making up this whole are. In order to communicate about the parts making up the material object it seems necessary to make reference to attributes such as colour, size, shape, solidity and weight.

The argumentation presented above does not, of course, represent a denial of the fact that in visual appearance the material object represents some sort of whole, since colour, size and shape are inextricably related to each other. We do not see colour *and* shape *and* size. The point I am making is that it is difficult to conceive of this whole in a way which does not involve some sort of abstraction. The fact that no abstraction seems to be involved when we perceive objects may be explained by presupposing a phylogenetically determined interaction between various sensory systems allowing the organism to receive stable information about the material object with a minimum of repeated stimulation. In connection with treatment of the material object I should like to call attention to the fact that in the present state of knowledge it seems to be more important to consider how *communication* about the material object takes place than to advance theories concerning the development of the perceiving of it.

As I have mentioned, in a later chapter I shall return to the question of communicating about the material object.

In connection with what has been said here about the material object, it should be noted that a description of the material object in physicalist terms cannot be given unless presuppositions are made concerning properties of the organism. Moreover it is problematic to argue, as has recently been done by Strawson (1959, p. 39), that belief in the separate existence of the material object is essential for the development of a four-dimensional spatio-temporal frame of reference:

It seems that we can construct an argument from the premise that identification rests ultimately on location in a unitary spatio-temporal framework of four dimensions, to the conclusion that a certain class of particulars is basic in the sense I have explained. For that framework is not something extraneous to the objects in reality of which we speak. If we ask what constitutes the framework, we must look to those objects themselves, or some among them. But not every category of particular objects which we recognize is competent to constitute such a framework. The only objects which can constitute it are those which can confer upon it its own fundamental characteristics. That is to say, they must be three-dimensional objects with some endurance through time. They must also be accessible to such means of observation as we have; and, since those means are strictly limited in power, they must collectively have enough diversity, richness, stability and endurance to make possible and natural just that conception of a single unitary framework which we possess. Of the categories of objects which we recognize, only those satisfy these requirements which are, or possess, material bodies — in a broad sense of the expression. Material bodies constitute the framework. Hence, given a certain general feature of the conceptual scheme we possess, and given the character of the available major categories, things which are, or possess, material bodies must be the basic particulars.

As has been made clear above, most probably the perceiving of the material object presupposes that space around man is in some way structured, while conversely the perceiving of direction, distance, and extension presupposes the existence of material objects. In other words it may not be possible to distinguish between the perceiving of space and the perceiving of the material objects. If this is so, it is hardly meaningful to say that the development of the three-dimensional frame of reference is dependent upon the material object.

Evidently, a fruitful theory of spatial perceiving must be based on a biological model. It is hardly fruitful — although frequently done — to base this study on a physicalist model. A well-known attempt in this direction was made by Gibson (1966). This attempt resulted in empty theoretical statements probably due to the fact that the philosophical issue of realism versus idealism was confused with the giving of an explanation of empirical data. (For critical reviews of Gibson's theory, see Saugstad, 1965; Praetorius, 1969; Lian, in press.)

Modern research workers have come to question the presupposition that the organism is passive in receiving information from the external world. In the first place they have found considerable nervous activity in the sensory systems even when these are not directly stimulated. Secondly they have found that nervous activity in the various sensory systems seems to be dependent upon the activity going on in other parts of the nervous system. The performance of the sensory systems is thus a result of an interaction with other parts of the nervous system. For example, in mammals the sensory systems seem to develop in an inadequate manner when the organism is not performing movements relative to the visual impressions received. Thirdly they have found that the development of sensory activities in many species including man follows maturational stages and that development is impeded or deviates from the normal if the organism is not properly stimulated when it has reached a certain maturational stage. This seems to indicate that the development of sensory activities is the result of a complicated interaction between the organism and its environment through phylogenesis. When this perspective is taken on perceiving, the characterization of perceiving as being a result of the passive reception of information seems to be misleading. It is more properly to be regarded as an activity, as I emphasized in the previous section. The conclusion arrived at by Hebb (1949, p. xvi) seems to be well warranted:

> The central problem with which we must find a way to deal can be put in two different ways. Psychologically, it is the problem of thought: some sort of process that is not fully controlled by environmental stimulation and yet cooperates closely with that stimulation. From another point of view, physiologically, the problem is that of the transmission of excitation from sensory to motor cortex. This statement may not be as much oversimplified as it seems, especially when one recognizes that the 'transmission' may be a very complex process indeed, with a considerable time lag between sensory stimulation and the final motor response. The failure of psychology to handle thought adequately (or the failure of neurophysiology to tell us how to conceive of cortical transmission) has been the essential weakness of modern psychological theory and the reason for persistent difficulties in dealing with a wide range of experimental and clinical data, as the following chapters will try to show, from the data of perception and learning to those of hunger, sleep, and neurosis.
>
> In mammals even as low as the rat it has turned out to be impossible to describe behaviour as an interaction directly between sensory and motor processes. Something like *thinking*, that is, intervenes. 'Thought' undoubtedly has the connotation of a human degree of complexity in cerebral function and may mean too much to be applied to lower animals. But even in the rat there is evidence that behaviour is not completely controlled by immediate sensory events: there are central processes operating also.

The point made by Hebb that psychological activities have in common that they involve an attitudinal or directional factor is central to the theory to be presented in this book, and in later chapters I shall elaborate upon it. Here I shall just mention that if all modes of psychological functioning have in common that an attitudinal or directional factor is involved, this factor must constitute a defining characteristic and must necessarily be presupposed in all methods applied to the study of psychological functioning. Consequently this factor cannot be treated as an explanatory principle regarded as existing independently and having no necessary connection with method, although this has been done consistently, both implicitly and explicitly, by research workers in psychology, Hebb included.

A theory of psychological functioning must account in a satisfactory manner for the relationship between the activity of perceiving and the activity of using language. In attempts to account for this relationship the difficulty of distinguishing between perceiving and thinking emerges as a fundamental one. If we cannot presuppose that man can have a private language, it is difficult to see how one would be able to distinguish between the two. In a later chapter I shall consider some of the difficulties met with in the drawing of a distinction between, on the one hand, perceiving, remembering, imagining and thinking, and, on the other, man's use of language.

CHAPTER 4

On the nature of perceiving, remembering, imagining and thinking (continued)

The tendency to believe that a fundamental distinction can be drawn between perceiving and thinking is deeply rooted in Western thinking, and seems to have been drawn by theoretical psychologists of all orientations. In order to arrive at a clearer conception of the relationship between perceiving and thinking, it may be of considerable help to examine the presuppositions underlying it in a historical perspective. Such an examination will reveal that Western thinkers from Descartes to Skinner have presupposed that somehow the sensory systems provide the material for man's thinking and acting. Thus it is presupposed that, on the one hand, man receives sensory impression and, on the other hand, he deals with (manipulates, operates upon, utilizes) these impressions in thinking and acting.

Historical remarks on the activity of perceiving

In introducing his idea of consciousness Descartes [1644, pp. 289-290] postulated that the mind had direct knowledge of the activity taking place in the sensory nerves. In a passage entitled 'What sensation is, and how it operates' he wrote:

> We must know, therefore, that although the mind of man informs the whole body, it yet has its principal seat in the brain, and it is there that it not only understands and imagines, but also perceives; and this by means of the nerves which are extended like filaments from the brain to all the other members, with which they are so connected that we can hardly touch any part of the human body without causing the extremities of some of the nerves spread over it to be moved; and this motion passes to the other extremities of those nerves which are collected in the brain round the seat of the soul, as I have just explained quite fully enough in the fourth chapter of the Dioptrics. But the movements which are excited in the brain by the nerves affect in diverse ways the soul or mind, which is intimately connected with the brain, according to the diversity of the motions themselves. And the diverse affections of our mind, or thoughts that immediately arise from these motions, are called perceptions of the senses, or in common language, sensations.

I shall turn to the Cartesian conception of mind in the next chapter. Here I shall only point out that Locke [1690, p. 78] elaborated this conception by postulating that the mind received sensory impressions in the form of sensations, and that these sensations were operated upon by the mind:

> Secondly, the other fountain from which experience furnisheth the understanding with *ideas* is the *perception of the operations of our own minds* within us, as it is employed about the *ideas* it has got; which operations, when the soul comes to reflect on and consider, do furnish the understanding with another set of *ideas,* which could not be had from things without. And such are *perception, thinking, doubting, believing, reasoning, knowing, willing,* and all the different actings of our own minds; which we, being conscious of and observing in ourselves, do from these receive into our understandings as distinct *ideas* as we do from bodies affecting our senses. This source of *ideas* every man has wholly in himself; and though it be not sense, as having nothing to do with external objects, yet it is very like it, and might properly enough be called internal sense. But as I call the other *sensation,* so I call this REFLECTION, the *ideas* it affords being such only as the mind gets by reflecting on its own operations within itself. By REFLECTION then, in the following part of this discourse, I would be understood to mean that notice which the mind takes of its own operations, and the manner of them, by reason whereof there come to be *ideas* of these operations in the understanding. These two, I say, viz. external material things as the objects of SENSATION, and the operations of our own minds within as the objects of REFLECTION, are to me the only originals from whence all our *ideas* take their beginnings.

The Lockian idea of operations of the mind, which was an attempt at elaborating the Aristotelian conception of knowledge (on this point in Aristotle, see O'Connor, 1964), has played a fundamental role in the development of conceptions of psychology. To this I shall return in Chapter 7 of this book. At this place I shall stress that the Cartesian-Lockian conception of mind led philosophers and psychologists to conceive of perceiving in terms of some content of mind.

The idea of immediate experience

The content of mind involved in perceiving was regarded as being immediate, i.e. as not representing an abstraction, as not involving thinking. This content was termed 'immediate experience'. As seen from the quotation given above, Locke regarded the sensation as representing immediate experience and Husserl later regarded some sort of whole or Gestalt as representing immediate experience.

While Husserl is in opposition to Locke with regard to the nature of the content of mind it must be noted that these two thinkers were in agreement on the fundamental point that perceiving could be conceived of in terms of some content of mind i.e. in terms of what has been referred to as 'immediate experience'.

The belief in a content of mind which was immediately given was made central in empirical psychology in the latter half of the nineteenth century as well as in the philosophy of science of the positivists. Apparently, as was emphasized by Heath (1967, b, p. 157) in a critical article on the use of the term 'experience', however one conceives of immediate experience it represents an abstraction:

> The 'given'. The uncertainty of sense experience leads, by this route, to a further important conclusion. Since perceptual illusion and mistake seem essentially to be the fault of the observer, he must himself contribute something to his experience by way of interference, interpretation, or construction. Experience must, in part at least, be the work of the mind. For all that, the individual certainly does not create or invent his experience and in certain respects is powerless to alter it at will; it seems, therefore, equally undeniable that some part of it is simply 'given' and is only thereafter subject to adulteration by its recipient. This given is generally referred to as the object of 'bare' or 'immediate' experience, in contrast to the more 'solid' or developed experience of which it is held to be an essential ingredient. The legitimacy of the contrast is seldom, indeed, disputed, for though immediate experience has often been denounced as a myth, the usual motive for doing so has been to stigmatize it as a mere abstraction got by analysis and not something that could occur, psychologically, by itself. *All* experience, on this view, involves interpretation, and it is thus senseless to suppose any unvarnished, direct acquaintance with the given. But since it would be equally senseless to suppose an interpretation with nothing to interpret, it is commonly admitted that an 'epistemic' given must nonetheless be present in experience, though impossible to view independently, since this would *ipso facto* be to construe it in some fashion under the auspices of thought.

The use of the term 'sensation'

As might be expected, the empiricists' attempts to account for sensations have been unsuccessful. (For a review of the various attempts, see the following review articles: on sensationalism by Alexander, 1967, c; on phenomenalism by Hirst, 1967, a; on sensa by Hirst 1967, d.)

The idea of the sensation as forming the basis of knowledge was central in British empiricism from Locke to Stuart Mill and later, as was noted in the introductory chapter, in Mach and the logical positivists. In the empirical study of perceiving founded by Helmholtz, Fechner, Mach and others (for a review of the early history of this study, see Boring, 1942) it was made the central theoretical concept, and when Wundt (1874, 1896) developed his framework for an empirical psychology, sensations along with feelings were the elements on which the framework rested.

As pointed out by Husserl [1913] and as emphasized by Gestalt psychologists, the sensation represents an abstraction. Thus, an impression of yellow — such as Locke used as an example of a sensation

— is usually present as belonging to the shape of some definite material object. If this is not the case, at least it appears as having an extension of some sort. Similarly a sensation of pitch appears as belonging to some definite tone or noise, and when an object is being held, a sensation of weight is experienced along with impressions of touch and temperature.

Like any sensory impression the sensation is dependent upon a variety of factors. Thus a sensation of yellow, as referred to above, is dependent upon contrast effects, the intensity and homogeneity of the light, the state of adaptation of the eye as well as upon spatial relationships in the visual field. Many types of sensations, perhaps all, are the result of interactions between two or more modalities. (On this point, see Fieandt and Moustgaard, 1977; Luria, 1973.) In the study of perceiving they are therefore introduced by reference to detailed specifications involving operational steps of various sorts.

The experiment in psychophysics as introduced in the early study of perceiving rests on the presupposition that the experimenter is capable by means of verbal instructions of directing the attention of the subject so that he reacts to one particular aspect of the total stimulation affecting his sensory organs. Thus for example the subject may be instructed to react to changes in hue and not to changes in the form, size, or saturation of some patch of colour. Similarly in an experiment in hearing, the subject may be instructed to react to changes in pitch and not to changes in loudness or duration of the tone. Using a more refined technique the experimenter may introduce variations in one single sensory attribute, e.g. hue, and reduce verbal instructions to telling the subject just to indicate the point when two sensory impressions appear as equal. But this technique presupposes that the experimenter is in possession of information concerning the relationships between hue and other sensory attributes so that variations can be introduced only in one attribute. Otherwise he could not obtain information about the effect of variations in one attribute, in this case in hue. When this presupposition is examined it will be seen that it rests on the results of experiments where the subject is instructed *verbally* to react to some definite sensory attribute. Therefore, all psychophysical experiments with human subjects rest on the presupposition that the experimenter is capable of directing the attention of the subject to some definite sensory attribute. This point is important not only because it contains a fundamental methodological principle for the study of perceiving, but also because it invalidates behaviourism as a philosophical doctrine. It demonstrates that activities engaged in by the organism cannot be adequately described unless properties of the organism of some sort are presupposed. This is what I meant when I (Saugstad, 1965) previously stressed that the events studied in psychology must be determined by a threefold reference. This point, which seems to be in line with the position taken by Wittgenstein (1953), will be elaborated in a later chapter.

The behaviourist may possibly object to the argument presented above by saying that it is possible to do the same type of experiment on individuals of species other than man and that these species cannot be said to possess language, the system of communication developed by man. The behaviourist would then be overlooking the fact that the expression 'the same type of experiment' can only have a meaning when reference is made to use of language. In the experiments on animals the experimenter has to follow specific training procedures in order to make the animal react to definite aspects of the situation. These training procedures are clearly developed so as to be analogous to the verbal instructions given to the human subject. One might say that the animal is taught to follow some of the rules of language. The belief in the sensation as representing some entity whose existence is independent of some definite context has probably led behaviourists astray in their thinking about the subject matter of psychology.

The mental element

In order to explain psychological functioning in terms of the model presented by Descartes one would have to ascribe various properties to the res cogitans or the mind. The British empiricists adopted the procedure of postulating mental elements which were believed to be determinable by reference to sensations. The Humian idea of an association, to be discussed below, allowed the theorist, so it was believed, to account for the activity of thinking in terms of previous learning in which the elements had been associated with each other. The empiricist model, which dominated Western thinking for about 200 years, is on the face of it a powerful model. The activities of perceiving remembering and thinking could be related to each other by postulating the sensation as the fundamental element and it allowed one to explain development in terms of simple principles of learning. In one version or another this model was taken over by early theorists in learning, such as Ebbinghaus, Thorndike and Pavlov. The difficulty with the model is first and foremost that it is meaningful only within the broader framework of the Cartesian belief in consciousness. As has already been noted, the relationship of the model to use of language is fundamentally unclear.

When it is realized that the idea of the sensation represents an abstraction it will also be realized that it is difficult to see how the

76

idea of mental elements might be invoked to explain thinking. This explanation would require that the mental element was so constituted that it represented sensations in some sort of pure form, in other words out of the context in which they appear in the activity of perceiving. Obviously it is difficult to conceive of this type of entity. Moreover the mental element would have to be so constituted that it could represent both the particular and the general case. This means that the model presupposed the existence of a theory which could account for how the particular and the universal could arise. And this theory, of course, was not to involve presuppositions about thinking because this might make reasoning circular. As made clear by Vygotsky (1962) a central problem to be dealt with by a theory of thinking is that of accounting for the universal, and, as is seen from the philophical discussions of the universal, this problem is not easy to deal with. (For a review of this discussion, see Woozley, 1967.)

It should be noted that in accounts given by British empiricists the activity of thinking was not necessarily uninfluenced by use of language, but it was held that it could take place without a necessary connection with this use. Speaking was believed to be preceded by thinking. Thus, in speaking, two activities were assumed to take place: (1) an activity of using language and (2) an activity of thinking (or of perceiving).

The relationship between the acquisition of use of language and thinking was never worked out in a consistent manner.

Evidently the empiricist account of thinking only makes sense as long as one believes that adequate definitions can be given of this activity. When it is realized that the ability to use the verbs 'to perceive', 'to remember', 'to imagine' and 'to think' correctly does not imply that the individual having this ability is also capable of defining these activities adequately, the empiricist explanation of thinking will probably lose its attraction.

In Chapter 5 I shall consider the problem of distinguishing between imagining and use of language. In that chapter I shall comment on the study of imagining.

The idea of an association

Hume [1739] elaborated the model presented by Locke to account for knowledge in terms of sensations by adding to it the idea of association. He held that the sensations (or the impressions or ideas left in the mind by the sensations) were associated with each other in such a way that various psychological activities could be accounted for. Thus the material object was regarded as various types of sensations associated with each other. Inspired by Newton, Hume wanted to found a science of psychology, but unlike the great scientist he was not concerned about the nature of the reality he studied and, as was emphasized by MacNabb (1967, p. 76) in a review article on Hume, he took over the older notion of an idea, the result being that his central terms 'idea' and 'association' were left hanging in the air:

> *The origin of ideas.* For the professed founder of a new experimental science, Hume began in a distressingly dogmatic and a priori manner. 'All the perceptions of the human mind resolve themselves into two distinct kinds, which I shall call impressions and ideas'. Exhaustive dichotomies always merit suspicion and this one is no exception. Hume did not in fact succeed in maintaining it. Impressions are supposed to be either sensations, passions, or emotions, but he soon introduced a number of familiar experiences which are none of these, for instance: the order in time of the five notes of a tune is not a *sixth* impression, but a *manner* in which the five impressions occur; an 'idea of an idea' is distinguished, not by the impressions which it represents but by the representation of a certain indefinable 'je-ne-sais-quoi'; belief is said to be neither part of the idea believed nor a distinct impression produced by that idea, but a special *manner* in which the idea is conceived.

In what follows this passage MacNabb showed how Hume arrived at his dichotomy by uncritically accepting from seventeenth century philosophy the idea of mind as an immaterial entity equipped with the power of representing the external world and of reacting in various ways to these representations. MacNabb traced the idea of an idea backwards in time from Descartes and Locke to the Christian Platonists and then finally to Plato himself. From Locke and Hume it was transmitted forward to Stuart Mill and other nineteenth century thinkers and from them to empirical psychology. The idea of an idea and its necessary adjunct, the association, which was said to connect the various ideas, thus has a very long history. When account is taken of the fact that the idea of an idea and of an association is woven into conceptions of consciousness, one can easily understand that empirical psychologists relying on operational definitions have not been capable of eliminating it from their theories.

In order for Hume's model to work, the two terms 'sensation' and 'association' would have to be determined independently. It is difficult to imagine how this could be done. For example, when it is stated that a material object represents sensations associated with each other, it is difficult to see what can be meant by a sensation independent of an association and vice versa. In what sense can one say that a stone, for example, represents an association between definite sensations of colour, size, shape, hardness and weight? Clearly, a material object does not represent *any* combination of sensations, but a combination of some definite type. This point was left out of consideration by Hume and his later followers. Apparently Hume conceived of an association on analogy with the way an adult individual learns the name of another person with whom he happens to be acquainted. On the one hand, there is the person, and on the other, the name, and these are then associated in the mind of the individual learning the name. It is difficult to see what would correspond to the name and what to the person when it is stated that a material object is an association of sensations.

As has been mentioned, the term 'association' has played a fundamental role in empirical psychology. It was made central in the theories of Wundt, Ebbinghaus, Freud, Thorndike and Pavlov. Freud also extended the idea of an idea to include mental elements which were regarded as unconscious, and the idea and its adjunct, the association, together constitute the cornerstone of his theory. Thorndike and Pavlov modified the idea of association so that instead of speaking of an association as a connection between two sensory impressions or ideas they conceived of it as a connection between a sensory impression (a stimulus) and a muscular contraction or movement on the part of the organism (a response). Thus, the idea of the association came to form the basis of the stimulus-response paradigm of the behaviourists. The use of the term 'association' was severely criticized by the psychologists of the Würzburg and Gestalt schools, by Lashley, and by a number of other theorists. (For a critical review of the use of the term 'association', see Humphrey, 1963.)

Thinkers of the associationist tradition formulated various principles or laws of association. Among these formulations the law of association by temporal contiguity assumed a central position. Briefly this law states that when certain conditions (theorists refer to different types of conditions) prevail, events occurring in temporal contiguity will be associated with each other. This idea of association in terms of contiguity has survived in spite of serious attacks. The survival of the term is only partly explainable by the fact that from Wundt to Skinner theoretical psychologists have tended to accept uncritically — in one version or another — empiricist philosophy. There can be no doubt that in some way the idea of association through temporal contiguity is needed in psychological theory. It is difficult to understand how one might account for development (phylogenetic as well as ontogenetic) without having recourse to this idea.

Unfortunately, there seems to be no simple answer available to the question of what is meant by an event when it is stated that two events are associated. Obviously the empiricist idea of sensory impressions — or the closely related behaviourist idea of stimuli and responses — as representing the events is too simple. Until the problem of what is meant by 'event' is clarified, statements concerning the principle of temporal contiguity must remain diffuse. So far it must be concluded that from Aristotle to the present little progress has been made in thinking about the idea of an association. The fact that the use of the term is so diffuse implies, of course, that little progress has been made in the study of remembering and learning. In a recent discussion of the use of the term, Deese (1968, p. 97) underlined this point:

> Nevertheless, I think we need to remind ourselves that the whole course of the experimental investigation of association, including nearly all of its most recent manifestations, has been determined in a fundamental way by the oldest of philosophies — i.e. arm-chair — doctrine. In fact, the fundamental assumptions of the study of associative processes have been untouched by nearly an entire century of empirical investigation. It is hard to think of another discipline in which so long a period of investigation has not been accompanied by a fundamental change of assumptions.

Husserl [1913] and, inspired by him, Gestalt psychologists criticized the idea of the sensation as given, arguing that the sensation represented an abstraction. Instead of positing the sensation as given they posited the structure (the whole or the Gestalt) as given. While the criticism of the idea of a sensation has undoubtedly been fruitful for research in the study of perceiving, the term 'structure' meets with the same difficulty as does 'sensation'. (For a further examination of this point the reader is referred to Hamlyn, 1971, and to my previous work, Saugstad, 1965.)

The Gestalt psychologists did not deny that the activity of thinking was affected by learning, but they failed to provide a frame of reference which would allow the theorist to describe and explain this learning. (For a criticism of this point the reader is referred to my previous article, Saugstad, 1958.) Piaget (1950, 1971) has rightly criticized the Gestalt psychologists for not understanding that it is unreasonable to believe that mental structures do not change in the course of ontogenesis. However, in presenting his own account of this development he too, like the Gestalt psychologists, posited mental structures as given entities. As Hamlyn (1971, p. 19) has pointed out, Piaget is subject to the same criticism as the Gestalt psychologists:

> First, however, let me sum up in a general way what I have been saying about Piaget's position. In effect I have put Piaget in that tradition of psychology, of which the Gestalt psychologists are the most obvious example, which comprises to one extent or another a reaction against the sensationalist/ associationist position. That position involved a mixture of philosophical and psychological issues, and the same must be true, in consequence, of the

reactions. The only real basis for the atomism of associationism was the doctrine of atomic sensations and ideas which it inherited from the British Empiricist philosophers such as Hume. The Gestaltists put in its place another theory of the 'given' derived from Husserl and ultimately Brentano. Piaget's own reaction is more in the Kantian or idealist tradition, but his theory is as much dependent on a philosophical position as were those of the others that I have mentioned. My own opinion is that the mixture of philosophical and empirical issues involves in each case a muddle, that the philosophical and psychological questions which are at stake are different from each other, and that there are no grounds for the belief that philosophical questions can be answered by appeal to empirical evidence or vice versa.

Attempts at measuring experience

In connection with the difficulty of making clear what may be meant by 'experience' and 'sensation' mention should be made of the attempts of empirical psychologists to measure sensations. Around the middle of the nineteenth century Fechner (1860) attempted to do this by an indirect procedure (by a determination of so-called 'just noticeable differences'). In view of the difficulties attaching to the use of the term 'experience' it is not surprising that psychologists still discuss the question of what is being measured. (For a review of this work, see Boring, 1950.) More recently Stevens (1960), working in the Titchnerian tradition in the USA, attempted to perform measurements by a more direct procedure. He told the subjects to indicate the value of various types of impressions by means of numbers on some number scale. Evidently Stevens overlooked the fact that the report given by the subject indicates both his impression of the sensation and his use of numbers. Clearly, although Stevens has held it to be so, this is not genuine measurement. (Cp. my (Saugstad, 1965) previous criticism of this procedure.) Ross (1964, p. 136) expressed his criticism by saying that by using this procedure we have characterized 'how subjects employ *numerals* (i.e., certain linguistic entities) as responses to certain stimuli, but we have not established any relations between these *stimuli* themselves.'

Remembering and thinking

On a variety of occasions the normal speaker is capable of distinguishing between the use of the verbs 'to remember' and 'to think'. He would ordinarily distinguish between the expressions 'he remembers the solution to a mathematical or a practical problem' and 'he is thinking it out'. On the other hand, it is evident that on many occasions he would not be able to say whether the use of one verb or the other would be the more appropriate. We use the verb 'to remember' when some previously acquired information or previously learnt performances are reproduced. In contrast the verb 'to think' is used when previously acquired information is utilized in ways which do not involve mere reproduction, as when judgements, decisions or plans are made or when problems are solved. Situations requiring thinking thus involve some aspect considered in some way to be novel. What is to be regarded as an aspect of novelty is dependent upon what species is considered, upon the ontogenetic development of the individual, and upon the capacity and previous training of the individual. For this reason it is difficult to assess this aspect of novelty and thus to draw a distinction between the activities of remembering and thinking. The difficulty may be illustrated by the following example. In the individual learning to multiply, the task of multiplying two figures requires much effort and is regarded as the result of an activity of thinking. In contrast, in the individual trained in multiplication, the same task requires little effort and is regarded as remembering. A number of other examples could be cited where the distinction between the activities of thinking and remembering seems to depend upon the amount of previous training. Actually the distinction between thinking and remembering may ultimately be found to rest on the amount of previous training in the individual. This makes it difficult to regard the distinction as fundamental.

The difficulty of determining what is to be meant by the expression 'element of novelty' is a major obstacle to progress in the study of problem solving. As I shall argue in a later chapter, problem solving must be regarded as a type of task which in some way represents a novelty for the individual.

With regard to the distinctions between the activities of imagining and thinking and imagining and remembering it is obviously difficult to find clear operational bases for such distinctions and I need not discuss them in any detail.

Concluding remarks on the relationship between perceiving, remembering, imagining and thinking

As was made clear at the beginning of this chapter, it is possible, at least to a certain extent, to distinguish between the activities of perceiving, remembering, imagining and thinking by conceiving of them as capacities of various sorts. However, as I have pointed out, this conception has limited usefulness, and, as was further argued, it is difficult to find other ways on which to base a distinction between these activities. If it is accepted that no clear basis for distinguishing between the four activities is available, it follows that it is not possible to define the terms 'perceiving', 'remembering', 'imagining' and 'thinking' in a manner fruitful for further research. In this connection I feel I should stress the fact that I am not denying that the study of perceiving has proved to be a fruitful area of research. What I am arguing is that unless more appropriate ways of conceiving of this study are found, it is extremely doubtful whether research workers will be capable of defining new perceptual characteristics so that they can be fruitfully studied. As was pointed out by Judd (1951) and Granit (1955), since the beginning of the nineteenth century few perceptual characteristics have been defined in psychophysical terms. The advancement in the study of perceiving has mainly consisted in an increased understanding of the anatomical structure and the psysiological processes involved in sensory functioning. Of course, this increased understanding may help research workers to make better guesses with regard to the nature of the interaction between the organism and its environment, but it is difficult to see how it could provide a reference system for dealing with this interaction. In Chapter 8 I shall deal with the belief in so-called 'physiological reductionism' which has led to the overlooking of the necessity of studying the interaction between the organism and its environment.

Moreover it would seem to follow from the conclusion arrived at here that there is no possibility of fruitfully relating the activities of perceiving, remembering, imagining, and thinking to one another in a more comprehensive theory, although this has been attempted, for example, in the developmental theories of Piaget and Vygotsky referred to in the previous chapter and also at a less explicit level in psychoanalysis.

On the nature of learning

While Gestalt psychologists concentrated their study on perceiving and attempted to explain remembering and thinking in terms of principles derivable from this study, behaviourist psychologists concentrated on the study of learning and attempted to explain remembering, thinking and use of language in terms of principles believed to be derivable from this study. I shall show that an approach in terms of learning can hardly be said to be more fruitful than an approach in terms of perceiving.

There can be no denying the fact that in some sense of the word the activities of perceiving, remembering, imagining and thinking as well as a variety of other activities are affected by learning. Still, it is difficult to understand how a study of learning — as has been maintained by behaviourists — can provide a fruitful basis for a study of these activities or for a general study of psychology.

Apparently theorists concerned with learning in the tradition of Thorndike and Pavlov took over the presuppositions made by the British empiricist philosophers concerning experience. The reasoning of the British empiricists would run somewhat along the following lines: Perceiving, remembering, imagining and thinking have in common that they are concerned with experience; in perceiving, experience is immediately received, in remembering it is reproduced and recognized, in imagining it is represented, and in thinking it is utilized. According to this way of reasoning it would be natural to believe that fruitful accounts could be made of these activities if principles could be established for the acquisition or learning of experience.

In the discussion undertaken above of the use of the term 'experience', experience was found to be a highly abstract or Platonic entity. Apparently by basing an approach to psychology on conceptions of experience as learnt one meets with fundamental difficulties. As might be expected these difficulties are not removed when, instead of speaking of the learning of experience, one simply speaks — as theorists in learning do — of learning. Obviously no clear determination of the term 'learning' is possible. Evidently unless we know how the various activities develop, it is difficult to say how they are learnt. Learning and ontogenetic development are clearly intimately related to each other. In order to understand ontogenetic development it is essential that we are capable of stating what the maturational as well as the other species-specific factors involved are. Theorists in learning, such as Thorndike, Pavlov, Guthrie, Hull, Spence, Estes and Skinner, to mention some of the most influential ones, have failed to see this point and as a result have been incapable of conceiving of psychology as the study of interactions between the organism and its environment. (For reviews of the work of these theorists, see Hilgard and Bower, 1966.)

The usual type of definition of learning, for example, the one offered by Hilgard and Bower (ibid, p. 2), presents the frame of reference within which the study of learning in the Thorndike-Pavlov tradition has been undertaken, and I shall consider this type, and in particular Hilgard and Bower's approach. Prior to presenting their definition they call attention to the fact that learning is dependent upon maturation and other species-specific factors, but this does not affect their definition, which runs as follows:

> Learning is the process by which an activity originates or is changed through reacting to an encountered situation, provided that the characteristics of the change in activity cannot be explained on the basis of native response tendencies, maturation, or temporary states of the organism (e.g., fatigue, drugs, etc.).

As has already been noted, according to this definition the change in activity is not to be explained on the basis of maturation. Hinde (1974) pointed out problems met with in attempts to define the term 'learning' without due consideration for questions of maturation. Smith and Bjerke (1974) in their book on ontogenetic development have emphasized that the theoretical interest attaching to a study of learning which excludes considerations concerning maturation must be of very limited interest. If one insists — as I shall — that psychology is concerned with interactions between the organism and its environment, one may seriously question whether the type of definition which has hitherto guided the work of theorists in learning can be regarded as being meaningful. Is it at all possible to conceive of learning without in some way also conceiving of ontogenetic development? In this connection attention should be called to the use of the term 'process' in the definitions offered by Hilgard and Bower. Obviously the use of this term contributes to the covering up of fundamental difficulties met with in the study of learning.

If we grant that learning cannot fruitfully be investigated unless ontogenetic development is in some way considered, it follows that learning cannot fruitfully be defined unless maturational factors are taken into account. This is so because the effect of environmental influences on the developing organism is obviously dependent upon the maturational stage reached by the organism.

Clearly, even if it is always dependent upon specific types of environmental influences, maturation is genetically determined and dependent upon species-specific characteristics. If one follows this line of reasoning, as Lenneberg (1967) has emphasized, learning cannot fruitfully be studied unless species-specific characteristics are taken into account.

In order to be fruitful a definition of learning should also take yet another aspect of development into account. Whatever the way one conceives of learning in the mammalian species, account must be taken of the problem of transfer. Evidently unless learning is conceived of in such a way that it is understandable how learning in what appears as one type of situation affects learning in what appear as other types of situations, no fruitful conception of learning can be attained. This is so because we can hardly conceive of learning in any type of situation unless we also conceive of learning which has taken place in previous situations as having affected the reactions of the organism. Theorists in learning in the Thorndike-Pavlov tradition have tended to treat transfer as extrinsic to the task of learning. In contrast Gestalt psychologists have emphasized the fact that the problem of transfer must be regarded as being central to the study of learning and they attempted in various ways to account for this problem. (For a treatment of this problem by Gestalt psychologists, see Koffka, 1935; Klüver, 1933.) Theorists in the Thorndike-Pavlov tradition have usually suggested that the problem of transfer can be accounted for by a specific principle, the principle of generalization. However, as Lashley and Wade (1946) made clear, principles to account for similarity are lacking. As I see it, the problem of stating what is meant by similarity, to which I shall return in a later chapter, cannot be separated from the problem of stating what is meant by identicalness, and this requires a reference system in terms of which it is possible to state what is meant by identicalness, similarity and dissimilarity.

It follows from what has been said above that learning cannot be exclusively treated as an environmental variable. Learning must also be regarded as an organismic variable. This point has been overlooked by behaviourist theorists from Watson to Skinner. In contrast Pavlov, who took as his point of departure the physiological reflex, developed his approach more in line with modern biological thinking. (In a later chapter I shall return to difficulties attaching to the Pavlovian approach.) However, Guthrie (1935) and Skinner (1938) extended the idea of the conditioned reflex to include all types of reactions affected by learning. This practice was adopted by later behaviourists and a similar extension was made by Soviet psychologists. (On this extension by Soviet psychologists, see Luria, 1961.) While this extension of the Pavlovian term 'conditioned reflex' ('conditioned response') has made it more widely applicable, it has had the unfortunate effect that the use of the term 'learning' has not been considered from the point of view of biological adjustment. Thus, what the term has gained in practical usefulness, it has lost in theoretical fruitfulness.

The fact that since the beginning of this century theorists in learning have continued to think that their conception of learning could be fruitful is probably due to their having accepted the following three beliefs: (1) Activities reasonably referred to as psychological are describable in terms of behaviour, (2) psychological activities can be accounted for in terms of the physicalist conceptions underlying the application of the stimulus-response paradigm, and (3) theoretical terms can be defined by reference only to operational procedures. In later chapters I shall show that all three beliefs are of a dubious nature. The acceptance of these beliefs by behaviourist psychologists has caused them to overlook the fact that fundamental problems in communication are met with in attempts to specify the types of events studied in learning. Below I shall give an example of the arbitrary manner in which behaviourist theorists have introduced their terms 'stimulus' and 'response', causing them to treat the problem of learning in an incoherent and inconsistent manner. Due to the fact that theorists in learning have been unwilling to examine the fundamental beliefs underlying their study, this example, even though it is a few decades old, must still be regarded as representative of treatment of the problems. In what he (1943, p. 70) called *Demonstration Experiment 1* Hull introduced his two terms by giving the following description of how a rat learnt to avoid an electric shock given through the floor of a two-compartment box, a box where the animal could jump from one compartment to the other:

> After some minutes the technician throws the switch which charges both the partition and the grid upon which the rat is standing. The animal's behavior changes at once; in place of the deliberate exploratory movements it now displays an exaggeratedly mincing mode of locomotion about the compartment interspersed with occasional slight squeaks, biting of the bars which are shocking its feet, defecation, urination, and leaps up the walls. These reactions are repeated in various orders and in various parts of the compartment; sometimes the same act occurs several times in succession, sometimes not. After five or six minutes of this variable behavior one of the leaps carries the animal over the barrier upon the uncharged grid of the second compartment. Here after an interval of quiescence and heavy breathing the animal cautiously resumes exploratory behavior, much as in the first compartment. Ten minutes after the first leap of the barrier the second grid is charged and the animal goes through substantially the same type of variable behavior as before. This finally results in a second leaping of the barrier and ten minutes more of safety, after which this grid is again charged, and so on. In this way the animal is given fifteen trials, each terminated by a leap over the barrier.

On the basis of this description Hull proceeded to assign meaning to his two central terms:

> It is evident from the foregoing that the final successful competition of the reaction of leaping the barrier (R_4) with the various futile reactions of the series such as leaping against the wooden walls of the apparatus (R_1) squeaking (R_2) and biting the floor bars (R_3) must have resulted, in part at least, from a differential strengthening of (R_4). It is also evident that each of these competing reactions was originally evoked by the slightly injurious effects of the current on the animal's feet (the condition of need or drive, D) in conjunction with the stimulation (visual, cutaneous, etc.) arising from the apparatus at about the time that the reaction took place. The stimulation arising from the apparatus at the time of the respective reactions needs to be designated specifically: leaping against the wall will be represented by S_A ; squeaking, by S_{A^I} ; biting, by $S_{A^{II}}$; and leaping the barrier, by $S_{A^{III}}$.

As will be seen, by this type of description Hull merely put labels on specific reactions made by the animal to its environment. In order to define his terms in such a manner that they could be used in a scientific theory, he would have had to have stated the conditions under which the animal makes the types of reactions labelled. The only thing that can be learnt from this description seems to be that Hull was capable of using language in a way understandable by the ordinary speaker. Evidently, as was made abundantly clear by Koch (1954), Hull's terms 'stimulus', 'response', 'learning', and 'reinforcement' were left hanging in the air.

Actually Hull's use of the terms 'stimulus' and 'response' as labels attached to particular reactions is characteristic also of present-day behaviourist psychology. This use, it will be seen, is based on an uncritical use of ordinary, everyday language. Koch (1964) designated it as a type of scholasticism. In a later chapter I shall argue that the term 'stimulus' is an abstraction which defies attempts at precise definition.

CHAPTER 5

Perceiving, remembering, imagining, thinking and use of language

In the previous chapter we noted the close relationship between the activities of perceiving, remembering, imagining and thinking. In addition to being related to each other these activities are also closely related to man's use of language. The activities of remembering, imagining and thinking and also — at least in certain respects — the activity of perceiving develop as the human individual acquires use of language. Use of language in turn is closely related to culture. The individual acquires use of language as he learns to participate in the various cultural activities and as he learns to participate in the various cultural activities he acquires use of language. The close relationship between, on the one hand, the activities of perceiving, remembering, imagining and thinking and, on the other, use of language and culture as well as the close relationship between use of language and culture make the study of psychological functioning difficult.

Prima facie one might believe that it ought to be easy to distinguish between the activities of perceiving, remembering, imagining and thinking, and use of language. In everyday discourse we distinguish between the use of the verbs 'to remember', 'to imagine' and 'to think', on the one hand, and 'to speak', on the other, and we certainly distinguish between, on the one hand, 'to perceive', 'to see', 'to hear', 'to feel' and, on the other, 'to speak'. However, when we consider the fact that the acquisition of use of language plays a fundamental role in the development of the activities of remembering, imagining and thinking, and also possibly in the development of perceiving, we realize that the distinction between these activities and the activity of speaking cannot be so clear-cut. Still, while admitting that perceiving, remembering, imagining and thinking and use of language are related in the normal adult individual, one might nevertheless believe that one could draw a distinction between the first three activities mentioned and use of language on the basis of phylogenetic and ontogenetic comparisons. A variety of species which may be said not to have language, the system of communication developed by man, are clearly capable not only of perceiving, but also of remembering and thinking. And before the human infant is capable of speaking it is apparently capable of perceiving, remembering and thinking and probably also of imagining. One might, therefore, believe that the distinction could be drawn firmly on the basis of phylogenetic and ontogenetic comparison.

Theoretical psychologists from Wundt to the present have — with hardly any exceptions — believed that the distinction could be made. Vygotsky (1962) must be credited for having understood that the drawing of the distinction was more problematic than was believed by the early Denk psychologists, the Gestalt psychologists, Piaget or the behaviourists.

On further examination it will be seen that the basis for making such a distinction is not so firm as is usually believed. Modern conceptions of biological evolution make it difficult to base the distinction between these activities on phylogenetic comparisons, and the more advanced conceptions of use of language make it difficult to distinguish between them on the basis of ontogenetic comparisons. The belief that the latter basis for drawing the distinction is valid seems to reflect the confusion of the activity of speaking with use of language. When we say that the child who does not speak is devoid of language we overlook the fact that the child is growing up in a culture which is dependent upon man's use of language. It is not a wolf-child which is learning to speak, it is a child brought up in human culture.

Apparently in order not to engage in empty speculation the theorist in psychology must carefully consider the questions involved in distinguishing between, on the one hand, the activities of perceiving, remembering, imagining and thinking and, on the other, man's use of language. Below I shall consider the following four types of comparisons which may possibly be used as a basis for distinguishing between, on the one hand, perceiving, remembering, imagining and thinking, and, on the other, use of language: (1) Phylogenetic comparison, (2) ontogenetic comparison, (3) comparison between normal and abnormal development and functioning and (4) comparison between different cultural languages. The examination will be mainly concentrated around the distinction between use of language and thinking. In a later section I shall consider the distinction between use of language and perceiving, remembering and imagining.

Thinking and use of language

Phylogenetic comparison

Vygotsky (1962), one of the few research workers who has attempted to think systematically through the questions raised by a scientific study of thinking, argued that use of language and thinking, or as he expressed it, speech and thought, could be distinguished in the following way: On the one hand, species exist in which thinking may be said to take place, but they may only communicate to a minor extent by vocalization. On the other hand, species exist which communicate by vocalization but it may be said that they only have a minor capacity for thinking. As was argued in the previous chapter, it is frequently problematic to compare specific activities in man with specific activities in species other than the primate species. For example, the fact that birds or other species communicate by vocalization but only have a minor capacity for thinking can hardly be regarded as an argument in favour of a distinction between speaking and thinking in man.

Lenneberg (1964, p. 642) pointed out that the similarities noted between use of language and animal communication rest on superficial intuition and in agreement with Hockett (1960) he stressed the fact that in the discussion of these similarities criteria of a biological nature are usually confused with criteria of a logical nature:

> Furthermore, the similarities noted between human language and animal communication all rest on superficial intuition. The resemblances that exist between human language and the language of the bees and the birds are spurious. The comparative criteria are usually logical instead of biological; and the very idea that there must be a common denominator underlying all communication systems of animals and man is based on an anthropocentric imputation.

With regard to the comparison between man and the other primates, it must be clear that even if it is accepted that thinking can take place in other primate species which only communicate by vocalization to a minor extent, this does not necessarily imply that thinking and use of language can be distinguished *in man*. In order that the thinking found in other primates should be taken to mean that thinking and use of language were distinguishable in man, one would have to show that the forms of thinking found in the other species were identical to those found in man. Apparently, while it is reasonable to believe that thinking in man and other primate species has fundamental points in common, it is difficult to argue either for or against the belief that they are identical. For example, do chimpanzees solve the practical problems they can manage in the same way as man solves what seem to be similar problems?

The argument for making a distinction between thinking and use of language in man on the basis of a comparison with other primate species is further complicated by the fact that, as evidenced by the descriptions of van Lawick-Goodall (1973), other primate species, as for example, in the case of the chimpanzee, communicate not

only to express emotions and motivations, but also to achieve coopera-
tion of various types. Thus in all probability the chimpanzee is also
capable of communicating in ways similar to that of man. Consequently not only his thinking, but also his ways of communicating
may be said to be similar to that of man. So one may say that the
chimpanzee has a capacity for thinking as well as a means of communication. In other words in the chimpanzee there may be a
correspondence between the capacity for thinking and the capacity
for communicating.

To conclude the discussion of the problem of distinguishing between
thinking and use of language in man on the basis of phylogenetic
comparison I shall point out that man's capacity for using language
must be more or less regarded as constituting a whole in which
activities such as perceiving, remembering, imagining and thinking
are integrated. Lenneberg (1964, p. 642) expressed the same point
in this way:

> Cognition is not made up of isolated processes such as perception, storing
> and retrieval. Animals do not all have an identical memory mechanism except
> that some have a larger storage capacity. As the structure of most proteins,
> the morphology of most cells, and the gross anatomy of most animals
> show certain species specificities (as do details of behavioral repertoires),
> so we may expect that cognition, too, in all of its aspects, has its species
> specificities. My assumption, therefore is that man's cognition is not
> essentially that of every other primate with merely the addition of the capacity
> for language; instead, I propose that his entire cognitive function, of which
> his capacity for language is an integral part, is species-specific. I repeat once
> more that I make this assumption not because I think man is in a category
> all of his own, but because every animal species must be assumed to have
> cognitive specificities.

By emphasizing the fact that use of language would seem to constitute
an integrated whole of a nature indicated above, I do not want to say
that perceiving, remembering, imagining and thinking in man do not
share similarities with these activities in primate and other species.
I only want to emphasize the difficulty of drawing the distinction
between these activities and use of language in man on the basis
of phylogenetic comparison. I fully agree with biologically oriented
research workers that in order to throw light on the nature of
use of language it is essential to compare this use to communication in other species. (For a review of comparative work on communication, see Hinde, 1974.) By noting similarities and dissim-
ilarities in communication between various species we may arrive
at a more fruitful characterization of use of language, but in order to
do so in a meaningful manner, we need a reference system to
make clear what is meant by communication and use of language.

Furthermore, it is useful to investigate how one may teach individuals of other species how to communicate, as has been done by research workers such as Mowrer (1960), Gardner and Gardner (1969) and Premack (1971).

In connection with the last point I must call attention to the fact that the difficulty of conceiving of learning in terms of the approaches discussed in the previous chapter makes it difficult to draw inferences from the results of such teaching. For example, the question of whether or not chimpanzees are capable of use of language cannot be discussed without a consideration of how human individuals acquire use of language. Evidently, the way use of language is acquired very probably represents an important characteristic of use of language. As is well known, the initial occurrence of speech occurs at some definite stage of ontogenetic development. As was made clear by Lenneberg (1967), this initial occurrence of speech represents a fundamental characteristic of man's use of language. The fact that individuals of other species can perform in ways similar to man after having been taught to do so cannot be taken as evidence of the fact that they are capable of use of language unless it is also demonstrated that this teaching has led to acquisition similar to the acquisition of use of language in general. In discussions of these problems, which have been illuminating in other respects, the point made here has not been sufficiently clarified. (For a review of the discussion of whether or not apes are capable of use of language, see Ploog and Melnechuk, 1971.)

Ontogenetic comparison

As has been mentioned above, one might believe prima facie that thinking and use of language can be distinguished on the basis of ontogenetic development. Among others Vygotsky (1962) and Piaget (1950) have accepted this basis for making this distinction. Actually the belief is not easy to support. On reflection it will be understood that it is difficult to state when a child begins to acquire use of language.

As the human infant grows it has contact with adult individuals. Thus, from birth on there is social contact. Through this social contact the child is affected by culture, and since human culture is inconceivable without language the child is of necessity affected by use of language from birth on. It is hardly meaningful to indicate, as has been done for example by Piaget (ibid), the point in ontogenetic development at which the child begins to acquire use of language. Ordinarily, of course, we do not think that the newborn baby is acquiring use of language, but upon reflection it will be understood that from birth on the child is adjusting to a social environment involving communication. The infant's smiling and crying along with a variety of other types of reactions must be regarded as ways of communicating. For this reason it is not possible to say at what point in ontogenetic development the child begins to acquire use of language.

It is important to note that the discussion above fundamentally concerns the problem of what constitutes use of language. At the present stage of knowledge it is hardly meaningful to say that use of language is so constituted that up to some specific point in ontogenetic development the child is without use of language. Apparently the belief in the possibility of distinguishing between use of language and thinking on the basis of ontogenetic development reflects inadequate conceptions of language. According to these conceptions use of language is to be regarded as consisting solely of a set of signs and a set of rules for the use of the signs. It is not seen that language is a means of communicating about specific types of events and that use of language cannot be conceived of as being independent of these events. When the human infant begins to conceive of these events it should probably be said that it is beginning to acquire use of language. To conceive of the acquisition of use of language beginning when the child begins to understand and use signs which seem to correspond to our morphemes is therefore probably misleading. Before the child begins to understand and use signs of this type, it has already interacted with the adult individual and this interaction will in all probability have affected the child's conceptions of the sign as well as its conceptions of the events communicated about.

The belief in a distinction between use of language and thinking on the basis of ontogenetic development seems, as I indicated earlier, to be based on the confusion of use of language with speech. As was emphasized by Lenneberg (1967), the understanding of language is not at all identical to the activity of speaking. An individual may be capable of understanding and communicating without speaking. For this reason we cannot say that a child whom we may regard as being without speech is not affected by use of language.

This last remark about use of language and speech should not be taken to mean that the initial occurrence of speech in the child is easy to determine. As was emphasized by Brown (1958) the activity of perceiving of phonemes is probably dependent upon a complicated interaction between the organism and the environment and it is obviously not easy to state in a satisfactory manner when phonemes are perceived and correctly produced. Still, it seems easier to determine an ontogenetic stage where the child can be said to have begun speaking than to determine a stage when the child can be

94

said to have begun acquiring use of language.

As will be understood, it is difficult on the basis of considerations of ontogenetic development to argue for a distinction between thinking and use of language.

The point being made is of course *not* that at the early stages of ontogenetic development the child might be characterized by saying that it is acquiring use of language but that it is not thinking. The point is merely that at present attempts to draw the distinction on the basis of ontogenetic development must be regarded as most arbitrary and highly unsuitable for forming the basis of a fruitful scientific theory.

Comparison of normal and abnormal development and functioning

Attempts at distinguishing between use of language and thinking on the basis of abnormal development and functioning meet with the same difficulty as attempts to distinguish on the basis of ontogenetic comparison. While comparisons of the development in individuals deaf from birth and normal individuals are of great theoretical importance it must be clear that such comparisons do not, as was suggested by Oléron (1957) and Furth (1966), allow us to compare thinking in individuals who do not have use of language with thinking in individuals who do. Individuals born deaf nevertheless grow up in a human culture and thus cannot be regarded as not being influenced by use of language. Not having learnt to speak they may be regarded as speechless, but as has been emphasized, being speechless is not the same as not being influenced by use of language.

The difficulty of disentangling use of language and culture from one another is also present in attempts to distinguish between use of language and thinking on the basis of certain types of abnormal functioning which are the result of brain damage. Humphrey (1963) claimed as a basis for the distinction that aphasic patients may be found who are incapable of speaking but apparently capable of thinking. This claim would only be warranted if use of language and speech could be regarded as identical. Evidently it cannot be claimed that the patients who had lost the capacity for speaking had also lost the capacity for engaging in culturally determined activities. Since they are capable of engaging in culturally determined activities they cannot be said to be unaffected by use of language when thinking.

Comparison between different cultural languages

The individual familiar with the use of more than one cultural language will know that in some instances at least it is possible to transmit

95

what seems to be exactly the same information in two different cultural languages. For example, it seems possible at least in certain instances to transmit exactly the same information in the English and the Norwegian languages. This suggests that use of language and thinking can be distinguished from one another. The argument, which has apparently convinced many, rests on two presuppositions: (1) that it is possible to determine when the same information is transmitted in two different languages and (2) that it is possible to determine when two cultural languages are to be regarded as different.

With regard to the first presupposition it is difficult to find criteria for determining what is to be meant by 'the same information'. The problem of determining what is to be meant by 'the same information' has more recently emerged in attempts to develop so-called generative grammars. For example, do the two sentences 'The man is building the house' and 'The house is being built by the man' transmit the same information? (For a review of this problem, see Lyons, 1971.) The problem has also emerged in attempts to develop so-called extensional logics. Here the problem (the problem of synonymity) has arisen in attempts to determine when two words or expressions are synonymous and consequently can be substituted for each other. (On the problem of synonymity the reader is referred to the article by Linsky, 1967, b.) Apparently it is difficult to determine what is to be meant by 'the same information' without making an appeal to intuition. This means that it cannot easily be decided whether the determination is made on the basis of familiarity with use of language or is the result of an activity of thinking which is independent of use of language.

With regard to the second presupposition it appears to be difficult to find criteria for determining when two languages are to be regarded as different. Of course we may note differences between the two languages with respect to phonological, morphological and syntactic rules. However, since the individual making the determination was familiar with one language when he learnt the other we cannot know whether the information transmitted in this other language is transmitted by the application of linguistic rules which on further examination could not be regarded as thinking. This means that in order to decide whether or not two languages should be regarded as different we would have to have more satisfactory conceptions of thinking than are at present available.

In conclusion we may say that the first presupposition seems to lead to considerations of use of language which reveal that our conceptions of use of language are unsatisfactory, and the second presupposition seems to lead to considerations of thinking which reveal that our conceptions of thinking are likewise unsatisfactory.

Linguists have debated whether or not existing cultural languages have fundamental features in common so that one might conceive of some sort of universal language common to all mankind.
Chomsky (1966, 1972) has recently revived this discussion. Apparently the problem of determining the meaning of common features
cannot be solved by an appeal to the linguist's intuition. Specific
criteria must be found in terms of which a comparison can be made.

As Chomsky (1972) has made clear, the belief in a universal
language would gain support if it could be shown that use of language
is a species-specific activity of such a nature that all types of human
languages would have certain features in common. Support for this
belief has been provided by Lenneberg (1967). However, we must
not overlook the fact that the problem of determining the meaning of
'difference' with regard to two different cultural languages cannot be
solved solely by an appeal to biology, as was apparently believed by
Lenneberg (ibid). It is necessary to arrive at criteria for determining
thinking which are not dependent upon an appeal to intuition. Otherwise the term 'biology' will be devoid of meaning.

The Whorfian thesis

On the basis of a comparison between some American Indian languages and the English language Whorf (1956) suggested that the structure of the cultural language with which an individual was familiar
would determine his thinking. As I shall make clear in Chapter 11, the
use of the term 'linguistic structure' is problematic. Moreover, it will be
understood that this thesis is not easy to test. As was made clear above
it is not easy either to determine when two different expressions represent different forms of thinking or to determine when two cultural languages may be said to be different. However, the thesis might be tested
indirectly in the following way: Individuals are found who have the
same cultural background but who are familiar with use of one or
the other of two different languages. If differences are found in
performance of a task which may reasonably be said to involve
thinking between the individuals familiar with use of one cultural
language as compared to the individuals familiar with use of the other
cultural language, one could perhaps conclude that the structure of the
cultural language determined the thinking of the individual. Attempts
have been made by Carroll (1964) to test this thesis. While the
results of this type of research may prove to be of theoretical interest,
it will be realized that it is problematic to find two groups who
may be said to have an identical cultural background but different
cultural languages. Of course use of language and culture are so
intertwined that it is difficult to demonstrate that individuals who

have acquired use of two different cultural languages have the same cultural background.

When it is realized that in some way perceiving in man reflects his biological relationships with the external world and further that use of language and thinking are closely related to perceiving, it will be clear that it is difficult in an adequate manner to state a thesis to the effect that thinking is relative to linguistic structure, as suggested by Whorf, or that thinking is relative to culture, as stated by Vygotsky (1962). While there can be no denial that in some way thinking is relative both to linguistic structure and to culture, it is also reasonable to believe that in some way man's thinking is independent of the structure of the specific languages and cultures existing.

Theories of thinking based on ideas of use of language

The intimate relationship between the activity of thinking and the activities of perceiving, imagining and remembering on the one hand, and use of language on the other, makes it difficult to state more specifically what is to be meant by 'thinking'. Grauman (1956) was correct when he said that present conceptions of thinking all seem to be embedded in comprehensive philosophical systems. In this state of affairs the theories of thinking presented must have limited usefulness. I have already commented upon the theory of thinking in terms of mental elements. Here I shall give some short comments on the Watsonian theory of thinking as subvocal speech and on the Vygotskyan theory of verbal thinking as internal speech.

In the early days of behaviourism Watson (1929) advanced the view that thinking might be conceived of as subvocal speech. This view, which aroused quite a lot of interest, only seems to be interesting as long as one fails to ask what is meant by speech. Speech, of course, must also be defined by the behaviourist as something meaningful. This raises the problem of how one might conceive of meaning without at the same time conceiving of thinking. As Graumann (1965) made clear the Watsonian thesis cannot be tested merely by investigating whether movements in speech organs may be registered while what is regarded as thinking is going on. It is also necessary to demonstrate that stimulation of the speech organs brings about what may be designated as thinking. This clearly brings one back to the problem of providing a definition of thinking. (For a review of the Watsonian thesis of thinking as subvocal speech, see Brown, 1958.)

Taking as his point of departure Piaget's idea of egocentric speech in the child, Vygotsky (1962) argued that at the stage when the child was engaged in egocentric speech the child was speaking to itself. This speaking to itself gradually became inner speech. By means of inner speech, verbal thought could arise as a union of speech and thought. Vygotsky's theory is intriguing and he was able to bring forward various types of evidence in support of it. But there can be no doubt that the difficulty of defining thinking seriously restricts the possibility of finding decisive support for it. As has been noted, Vygotsky (see p. 48) recognized a prelingual type of thinking. Because it is difficult to see what can be meant by this type of thinking it is also difficult to see what can be meant by verbal thinking as representing a union of this type of thinking and inner speech.

Perceiving and use of language

The close relationship between thinking and speaking and between thinking and use of language seems to be more or less evident, and from the days of Hobbes to the present speculative theories of various sorts have been advanced to account for the relationship. (For an historical account as well as a critical review of the speculations, see Aune, 1967.) In contrast perceiving and speaking and perceiving and use of language have been regarded as clearly distinguisable. It is probably mainly to the credit of Wittgenstein (1953) that modern thinkers have seriously begun to question this latter distinction. If it is accepted that thinking and use of language cannot be clearly distinguished from one another, and further, as argued in the previous chapter, that thinking and perceiving cannot be clearly distinguished either, it would seem to follow that perceiving cannot be clearly distinguished from use of language.

The belief in a fundamental distinction between perceiving and use of language is probably based on considerations regarding the role played by learning and social interaction in the development of perceiving on the one hand, and the acquisition of use of language on the other. With regard to the role played by learning one might think that the development of perceiving was mainly a result of maturational factors while the acquisition of use of language was mainly a result of learning. Actually the development of perceiving, as has been emphasized, is the result of a complicated interaction between the organism and its environment and thus involves learning. Moreover, what has recently begun to be evident is that the acquisition of use of language in the child is highly dependent upon maturational factors. (On this point reference should be made to Lenneberg, 1967.) So clearly the development of perceiving and the acquisition of use of language in the child depend both on learning and on maturational factors.

With regard to the role played by social interaction, evidence is accumulating to support the view that the activity of perceiving develops as a result of an interaction between the human infant and the mother or some other adult individual in close continuous contact with the infant. Fundamentally the development of the capacity for perceiving may be dependent upon social contact. Conversely, it should be noted that social interaction is fundamentally dependent upon the activity of perceiving. The term 'social' is without meaning unless it has some reference to the activity of perceiving. According to this way of reasoning, an attempt to distinguish between perceiving and use of language in terms of social interaction will be seen to meet with difficulties.

Thus in terms of empirical evidence it is hardly reasonable to draw a hard and fast line between perceiving and use of language.

When the distinction between perceiving and use of language is considered along more general lines of reasoning the distinction becomes a dubious one. In the first place, if the distinction was a clear one it would be reasonable to believe that one might be capable of defining sensory impressions, or percepts of various sorts, without the necessity of reference to use of language. This in fact is the empiricist position, according to which all knowledge is reducible to perceptual impressions of some sort. Evidently this definition would have to be made in an ostensive manner. As was made clear by Hamlyn (1967, c, pp. 504-505), it is difficult to understand how in making his definition the empiricist can avoid presupposing use of language:

> The thesis that all the materials for knowledge are derived from experience may seem more plausible. Yet, despite the number of philosophers who have maintained this thesis, it is not altogether clear what it means. The version of the doctrine held by Locke and Aquinas looks like a psychological account of the origin of our ideas; in logical dress it amounts to the view that all our concepts or all the words which we use are definable in terms of those which are ostensively definable. Whether or not there are any a priori notions outside logic and mathematics, it certainly seems implausible to say that logical and mathematical notions may ultimately be definable ostensively. More important, the notion of ostensive definition is itself suspect. How could one understand what was going on when a noise was made, accompanied by a pointing to something, unless one knew the kind of thing which was being indicated and, more important perhaps, was aware that it was *language* that was being used? In other words, much has to be understood before this kind of definition can even begin. The notion that words can be cashed in terms of direct experience without further presuppositions is, thus, highly suspect. This is not to say that there are no distinctions to be made between different kinds of concepts or words, but merely that the distinctions in question cannot be made by means of any simple distinction between empiricism and rationalism.

In order to avoid presupposing use of language the empiricist would have to postulate that it is possible to communicate about sensory impressions or percepts of various sorts in terms of a private language, i.e. a language which was private in the sense that it could not possibly be understood by another individual. This has actually been the position taken by empiricists from Locke and Hume to Russell and Carnap.

In the previous chapter it was noted that Locke elaborated the Cartesian conception of perceiving. It will be seen that according to Descartes only the mind could have direct knowledge of the sensory impressions received. This knowledge must therefore be private in nature. Privacy, as emphasized by Peters and Mace (1967), is thus the hallmark of Cartesianism. As was seen from the quotation given in the previous chapter, Locke took over the idea of privacy and transmitted it to the succeeding philosophers in the empiricist tradition. From the British empiricists the idea of privacy was transmitted to Mach and the logical positivists. Furthermore it should be noted that the idea underlies the conceptions of consciousness presented by Husserl and later developed by existentialist philosophers, and finally that behaviourism rests on the presupposition that a distinction can be drawn between private and public experience.

The idea of privacy seems to have been taken more or less for granted until Wittgenstein challenged it in his later period. Wittgenstein presented a number of arguments against presuppositions made in attempts to find a basis for the idea. For example, he questioned the presupposition that identity between two successive sensory impressions could be established by an appeal to a faculty of remembering which was of a private nature and the presupposition that rules might be of a private nature. Identity and rules would have to be established by criteria which were inseparable from what he referred to as 'man's way of life'. Use of language could thus not be regarded as contingent on the objects or on the attributes of the objects of the external world or on emotions or motivational states of various types. (For reviews of the thesis that man can have no private language, see the symposium on Wittgenstein's *Philosophical Investigations* edited by Pitcher, 1966, and also the review article by Castañeda, 1967.)

Even if Wittgenstein may not have argued conclusively against the idea of a private language, there can be no doubt that it is more difficult to argue for this idea than is believed by philosophers and psychologists. Therefore, one may seriously question whether it can be fruitful to base a scientific psychology on an idea as dubious as that of a private language. Particularly in the study of use of language, perceiving, remembering, imagining and thinking it is probably of the utmost importance that the research worker painstakingly examines his position from the point of view of whether or not he is capable of communicating about the types of events he has postulated for his study. As has previously been mentioned, a reference to behaviour or operational definitions does not guarantee that he will be capable of doing so. In the study of psychology, the idea of privacy may actually constitute an obstacle to progress similar to that of the phlogiston theory prior to Lavoisier.

As was mentioned above, Descartes made privacy the hallmark of consciousness. It is important to emphasize the fact that this is closely related to the Western belief in the inner man and the mind—body dualism and in this connection that the ancient Greek philosophers (on this point, see Peters and Mace, 1967) do not seem to have drawn the distinction. On the other hand, one may lose hold of the problem if one one-sidedly attributes the idea to the Cartesian tradition, as Ryle (1949) seems to have done. As Malcolm (1966, pp. 66-67) has suggested, the belief in privacy comes naturally to anyone who philosophizes over the relationship between perceiving and use of language:

> It is worth mentioning that the conception that it is possible and even necessary for one to have a private language is not eccentric. Rather it is the view that comes most naturally to anyone who philosophizes on the subject of the relation of words to experiences. The idea of a private language is presupposed by every program of inferring or constructing the 'external world' and 'other minds'. It is contained in the philosophy of Descartes and in the theory of ideas of classical British empiricism, as well as in recent and contemporary phenomenalism and sense-datum theory. At bottom it is the idea that there is only a contingent and not an *essential* connection between a sensation and its outward expression — an idea that appeals to us all. Such thoughts as these are typical of the idea of a private language: that I know only from my *own* case what the word 'pain' means (293, 295); that I can only *believe* that someone else is in pain, but I *know* it if I am (303); that another person cannot have *my* pains (253); that I can undertake to call *this* (pointing inward) 'pain' in the future (263); that when I say 'I am in pain' I am at any rate justified *before myself* (298).

Thus both epistemological examinations such as those undertaken by Wittgenstein (1953) and modern research on the development of perceiving and use of language in the human infant indicate that the relationship between perceiving and use of language is extremely complicated. On the one hand, the acquisition of use of language presupposes an organization or structuring of the stimulation impinging on the sensory organs, and, on the other, the acquisition of use of language in important respects contributes to the organizing or structuring of the stimulation impinging on the sensory organs. The complexity of this interaction is illustrated by the fact that the perceiving of speech presupposes a complicated structuring of the auditory stimulation. When it is argued that use of language structures this stimulation it must be kept in mind that the perceiving of speech presupposes a structuring of the auditory stimulation, and, for all we know, the structuring of the auditory stimulation may be dependent upon the structuring of stimulation impinging on sensory organs other than the ear. Research workers such as Vygotsky (1962) and Luria (1961), who may otherwise be said to have contributed to what seems to be a more balanced view of the relationship between perceiving and use of language by stressing the role of language, seem to have overlooked this point.

In a discussion of the relationship between perceiving and use of language, mention should also be made of the fact that both perceiving and use of language have important motor aspects. The human infant learns about the external world by moving in it and by manipulating material objects, and he produces speech by complicated sequences of muscular contractions. An adequate account of the relationship between perceiving and use of language can hardly be given unless this motor aspect is taken into account.

Remembering and use of language

The difficulty of distinguishing between the activity of perceiving and use of language, as has been discussed above, also makes a distinction between remembering and use of language difficult. If what is perceived must be communicated about by using language, one must in all probability also communicate about what is remembered by using language.

Actually, the problem of what can be said to be remembered is a fundamental one. It will be understood that unless a test is made of what is perceived or learned in a memory task, it is not possible to say with any preciseness what has been remembered. This seems to be the conclusion arrived at by modern theorists concerned with remembering. Thus, Norman (1969, p. 125) concluded: 'Up to this point we have read and discussed a variety of phenomena and mechanisms associated with attention and memory. But we have avoided one basic issue: just what is stored? Unfortunately there are no answers.'

Obviously, if the research worker is to be able to deal with remembering in a rigorous manner, he will have to determine a unit in terms of which remembering can be described. The study of remembering was decisively influenced by the pioneer work of Ebinghaus [1885]. He believed — and made others believe — that he had constructed a unit in terms of which remembering might be determined. The unit he suggested, which, as is well known, consisted of two consonants with a vowel placed between the two consonants, was more or less explicitly assumed to have no meaning. Ebinghaus conceived of remembering as a more or less passive storing of material according to laws of association. It needs only a moment of reflection to realize that his so-called nonsense syllable is closely connected to use of language, and thus that in a variety of ways it can be ascribed meaning. If the nonsense-syllable is read aloud to the subject, the syllable will consist of phonemes which are related to use of language in innumerable ways. If the nonsense syllable is read by the subject, it will consist of letters which are related to language as it is written and, of course, also to the phonemes of the cultural language used by the subject. Thus, Deese (1968, pp. 100-101) stated that the difficulties involved in determining the nature of the unit in experiments on remembering were insurmountable:

> In the first place, there are difficulties in determining exactly what a single item is, as I have pointed out before (Deese, 1961). In fact, the difficulties are insurmountable. I cannot refer to a general proof here; however, a demonstration of the limitations is possible. The nonsense syllable, as the work by Underwood and his students on response integration testifies, is not a single item. We might suppose — at least for Underwood's late adolescent subjects — that a single letter would constitute a single item. Therefore, each nonsense syllable, before response integration, is defined as a chain of three items having some contingent probability between them. The recognition of individual letters, phonemes, syllables or any unit at any level of analysis requires a knowledge of the deeper linguistic structures (see Chomsky, 1964).

As has been made clear, a list of nonsense syllables can be learned by using different strategies. For example, the nonsense syllables may be grouped in various ways, identified with definite words or brought into various types of constructed contexts, etc. This means that it is difficult to state what has been remembered in some definite task. To say that some definite type of material is learned in the way that connections are established between stimuli and responses is of little help in explaining learning and remembering. The terms 'stimulus' and 'response' can only be specified by reference to operational procedures, but not in a general manner. After having examined a variety of approaches to the study of learning and remembering Horton and Dixon (1968, p. 578) arrived at the following pessimistic conclusion: 'After all, if we don't have any idea what a stimulus is, how can we possibly talk about associations being formed between stimuli and responses?'

In Chapter 9 I shall deal more extensively with the stimulus—response paradigm of the behaviourists and with the problem of saying in what sense a word or a verbal utterance represents a stimulus. At this point I shall restrict myself to emphasizing the fact that in terms of the stimulus—response paradigm is not possible to describe adequately what has been learned and what remembered.

In opposition to Ebinghaus, Bartlett (1932) underlined that remembering was the result of a construction on the part of the organism. As was mentioned in Chapter 4, Neisser (1967) and others have elaborated on this important idea. Bartlett (ibid), also in contrast to Ebinghaus, emphasized the fact that tasks designated as tasks in remembering involved other activities, such as imagining and thinking. This point has been emphasized by modern research workers (see, for example, Reitman, 1970; Paivio, 1971). While accepting the two points made by Bartlett I shall have to call attention to the fact that Bartlett found no way of dealing with the problem of what was remembered. Thus, in a well known type of investigation he read a story to his subjects and then after various intervals of time had them reproduce the story as they remembered it. Apparently, Bartlett introduced no technique for arriving at a description of how the story was understood (learned) by the subject.

A number of modern research workers have approached the study of remembering in terms of what is called an 'information processing theory'. In this approach it is stressed that remembering is not simply the reproduction of some previously experienced or learned material, but involves a construction. In this construction perceiving, remembering, imagining and thinking interact. While this conception of remembering seems to be in closer contact with reality than previous ones, it has the weakness that the term 'information' is left undefined. Research workers adhering to this approach restrict themselves to specifying the term 'information' by referring to operational procedures, and, as a result, the approach provides no reference system for a scientific study of remembering. The following quote from Norman (1970, p. 2) in an introduction to the modern theoretical study of remembering illustrates the diffuseness of the information processing approach:

> The general picture of human information processing is this. First, newly presented information would appear to be transformed by the sensory system into its physiological representation (which may already involve a substantial amount of processing on the initial sensory image), and this representation is stored briefly in a sensory information storage system. Following this sensory storage, the presented material is identified and encoded into a new format and retained temporarily in a different storage system, usually called short-term memory. Then, if extra attention is payed to the material, or if it is rehearsed frequently enough, or if it gets properly organized, the information is transferred to a more permanent memory system (or, in some models, the rate at which it decays decreases substantially). In general, the capacity of this more permanent storage is so large that information that is stored there must be organized in an efficient manner if it is ever to be retrieved. Then,

finally, when it is necessary to retrieve information from memory, decision rules must be used, both to decide exactly how to get access to the desired information and then to decide exactly what response should be made to the information that has been retrieved.

Imagining and use of language

While psychologists in the latter half of the nineteenth century and in the first decades of the twentieth century took an interest in the study of imagining, little attention was paid to this activity by psychologists of a behaviourist orientation and in general by psychologists in the period from about 1920 to about 1960. In the 1960's there was a revival of the study of imagining. Perky's (1920) early experiment, which demonstrated that under certain conditions perceiving and imagining are not distinguishable from one another, was duplicated and the conclusions from the experiment elaborated and extended (Segal, 1972). The problem of eidetic imagining was reinvestigated (Haber and Haber, 1964). A number of studies were made concerning the role played by imagining in remembering, learning and thinking. (For a review of this work, see Paivio, 1971; Kaufmann, 1975; Kessel, 1972; Pylyshyn, 1973.)

The modern work on imagining tends to treat imagery as entities existing in consciousness. Thus, imagining as an activity takes place in consciousness and is regarded as being partly or entirely independent of man's use of language. As was made clear by Pylyshyn (1973, p. 2) attempts to determine images as a content of consciousness raise a number of questions:

> Any analysis in the nature and role of imagery is fraught with difficulty. The concept itself proves to be difficult to pin down. Is a visual image like some conceivable picture? If not, then in what way must it differ? If it is like a picture in some ways, then must it always be a picture of some specific instance, or can it be generic (if such a notion is intelligible)? Could it, for example, represent abstract relations or must the relations in the image be of an iconic or geometric variety? Is an entire image available at once — as a spatially parallel static picture — or do parts of it come and go? If parts can be added and deleted at will, must such parts be pictorial segments (e.g., geometrically definable pieces or sensory attributes such as color) or can they be more abstract aspects? Could one, for example, conceive of two images of the identical chessboard with one image containing the relation 'is attacked by' and the other not containing it? If so, then in what sense could a relation be said to be 'in the image'? Must images in some important sense be modality specific, as implied by such phrases as visual image, auditory image, etc.? And finally, must images always be conscious? Can one, for example, make intelligible the notion of an unconscious visual image?

Apparently, serious difficulties are raised in attempts to state what is meant by mental images or imagery without reference to use of language. This means that investigations in this area probably only demonstrate that imagining plays different roles in different types of tasks and that the capacity for imagining, just like the capacity for thinking, may vary from individual to individual. Results of this type are not without interest. One outcome of modern research on imagining seems to be the discovery of the fact that imagining plays a greater role than had previously been thought in the mastery of a variety of tasks. The importance of developing the activity of imagining may have been greatly underestimated in modern education. As long as no independent determination can be made of mental images or imagery, it is difficult to argue for the functional significance of mental images in the mastery of various tasks. Thus, without denying that individual differences in the capacity for imagining may be positively correlated with a capacity for solving various types of problems, as was found by Kaufmann (1975), I shall insist that these correlations simply demonstrate that the capacity for imagining affects problem solving performance.

Because much research has been concentrated around the hypothesis that images and what are referred to as 'verbal processes' can be regarded as alternative modes of symbolic representation, I shall consider this hypothesis, which was presented by Paivio (1971, p. 8):

> Images and verbal processes are viewed as alternative coding systems, or modes of symbolic representation, which are developmentally linked to experiences with concrete objects and events as well as with language. In a given situation, they may be relatively directly aroused in the sense that an object or an event is represented in memory as a perceptual image and a word as a perceptual-motor trace, or they may be associatively aroused in the sense that an object elicits its verbal label (or images of other objects) and a word arouses implicit verbal associates or images of objects. In addition, it is assumed that chains of symbolic transformations can occur involving either words or images, or both, and that these can serve a mediational function in perception, verbal learning, memory and language.

The hypothesis formulated here raises a plethora of problems. What is the basis for the use of the terms 'image', 'coding system', 'symbolic representation', 'experience', 'event', 'trace' and 'association'? Paivio amassed experimental results of various types in support of his hypothesis. Here I shall only consider one type of evidence regarded as essential for maintaining the hypothesis. Paivio found that words of a more concrete nature elicited reports of more imagery than words of a more abstract nature. When these results are considered in terms of the nature of the tasks performed, they seem to be explainable in a simple manner. For example, if a person is instructed to imagine various types of stones, or various types of situations in which some definite stone may occur, the individual will give a report which will be interpreted as containing more imagery than reports given to an abstract word such as 'justice'. Evidently, it is easier to imagine instances of a stone than of justice or to imagine situations involving stones than situations involving justice.

So far no evidence of a decisive nature proving that a fundamental distinction can be drawn between the activity of imagining and use of language seems to have come forth. In order to argue in a decisive manner for the hypothesis presented above, one would have to demonstrate that communication was possible without necessary reference to use of language. It will also be seen that in the hypothesis the use of the term 'symbol' is highly problematic. (I shall return to this use in Chapter 11.)

Concluding remarks

The previous examinations have made it clear that it is difficult to draw a clear distinction between the activities of perceiving, remembering, imagining and thinking, on the one hand, and use of language on the other. The difficulty seems to be so fundamental that it is hardly possible to base a fruitful study of psychological functioning either on everyday use of language or on any or all of the four activities.

The examinations undertaken above suggest that a close relationship between the four activities and use of language exists, but it should be noted that this does not show that identicalness is involved. The fact that it is difficult to make a clear distinction does not warrant the conclusion that the four activities and use of language are identical. Whether or not the activity of thinking — carried out in situations where we do not speak — represents use of language, we cannot at present decide. Moreover we are in no position to say that the activity of thinking in man is not closely related to the activity of thinking in individuals of other species. Furthermore we are in no position to say that the activity of thinking in a child which has not yet begun to speak is identical to use of language. Evidently it would be unreasonable to deny the possibility that in some way the four activities may be independent of use of language. As long as this possibility cannot be excluded it seems difficult to deny that in some way it might be possible fruitfully to conceive of use of language in terms of the four activities. It must be borne in mind that, on the one hand, it would not be meaningful to ascribe logical priority to use of language over the four activities. This is so because we cannot say what we mean by use of language unless we presuppose that individuals communicating by means of use of language have a capacity for perceiving, remembering, imagining and thinking. On the other hand, it is difficult to understand what can be meant if these capacities (or activities) are construed as being independent of use of language. For further discussion it is important that we conceive of use of language in such a way that we do not exclude perceiving, remembering, imagining, thinking, use of concepts and notions of intelligence. On the whole, if we start out with a conception of use of language which is not sufficiently inclusive, we will end up with a theory which is defective. In this connection it should be noted that linguists tend to make this exclusion. Psychologists and biologists, on the other hand, tend to conceive of use of language as a way of communicating which is independent of the production of the phonemes which make up one of the bases for use of language. Thus in the discussion of whether apes could be credited with a capacity for use of language (for this discussion, see Ploog and Melnechuk, 1971) it was agreed that it was not necessary for human vocalization to be produced by an organism in order for it to qualify as having language. One may well ask how one could possibly test the hypothesis that human individuals could have a language which was not based on vocalization.

CHAPTER 6

On the nature of concepts, problems and intelligence

On the nature of concepts

The difficulties involved in distinguishing between on the one hand the activities of perceiving, remembering, imagining and thinking and, on the other hand, use of language are met with in attempts to conceive of concepts as existing independently without necessary reference to use of language. The term 'concept' has been a controversial one all through the history of Western philosophy. Thus, in a critical article on the treatment of the term 'concept' in philosophy, Heath (1967, a, p. 177) wrote:

> Concept is one of the oldest terms in the philosophical vocabulary, and one of the most equivocal. Though a frequent source of confusion and controversy, it remains useful, precisely because of its ambiguity, as a sort of passkey through the labyrinths represented by the theory of meaning, the theory of thinking, and the theory of being. Logic, epistemology, and methaphysics have all accordingly found use for it in one capacity or another.

During the last 50 years empirical psychologists have exerted considerable activity in investigating what has been called the attainment, achievement, or formation of concepts. Unfortunately, instead of attempting to elucidate the nature of concepts, they have clung to one philosophical tradition or another. In general both psychologists who conceive of their subject matter in terms of consciousness and behaviourists have treated concepts as extra-linguistic entities, and as a consequence the empirical study of concepts, referred to as concept formation, concept learning, or concept attainment, has remained a confused area of study. Below I shall consider various approaches to this study.

One of the first to investigate concepts empirically was Hull (1920). His study has been influential and will be considered a little more closely. Hull (ibid, pp. 5-6) listed what he referred to as three types of generalizing abstraction. About the third type, on which he concentrated, he wrote:

> In schematic outline the external factors conditioning this process may be briefly stated as follows: A young child finds himself in a certain situation,

reacts to it by approach say, and hears it called 'dog'. After an indeterminate intervening period he finds himself in a somewhat different situation, and hears that called 'dog'. Later he finds himself in a somewhat different situation still, and hears that called 'dog' also. Thus the process continues. The 'dog' experiences appear at irregular intervals. The appearances are thus unanticipated. They appear with no obvious label as to their essential nature. This precipitates at each new appearance a more or less acute *problem* as to the proper reaction. This problem largely monopolizes the focus of consciousness. Meantime the intervals between the 'dog' experiences are filled with all sorts of other absorbing experiences which are contributing to the formation of other concepts. At length the time arrives when the child has a 'meaning' for the word dog. Upon examination this meaning is found to be actually a characteristic more or less common to all dogs and not common to cats, dolls and 'teddybears'.

This quotation from Hull reveals that he came to make two dubious presuppositions. In the first place he presupposed that a concept can be defined in terms of common characteristics. Secondly he presupposed that words can be defined in an ostensive manner. I shall return to the latter presupposition in Chapter 10.

Concerning the former presupposition that a concept can be defined in terms of common characteristics, it is obscure what can be meant by this statement. If we take the concept of 'colour', what are the common characteristics of visual impressions that make us say that they have colour? Apparently when we use a word or expression indicating a concept, we are not able to state what the basis for this use is. Osgood (1953, p. 668), one of Hull's followers, understood that something was wrong about this conception of a concept. He said that Hull merely studied the development of labelling. This may be true, but not necessarily. A fundamental problem arising in this study is how to distinguish between the learning of a new concept and the learning of how to label an already acquired concept. I shall return to this point in the second part of this book.

Osgood (ibid) proceeded to point out that attempts at defining concepts in terms of perceptual relations did not avoid the difficulty mentioned above. Instead he suggested that concepts could be defined in terms of a common mediating response:

> *Common mediation process.* But are common perceptual relations any more essential to concept formation than identical elements? Must there be any similarity at all in the external stimulations? What perceptual commonness exists among mittens, hats, and neckties (they are all 'clothing')? Among crawl, swim and fly (they are all 'locomotion')? Among France, Japan and Russia (they are all 'nations')? It would seem that the only *essential* condition for concept formation is the learning of a common mediating response (which is the meaning of the concept) for a group of objects or situations, identical elements and common perceptual relations merely facilitating the establishment of such mediators. Several recent experiments on concept formation fit this view.

111

The attempt to define a concept in terms of a common mediating response meets with serious difficulties which will be discussed in the next chapter under the section Verbal Behaviour. At this juncture I shall just comment on a suggestion by Kendler (1961, p. 447). She stated that the acquirement of a concept could be conceived of as the giving of a common response to a set of dissimilar stimuli. Apparently Kendler confused two different questions: (1) The question of determining an operational criterion for ascertaining that the subject in a laboratory situation has attained some definite concept, and (2) the question of the nature of concepts. Kendler's definition, which was also adopted some years later in a review article by Kendler and Kendler (1968), may answer the first question, but not the second. Concerning the second question one may ask what, for example, the common response given to the concept of 'colour' is. Alston (1964, p. 26) commented on attempts to account for the meaning of words in terms of a common response by asking what, for example, is common to the situations in which the following utterances containing the word 'shirt' are made:

Bring me my shirt.
This shirt is frayed.
I need a new shirt.
Shirts were really worn before the fourteenth century.
What a lovely shirt!
Do you wear a size 15 shirt?

This comment by Alston is relevant to the definition suggested by Kendler. Evidently concepts cannot be defined either in terms of common characteristics or in terms of common responses.

In the quote from Hull given above, it was noted that Hull introduced his discussion of the nature of concepts by referring to the child's learning of some definite concept. This reference to the learning of concepts in the child is characteristic not only of behaviourists, but also of psychologists who conceive of subject matter in terms of consciousness. It will be understood that if a concept can be defined neither in terms of a common characteristic nor in terms of a common response, it is difficult to see what can be meant by 'learning' in this connection.

In the previous chapter difficulties attaching to the use of the term 'learning' by theorists in psychology were discussed. Apparently in the empirical study of concepts both the term 'learning' and the term 'development' may serve as cloaks to hide our ignorance. In connection with the behaviourist's account of the acquisition of concepts, it should also be noted that in it it is usually

112

presupposed that the types of learning on which behaviourists have based their accounts, are relatively simple. As pointed out by Leeper (1951), the descriptions given by human adults of the procedures adopted when they serve as subjects in studies of the use of concepts may apply to the procedure adopted by animals in the simpler type of learning situation mentioned above. The tasks involved in classical conditioning, the various types of instrumental conditioning, and trial-and-error learning studied by theorists in learning, may require that the animal forms hypotheses and tests them out as the human individual seems to do. This was the position taken by Krech (1932) when he spoke of hypotheses in rats learning to run mazes. The distinction between learning in simpler situations and learning in more complex situations may be highly arbitrary.

In his extensive review of theoretical statements and results of the empirical study of concepts, Johnson (1972, pp. 32-33) attempted to avoid the difficulties inherent in stating what is meant by 'a concept' by saying that a concept can be regarded as a hypothetical construct, specifically an ability construct. The concept as an ability construct was characterized in this way: 'A concept, then, is an abstraction, and achievement of the concept is demonstrated by use of the abstraction for classification, communication, and problem solving, according to the standards of the culture'.

Apparently Johnson was correct in stating that the use of concepts in a human individual can only be inferred from the way an individual within some definite culture makes abstractions, communicates, and solves problems, but this then disqualifies the statement as a description of a problem area in scientific psychology.

The acquirement of a concept must be seen as relative to the general development of the individual. This means that it is dependent upon ontogenetic development as well as on the specific cultural activities of the individual. In a criticism of Piaget's use of the term 'concept' in his developmental studies, Hamlyn (1971, p. 6) expressed the relative nature of the concept referred to here by relating the acquirement of concepts to general understanding in the individual:

> To have a concept is to have a certain form of understanding; to have a concept of X is to understand or know what it is for something to be an X. (To this extent understanding is a form of knowledge, and a thesis about concepts and understanding can properly be part of a theory of knowledge.) The knowledge of what it is for something to be an X can be manifested in a great variety of ways, although the range of ways in question will to some extent be delimited by the kind of concept that X is.

What must be clear is that understanding and thus the use of concepts in man cannot be conceived of as having an existence independent of man's use of language. In emphasizing this point it must be mentioned that this view of the use of concepts in man does not preclude that one can meaningfully speak of concepts in individuals of other species, as was made clear in the article by Heath quoted above.

Actually, as early as about 1930 Vygotsky (1962, p. 56) realized the intimate relationship between use of language and concepts. In a criticism of Ach's (1921) early empirical studies of use of concepts he wrote:

> All the higher psychic functions are mediated processes, and signs are the basic means used to master and direct them. The mediating sign is incorporated in their structure as an indispensable, indeed the central, part of the total process. In concept formation, that sign is the *word,* which at first plays the role of means in forming a concept and later becomes its symbol. In Ach's experiments this role of the word is not given sufficient attention.

The view that use of concepts cannot be treated without consideration of man's use of language is also slowly creeping into Western psychology. Thus, in a recent review of positions in and results of empirical research on use of concepts Kendler and Kendler (1968, p. 210) arrived at the following conclusion:

> These theoretical issues are influencing specific experimental problems and shaping general research programs. A frank recognition among most investigators is that, to some extent, future theoretical progress must await advances in our understanding of the relationship between conceptual behavior and verbal and developmental processes as well as the design of new experimental techniques to tap the wide variety of concepts humans do learn and use.

The fact that man's use of concepts must be inferred from his use of language and is thus closely related to his culture should not be taken to mean that concepts can be conceived of as arbitrary man-made constructs. Vygotsky seems to have thought so and Bruner and co-workers (1956, p. 232) explicitly stated this as their belief:

> The categories in terms of which we group the events of the world around us are constructions or inventions. The class of prime numbers, animal species, the huge range of colors dumped into the category 'blue', squares and circles: all of these are inventions and not 'discoveries'. They do not 'exist' in the environment. The objects of the environment provide the cues or features on which our groupings may be based, but they provide cues that could serve for many groupings other than the ones we make.

Man's use of concepts reflects his conception of the external world. Thus, the conception of material objects and their attributes, colour, form, size, etc., must be regarded as the result of an interaction between the human organism and its environment. In some

114

way then, man's understanding reflects his relationship to the external world, and it would be unreasonable to believe that concepts can be regarded as exclusively man-made.

The acceptance of the point made above implies that in order to come to grips with the problem of what constitutes man's concepts, it is essential to make clear in what sense man's understanding reflects his relationship to the external world. In Part 2 of this book I shall discuss this fundamental problem.

On the nature of problems

Problem solving represents another main area of empirical research on thinking. Like the study of use of concepts considered above, research on problem solving meets with fundamental problems of definition. The main difficulty in making theoretical statements on problem solving originates in the difficulty of saying what is meant by 'novelty'.

As was made clear in the preceding chapter we distinguish in ordinary use of language between remembering and thinking, even if this distinction is often not easy to observe. Apparently if some definite task is mastered by an individual by an activity which may be described as remembering, we should not regard this as problem solving. In some way the task must involve some aspect of novelty for the individual.

The question arises: Is it possible to specify this aspect of novelty without considering in detail the previous training or experience of the individual? On the one hand, it must be clear that it does not make sense to speak of a problem unless the individual is in some way capable of solving what is regarded as the problem. To take some simple examples, the problems dealt with by mathematicians and nuclear physicists are not problems for the ordinary citizen. Clearly the ordinary citizen lacks the training or the experience of the mathematician or physicist and is thus unable to understand what the problems involved are. On reflection it will be understood that the formulation of any problem is relative to the training or the experience of the individual. What is meant by 'a problem' must thus be considered as being dependent upon the general culture as well as the sub-culture into which the individual has grown. Furthermore what is meant by 'a problem' must also be considered as dependent upon the ontogenetic development of the individual. What are considered problems for adults cannot be considered problems for children, unless specific conditions prevail. When ontogenetic development is taken into consideration, it will be understood that every task mastered by a human adult which requires training, at one stage or another must have represented a problem to the child. Since we can scarcely conceive of any task mastered by the human adult which is uninfluenced by training, any task may be said at one time to have represented a problem for the human individual. Evidently, then, a problem must be defined relative to the training or experience of the individual.

On the other hand, as has been mentioned, problem solving cannot be said to take place when the individual merely reproduces what he has previously learnt. This means that we shall have to state when an individual uses his previous training or experience in a new way. If the expression 'a new way' could simply be determined by ascertaining that the problem situation was in some way different from situations previously dealt with by the individual, no serious difficulty would be involved. Evidently by taking the expression 'new way' in this sense, we would not have ascertained that the individual could not have utilized some previously acquired concept or principle to solve the problem, and we could not speak of a new way to handle the difficulty. The research worker would have to find a way of determining when a concept or principle is used in a new way by the subject. In order to do so he would have to state what is meant by a 'concept' or 'principle'. In the previous section on use of concepts we arrived at the conclusion that the use of some definite concept by an individual implied that he had a certain understanding and that it was difficult to conceive of this understanding as being independent of his use of language. So apparently we would have no simple way of stating what was meant by a 'concept'.

On reflection it will be understood that attempts to state what is meant by a 'principle' would lead us into similar difficulties as those involved in stating what is meant by a 'concept'. When we speak of principles we imply some sort of generality in application. Attempts at determining this generality would lead us into questions of understanding and use of language as was the case for concepts.

Moreover it will be noted that the research worker would not evade the difficulty by defining problem solving as an activity during which some novel principle was learnt. This was suggested by Gagné (1966, p. 132):

> The definition suggested by this discussion is this: Problem solving is an inferred change in human capability that results in the acquisition of a generalizable rule which is novel to the individual, which cannot have been established by direct recall, and which can manifest itself in applicability to the solution of a class of problems.

This suggestion by Gagné is valuable because it directs attention to an essential aspect of the question which seems to have been neglected, namely the fact that new rules or principles are formulated as the individual develops. Unfortunately this definition meets with the same difficulties as those dealt with above. In order to state what can be meant by 'a novel principle' we shall have to understand what is meant by a 'principle' or 'rule'. At this point the reader might object that references to the history of the advanced sciences make clear that novel principles have repeatedly been formulated, and that for this reason it ought to be possible to determine what can be meant by a novel principle. Without denying that this is the case, it should be pointed out that a characteristic of good scientific systems is that they are so constructed that they allow the research worker to decide on what constitutes novelty. Language as ordinarily used and as used in psychology does not allow of this decision.

Furthermore it will be understood that the definition discussed here is too narrow. We still speak of problems even if no novel principle seems to be present.

In the above discussion the difficulties met with in attempts to ascertain novelty have been considered from the point of view of the research worker. One might ask if the subject might not be able to decide whether or not he was using a novel concept or a novel principle? The research worker might simply ask him to decide whether novelty was present. It is difficult to see how the subject could do so unless he was able to state what was meant by a concept or a principle. Apparently he faces the same difficulty as the research worker.

Empirical psychologists have tried to overcome the difficulties referred to above by presenting various types of operationally definable criteria with regard to what constitutes a problem. Humphrey (1963, p. 312) stated: 'A problem is a situation which for some reason appreciably holds up an organism in its efforts to reach a goal.'

In addition to being ad hoc the definition is of little usefulness since it does not specify the types of conditions which must be present in order that one might say that the individual is not simply held up by what might be regarded as accidental circumstances, such as physical or physiological conditions.

Woodworth and Schlosberg (1954, p. 814) defined 'problem' in the following way: 'A problem, we may say, exists when O's activity has a goal, but no clear or well-learned route to the goal.'

While emphasizing the aspect of novelty, this definition is inadequate because it is based on an analogy which is more or less empty. Obviously it is not easy to state what is meant by a 'route' in an intellectual task. Johnson (1972, pp. 133-134), defined 'problem' in the following way: '... a problem arises when a person is motivated toward a goal and his first attempt to reach it is unrewarding.'

In addition to being ad hoc, as was the case for the definition suggested by Humphrey, Johnson's definition is too wide. A large variety of situations may be imagined in which the first attempt to reach the goal is unrewarding and which are nevertheless not reasonably to be considered problem situations. One could, for example, think of situations such as blowing out a burning match, the putting of a key in the lock of the front door in dim light, or the attempt to proceed uphill on a slippery road. In such cases the first attempt may be unrewarding, but they will not be included among problem situations.

In elaborating on his definition Johnson called attention to various uses of the term 'motive'. There is the problem of what is called external motivation in contrast to internal motivation. There is also the difficulty — not discussed by Johnson — that motives and sets are not easily distinguishable from one another. A fundamental characteristic of development in the mastering of intellectual tasks is that the ability to maintain various sets over a longer period of time increases. This ability to maintain a set not only distinguishes the performance of the expert (mathematician or physicist) from the non-expert, but also the performance of the human adult from the performance of the child. Thus, the use of the terms 'motive' or 'goal' cannot be considered without reference to the training and experience of the individual. Johnson attempted to deal with the problem of novelty by specifying intra-individual variability, inter-individual variability and the length of time required to solve problems. In view of what has been said above, it will be seen that these specifications are of limited usefulness.

In view of the fact that there is such a vast variety of problems, one would not expect that performance in problem solving could be adequately accounted for by the presupposition of a general problem solving ability. This position is supported by reviews of research literature by Vinacke (1974) and Bourne, Ekstrand and Dominowski (1971, p. 98). The last-mentioned research workers concluded:

> As should now be obvious, there is an enormous variety of problems, and it would be naive to expect that some people are consistently better or worse for all possible problems. Each type of problem doubtless requires different kinds of behavior, thus individual differences in performance will not be stable from one problem type to the next, and the correlates of problem-solving efficiency will change with the problem.

However, even if the question of the role of a general problem-solving ability is not yet satisfactorily answered, it should be noted that the finding of a problem-solving ability or a reasoning factor (on these points, see Johnson, 1972; Raaheim and Kaufmann, 1974) could hardly provide evidence that problem solving, as hitherto defined, represents an activity which can be shown to have clearly definable characteristics. When it is taken into account that the solving of all types of problems presupposes previous training or experience, it is to be expected that some sort of general ability can be inferred from the performances of different individuals on different types of problems.

It follows from the examination undertaken above that existing frames of reference do not allow the research worker to define problems in a fruitful manner. Terms such as 'concept' and 'principle' which may be needed for the definition are not easy to define. Moreover an adequate description of the previous training or experience of the individual who is to solve the problem necessitates an adequate description of the use of language in the individual. The latter description requires an adequate theory of use of language. The lack of a frame of reference will have as a result that the problem situation chosen by the research worker will not allow him to generalize to other types of problem situations.

As could be expected, theorists concerned with problem solving have concentrated on the question of how to handle previous training or experience. Theorists in learning, such as Watson (1929), Guthrie (1935), Hull (1943), Spence (1951), Skinner (1969), Osgood (1953), Staats (1970), to mention some of the most influential ones, have maintained that their principles of learning could be extended so as to account for problem solving. In Chapter 3 I made clear that the use of the term 'learning' by theorists in learning had remained vague and diffuse. For this reason it is difficult to assess their claims. In Chapter 9 the mediation hypothesis suggested by later behaviourists to account for man's use of language will be examined.

Owing to the inadequate frames of reference, empirical psychologists who take as their point of departure one of the existing theories of learning can hardly demonstrate more than the fact that previous learning affects performance on problem solving. This point, which is regarded today as commonplace, was important in the early history of psychology. Earlier theorists, such as some Gestalt theorists, for example, Wertheimer (1945) and Köhler (1929), had no place for the role played by learning in problem solving. (For criticism of the Gestalt work on problem solving, see Saugstad, 1958.)

A more direct approach to the problem of accounting for problem solving in terms of previous training or experience was taken by

Maier (1930). Oriented toward Gestalt theory, he attempted to demonstrate that successful problem solving involved more than having what might be regarded as the necessary previous experience. I (Saugstad, 1957) criticized his attempt, pointing out that when proper controls were introduced Maier's experiment would give results which allowed of the opposite conclusion.

In an attempt to assess previous training or experience I (Saugstad, 1955; 1958) conceived of problems of a practical type as consisting of components whose determination was arrived at in the following way: If one is to reach the solution to a problem various material objects have to be used in specific ways. In other words, they have definite functions in the solution of the problem. These functions should be regarded as the components mentioned above. The following procedure was adopted. Prior to the presentation of the problem the subjects were asked to state how they might use the objects in problem situations they could imagine. In this way their previous experience was assessed. Since it turned out that the subjects who had stated the necessary uses or functions for the objects tended to solve the problem when this was afterwards presented, I thought it possible to define a problem in terms of the uses or functions of material objects. The results of this procedure demonstrated that problems ought not to be conceived of as the type of whole or structure postulated by Gestalt psychologists, that probably sets did not operate as suggested by many theorists, and that the procedure of having the subjects state the uses or functions of material objects might be used as a test of creativity, as was done some years later by Guilford (1967) and co-workers. However, in conceiving of problem solving in this way, I overlooked the fact that functions must be seen as means-end relations and thus would have to be defined relative to definite problem situations. This would lead me back to the question of the definition of 'problem'.

Raaheim (1961, 1974) modified the procedure described above in that he presented subjects with problems in a general form, i.e. without telling the subjects which material objects were at their disposal. He found that subjects tended to proceed according to their verbal statements. The verbal statements could be interpreted in such a way that subjects conceived of problem situations in terms of what might reasonably be regarded as situations familiar to them. He defined 'problem' as a situation which in some way deviates from a familiar situation. While this demonstration may have highlighted various aspects of creative thinking, the approach is limited by the fact that it is difficult to see how one could give a fruitful definition of the terms 'familiar situation' and 'deviation from a familiar situation'.

In the results obtained by Raaheim and me (Saugstad, 1955; Saugstad and Raaheim, 1957) there is a clear trend which is of some interest relative to the problems dealt with in this book. Since this trend has not been emphasized in previous reports, I shall call attention to it here. In the experiments mentioned in the previous paragraph the subjects performed in the problem situations in a manner which could be predicted with close to complete accuracy on the basis of the statements made prior to their being presented with a problem situation. This agreement between statements made prior to the problem situation and performance on the problems is also found in Raaheim's (ibid) research. This demonstrates that the correspondence between use of language and thinking is very close. At least this was found to be so in adult human individuals. As will be remembered, prior to being presented with a problem, the subjects were asked to state all the functions they could imagine for a number of material objects. The results obtained by this procedure could serve as an accurate predictor of performance in complicated problem situations. The hypothesis that thinking is closely dependent on use of language is thus supported by the results of these experiments. However, it should be noted that the thesis advocated in this book does not concern the empirical relationship between the activities of perceiving, remembering, imagining and thinking, on the one hand, and use of language, on the other hand. The thesis presented here is that it is difficult to conceive of the activities mentioned in such a way that they could be communicated about without reference to use of language.

In more recent years a number of research workers have approached the study of problem solving by attempting to write programs for computers which simulate problem solving activity. These attempts may help us to understand this activity because the computer has the advantage over the human individual that one can assume with a very high degree of certainty that it has accurately followed a definite strategy for solving the problem, and further that it actually has utilized the information at its disposal. What limits this type of research is, of course, that the performance of the computer cannot be better than the program written by research workers. In our present state of knowledge it is doubtful whether research workers can write programs which allow one to test significant theoretical statements. Thus Newell and Simon (1972, p. 72) took as their point of departure the following definition of 'problem', which is permeated by a number of fundamental difficulties:

A person is confronted with a *problem* when he wants something and does not know immediately what series of actions he can perform to get it. The desired object may be very tangible (an apple to eat) or abstract (an

121

elegant proof for a theorem). It may be specific (that particular apple over there) or quite general (something to appease hunger). It may be a physical object (an apple) or a set of symbols (the proof of a theorem). The actions involved in obtaining desired objects include physical actions (walking, reaching, writing), perceptual activities (looking, listening), and purely mental activities (judging the similarity of two symbols, remembering a scene, and so on).

In view of the discussions presented in this chapter and those preceding it one must ask: What is meant by 'to know' and 'immediately' in this connection? And further what is meant by 'a physical object', by 'perceptual activities' and 'purely mental activities'? In a later chapter difficulties attaching to the use of the term 'symbol' will be discussed. Also mention should be made of the fact that, as was made clear for example by the mathematician Poincaré [1902], from the point of view of an empirical study of thinking the term 'proof' is not easy to introduce in such a manner that it can be consistently used in connection with *different* types of task. Obviously many of the questions raised here concern the reference system and cannot be answered by reference to the results of empirical research.

In addition to the fundamental weaknesses pointed out here it should be noted that Newell and Simon (ibid, p. 73) conceived of information in a crude Cartesian manner and of logic as representing a realm independent of use of language. The statement that the human individual interprets some information apparently presupposes that there must be some homunculus located inside the individual's head who is engaged in evaluating and judging. Gagné (1966, pp. 133, 134) emphasized the fundamental difficulties met with in attempts to specify the relationship between a physical description and the concepts used by the human individual:

> In contrast, then, to simpler forms of learning, the stimulus situation for problem solving needs to be described in terms of the concepts (classes of objects or events) of which it is composed. This may be the reason why it is possible to think of problem solving as a task of 'information processing'. If one can assume that the physical stimuli are first conceptualized (and thus that they convey information), it is reasonable to suppose that the next step is one of processing this information. It needs to be pointed out, however, that assuming the stimuli for problem solving to be concepts does not at all help to explain how they got that way. There still remains the very difficult job of accounting for the transformation of card spots into numbers, or matchsticks into squares, or printed marks into letters and words. In other words, a process of 'stimulus processing' underlies the formation of concepts, which in turn become the stimuli to be considered in problem solving.

Apparently, our ignorance about how we use language sets serious limits on the writing of programs which may allow the research worker to test significant theoretical statements.

122

In connection with the ignorance of our use of language it should be noted that the difficulties arising as a result of this ignorance cannot be overcome by selecting problems from mathematics or logic, or other branches of science. On the contrary, the difficulties seem to become more acute because we are not capable of stating how these branches of science are related to man's use of language. It would be naive to presuppose that these branches represented domains of an extra-linguistic nature. Of course, in order to study thinking as carried out within the various branches of science as well as that involved in the playing of games such as chess, one must have a reference frame outside these sciences or games. Too often philosophers and psychologists have believed that conceptions of consciousness can provide such a frame of reference.

The weaknesses pointed out in the study of the various approaches to the empirical study of problem solving would seem necessarily to lead to the belief that progress in this area must have been small. Apparently this belief is shared by a number of experienced workers in this area. Thus both Gagné (ibid) and Johnson (ibid) who, as we have seen, discussed the difficulties met with in attempts to define 'problem' gave expression to this belief. The latter (Johnson, 1972, p. 18) stated his belief in this way:

> We must admit that, in the accuracy of their predictions, psychological theories are not very successful. Predictions based on current theories are only slightly more accurate than those based on the intuitions of an intelligent layman. But psychological theories, including theories of thinking, generate interesting experiments and promise greater understanding in the future. Such theories have some value in explaining the behavior of the subject of an experiment; they have greater value in explaining the behavior of the experimenter who designs the experiment and interprets the results.

The present writer is more negative in his evaluation of the work done because he believes that what is lacking is a reference system which may allow the research worker to decide which experiments are interesting.

The study of intelligence

In the introductory chapter in the section entitled *An historical sketch of approaches to psychology* I mentioned that Galton (1883), the pioneer in the study of intelligence, did not appear to have had very clear ideas about the study he initiated. Galton seems to have believed that man's adjustment to his environment essentially depended upon the acuity of his senses because the tests he designed to measure what he referred to as human faculties were mainly tests for sensory acuity. Unfortunately he did not correlate performance on one test with performance on other tests in the individuals he tested. Nor did he correlate performance on the tests with performance on scholastic tasks. This was first done by Wissler (1901), about two decades after Galton published his ideas about tests and human faculties. Wissler found zero or low correlations. Binet (1905) reoriented the study of human faculties. His aim was to construct tests which might predict scholastic achievement in children in elementary schools. He took as his point of departure what according to his reasoning might be regarded as the abilities underlying this achievement. As has been admitted by Guilford (1967), later theorists within the testing movement were little concerned with questions pertaining to the nature of the subject matter studied. As I argued in the introductory chapter, this lack of concern reflects positivist thinking about the nature of reality and science. The study of intelligence, as the study was named in the 1890's, came to be conceived of more or less as a study of scholastic achievement regarded as some sort of totality. Guilford (ibid) attempted to extend this conception so that the study of intelligence could aim at accounting for all conceivable abilities important in accounting for man's adjustment to culture.

Whatever the way one conceives of the procedures followed by research workers within the testing movement, a description of these procedures must include statements of the presuppositions underlying the introduction of the individual tests as well as the assemblies or batteries of tests. What has become apparent today is that performance on all available tests is heavily influenced by learning and thus by culture. This means that the introduction of the tests presupposes conceptions of the nature of human culture. Clearly the difficulty of conceiving of human culture in a fruitful manner restricts the usefulness of the procedure, and the weakness in the thinking of the research workers in this area of research is mainly to be found in the fact that this point has never been seriously considered. In this connection it should be noted that cross-cultural studies of intelligence meet with serious difficulties because performance on a given type of test depends upon familiarity with specific tasks. For example, individuals who belong to a culture in which fishing, sailing and navigation are of little significance will answer questions pertaining to these activities less well than individuals belonging to a culture where these activities are of great significance.

Conceptions of human culture are necessarily closely related to conceptions of man's use of language. In testing procedure, conceptions of man's use of language are based on an intuitive understanding. This intuitive understanding directs procedure in the following ways: (1) It determines the choice of tests made by the theorist, (2) it determines the constructions of the individual tests, and (3) it forms the basis for the interpretation of the answers given to the questions by the individuals tested. When it is taken into account how enormously complex man's use of language in all probability is, the limitations of testing procedure become apparent.

To illustrate how dependent testing procedure is upon the understanding of use of language in the normal adult individual, I shall quote from one of the most advanced theorists in the study of intelligence. In his structure of intellect model, Guilford (1967, p. 62) referred to factors which involved 'operations'. Among such factors perceptual, memory and reasoning factors had previously been recognized. Guilford found that additional factors were needed. To these factors he made reference in the following manner:

> It became obvious that in addition to memory and evaluation, new operation categories were needed. Reasoning proved to be a poor categorical concept because it could not be uniquely defined. Creative-thinking abilities seemed to have properties of their own, involving fluency, flexibility and elaboration abilities; so a class of factors was given the title of 'divergent-thinking' abilities. The representative tests are all of completion form, and the examinee makes a good score for the number and variety of his responses and sometimes for high quality. It was recognized that there were other tests in which the examinee has to generate his own answer to each item but that it must satisfy a unique specification or set of specifications. A set of these abilities, parallel to the divergent-thinking abilities, suggested the title of 'convergent thinking'; in accordance with the information given in the item, the examinee must converge upon the one right answer. To avoid the ambiguity of the term *thinking,* the later substitution of the term *production* was made. Thus, two operation categories, divergent production and convergent production were adopted.

It will be seen from this quotation that the research worker has to rely heavily on his understanding of use of language to evaluate number and variety, and high quality of responses to questions in a test. In addition it must be clear that the introduction of the new factors suggested here is dependent upon the ordinary use in language of the words 'perceiving', 'remembering' and 'reasoning'.

In connection with the points made here concerning the limitations of the testing procedure, attention should be called to the fact that it is difficult to conceive of ontogenetic development in terms of the results of this procedure. In Chapter 2 of this book I mentioned the difficulty of conceiving of development in terms of a global intelligence score. Apparently, even if intelligence is conceived of in terms of the large number of abilities suggested by Guilford, it is not easy to imagine earlier stages in ontogenetic development where one might find activities corresponding to those described by the testing procedure. Hunt and Kirk (1971, p. 286) commented upon the problem of conceiving of development in terms of factors in the following way:

In fact, except for some of the abilities of Guilford (1967) which derive in large part from his intuition, factored abilities lack for us intuitive reality. They are of little use in observing and understanding the behavioral development of a child. They are of little use in choosing the circumstances best calculated to foster the development of new levels of ability in children. We contend that the traditional concept of intelligence as a continuous variable measurable by mental age and the IQ and conceived as a forcelike general ability has been of highly limited use in education and in the study of the nature of psychological development. We contend that the very existence of these measurement concepts of mental age and IQ and g have stood in the way of serious consideration of the concept of intellectual development as a hierarchy of learning sets which underlie a sequential epigenesis in the structure of information processing. We contend that this traditional view of intelligence has stood in the way of investigating the behavioral landmarks in intellectual development and the kinds of encounters with circumstances upon which their development depends.

In connection with the problem discussed above, mention should be made of the fact that the so-called non-verbal tests should not be regarded as being uninfluenced by man's use of language. They are non-verbal in the sense that solutions to the problems presented do not require reactions of a verbal nature. But without denying that information of theoretical significance may be obtained by comparing performance on non-verbal tests with performance on verbal ones, it must be clear that both the constructor of the non-verbal test and the individual taking the test are familiar with use of language. Moreover in order to be able to perform on a non-verbal test the individual taking the test must ordinarily receive complicated verbal instructions. There is thus no basis for maintaining that thinking and use of language can be distinguished by reference to differences in performance on non-verbal and verbal tests.

Of course, the fact that testing procedure is so heavily influenced by conceptions of culture and of intuitions about man's use of language, does not preclude the fact that important relationships can be — or have been — established between the various types of tasks forming the basis of the tests. Apparently, it is at least to some extent possible to evaluate the consistency of the interpretations given (of the tasks performed) on the basis of the results of testing procedure. (On this point see the critical evaluations of the results of testing procedure by Anastasi, 1958; Cronbach, 1960; Guilford, 1967.)

In connection with the problem of evaluating the results of testing procedure mention should be made of the fact that this procedure rests on a type of reasoning about similarity between tasks which should probably be regarded as a significant methodological innovation. A central idea underlying the procedure is that performance on tasks which are similar in nature will tend to correlate positively

126

among individuals with a similar background. Apparently it is possible that conceptions of similarity may be fruitfully explored in this way.

By way of conclusion I should like to point out that the fruitfulness of the study of intelligence is dependent upon the fruitfulness of the intuitions which underly conceptions of culture and use of language. As has been made clear it cannot be precluded that these intuitions may prove to provide a useful framework. On the other hand, it is also possible that these intuitions are the results of more or less empty speculation. It should be noted that the use of the term 'intelligence', which according to Guilford (1967) was introduced in the 1890's, does not seem to correspond to the use of any word in any cultural language. If, as it is reasonable to suspect, use of language represents the reality to be explored in the scientific study of psychology, this may be taken to indicate that the idea of intelligence is an abstraction which must be regarded as being only loosely related to reality. Possibly the introduction of the term 'intelligence' was made on a basis similar to the introduction of the term 'consciousness' by Descartes, i.e. based on empty speculation emanating from the lack of coherence and consistency in some particular metaphysical outlook.

CHAPTER 7

Psychology as the study of consciousness

In the previous chapter I argued that it was difficult to draw a clear distinction between perceiving, remembering, imagining and thinking on the one hand, and use of language on the other hand. When this distinction is abandoned — and this I think is essential if a fruitful scientific psychology is to be developed — it will be understood that it is difficult to argue for the existence of domains of events of an extra-linguistic nature.

Conceptions of material objects and their attributes, moving bodies and living individuals must then in some way depend upon use of language. By beginning an argument by postulating events of an extra-linguistic nature, we will inevitably become entangled in the problem of a private language and will not know whether we are communicating, or simply mis-using language.

In developing their systems, Western thinkers have postulated various domains of events of an extra-linguistic nature and psychologists have more or less uncritically accepted various beliefs in domains of this sort. Of decisive importance for the study of psychology has been the belief in a domain of events belonging to consciousness or mind. In turn the postulation of consciousness led to the postulation of the unconscious. As was mentioned in the introductory chapter, the idea of the unconscious limits the role attributed to consciousness, but since it builds upon it the points of criticism raised against the idea of consciousness apply to it. Moreover, behaviourism — just like psychoanalysis — does not represent a rejection of the idea of consciousness either. Behaviourists rejected the belief that consciousness is the subject matter of psychology, but not the idea of consciousness. Thus they accepted the distinction between public and private data and in this way entangled themselves in problems of consciousness. (On this point, see Spence, 1948; Skinner, 1964.) Here the behaviourist position is in line with that of the logical positivists. (On this point in logical positivism, see the article by Passmore, 1967, a.)

128

Problems of consciousness

Conceptions about consciousness are intimately related to ideas about an inner man and to ideas of the privacy of percepts, memories, images, thoughts, feelings and impulses to act. These ideas were developed in the philosophies of Plotinus and St. Augustin (on this point, see Pongratz, 1967), but as Peters and Mace (1967) made clear, these ideas are traceable to Philo, who lived in the first century before Christ. However, as Peter and Mace (ibid, p. 4) made clear, the idea of privacy is not found in Greek philosophy:

> It is difficult for modern Western man to grasp that the Greeks really had no concept of consciousness in that they did not class together phenomena as varied as problem solving, remembering, imagining, perceiving, feeling pain, dreaming and acting on the grounds that all these are manifestations of being aware or being conscious.

Having emphasized this point, Peters and Mace went on to show how the idea of private experience developed as a result of the increase of interest in individual experience following the breaking up of the self-sufficiency of the city states.

The idea of an inner man was made central in medieval thinking about man. When Descartes developed his system he elaborated this idea into a philosophy of mind and consciousness. (For a review of Descartes' philosophy, see Williams, 1967.) The philosophy of Descartes greatly influenced Western thinking. The idea of consciousness was given prominence in the philosophies of Leibniz, the British empiricists, in Kant, Hegel, Brentano, in the logicians inspired by Stuart Mill such as Frege, Russell and Carnap, and in Husserl and the phenomenologists of the twentieth century. It has permeated the thinking of theologians, linguists, sociologists, and, last but not least, that of psychologists.

However, even if the great influence exerted by Descartes is accepted, it is, as was mentioned in Chapter 5 (p. 102), hardly reasonable to attribute the idea of an inner man and consciousness solely to him.

This point is of some importance, because one might otherwise believe that the problem of privacy is eliminated by a criticism of Cartesian philosophy. The problem seems to remain, even if instead of speaking of conscious or internal elements one speaks of dispositions to react, as has been done by Ryle (1949), Aune (1967) and others. An account must then be given of how the various dispositions to react are related to use of language. (Cp. here the article on behaviourism by Taylor, 1967.) Nor is the problem removed when thinking is conceived of as being in dialectical opposition to perceiving, as was done by Vygotsky (1962) and Luria (1961).

Characteristic of the various conceptions of consciousness is the belief in certain types of inner events whose existence is held to be independent of use of language. Locke [1690, Bk. III, p. 12] presented this belief in a way which is not only characteristic of British empiricism up to Russell and Moore, but also of Continental philosophers from Descartes and Leibniz through Kant and Hegel to Brentano and Husserl and the phenomenologists of the modern era:

> The use men have of these marks being either to record their own thoughts for the assistance of their own memory or, as it were, to bring out their *ideas* and lay them before the view of others: *words, in their primary or immediate signification, stand for nothing but the ideas in the mind of him that uses them,* how imperfectly soever or carelessly those ideas are collected from the things which they are supposed to represent. When a man speaks to another, it is that he may be understood; and the end of speech is that those sounds, as marks, may make known his *ideas* to the hearer. That then which words are the marks of are the *ideas* of the speaker; nor can anyone apply them as marks, immediately, to anything else but the *ideas* that he himself hath, for this would be to make them *signs* of his own conceptions and yet apply them to other *ideas,* which would be to make them signs and not signs of his *ideas* at the same time, and so in effect to have no signification at all. Words being voluntary signs, they cannot be voluntary signs imposed by him on things he knows not. That would be to make them signs of nothing, sounds without signification. A man cannot make his words the signs either of qualities in things or of conceptions in the mind of another, whereof he has none in his own. Till he has some *ideas* of his own, he cannot suppose them to correspond with the conceptions of another man; nor can he use any signs for them: for thus they would be the signs of he knows not what, which is in truth to be the signs of nothing. But when he represents to himself other men's *ideas* by some of his own, if he consent to give them the same names that other men do, it is still to his own *ideas:* to *ideas* that he has, and not to *ideas* that he has not.

The above quote from Locke expresses in a direct and crude form the central belief in Cartesianism that the content of consciousness can be regarded as having a separate existence independent of use of language. As an illustration of the firm grip this belief has had on Western thinkers, one can compare the Lockian statement to the following one made by Wundt (1907, p. 349), where the latter expressed his ideas about the possibility of investigating thinking experimentally. It will be noted that in essence the belief expressed here is identical to that of Locke:

> Bei solchen Selbstbeobachtungen wurde mir nun vollkommen klar, dass man einen Gedanken nicht erst bildet, während man den Satz ausspricht, sondern dass er, bevor wir nur zum ersten Worte ansetzen, als Ganzes schon in unserem Bewusstsein steht. Dabei findet sich allerdings zunächst keine einzige der Wort- oder sonstigen Vorstellungen, die sich bei dem Durchlaufen und dem sprachlichen Ausdrucke des Gedankens bilden, in dem Blickpunkte des Bewusstseins, sondern erst in dem Moment, wo wir den Gedanken entwickeln, werden nun seine einzelnen Teile sukzessiv zu deutlichem Bewusstsein erhoben.

In modern psychology the Lockian idea of the existence of a distinction between the content of consciousness and use of language is echoed when — as was noted in the previous chapter — in their study of concepts empirical psychologists draw a distinction between concepts and use of language.

The examination previously undertaken of the relationship between the activities of perceiving, remembering, imagining and thinking, on the one hand, and use of language, on the other, showed that it is questionable whether percepts, memories, images, thoughts, or processes can be communicated about without reference to use of language. Even if one were forced to admit that the possibility that one might be able to refer to consciousness of some sort which was independent of use of language cannot be excluded, there seems to be no way of conceiving of a means of communicating about such mental content. This being so the postulation of the existence of conscious experience in the form of mental elements, structures, processes, intentions, or meanings must of necessity represent empty speculation.

A main reason why the idea of consciousness as a domain of events whose existence is independent of use of language has had such a firm grip on Western thinking may be found in the fact that man's use of language may easily appear as mysterious. By postulating the entity of consciousness containing the percepts, memories, images and thoughts of man it has been believed that a satisfactory and non-mysterious explanation of this use has been provided. It is easy to see that this belief may have fatal consequences for empirical psychology. Fundamentally it represents a confusion of description and explanation. Even if it is granted, as was done in Chapter 1 of this book, that descriptions and explanations cannot be clearly distinguished from one another in scientific theory, science cannot be advanced by substituting explanations for descriptions. This seems to have happened in the early as well as the later psychology of consciousness, and also in behaviourism. In the following pages I shall briefly indicate some of the difficulties met with in introspective psychology, in phenomenology and in psychoanalysis as a result of concentration on the idea of an inner man and consciousness.

The introspective method

The early empirical psychologists held that they were investigating consciousness by the so-called introspective method. Wundt referred to the method as *Selbstbeobachtung*. Since he never seems to have attempted to account systematically for his use of the term *Selbst-beobachtung,* it is hardly of significance to consider possible distinctions between the introspective method and the method of *Selbst-beobachtung.* The main point is that Wundt held that immediate experience was the proper subject matter of psychology. On this point his contemporary Brentano [1874] and Brentano's student, Husserl, and the later phenomenologists were in agreement with Wundt. The idea that the subject matter of psychology was what could be *observed,* was later transmitted to Watson and the behaviourists. Therefore, not only phenomenology but also behaviourism has this fundamental presupposition in common with Wundtian psychology. Since introspective psychology has been revived it is still important for the modern theorist in psychology to consider the introspective method.

The generations of psychologists succeeding Wundt have for various reasons by and large rejected the introspective method. One point of criticism raised against it is that it does not allow of an adequate operational specification. That this point is significant, is illustrated by an examination of the account given of the method by Wundt's student Titchener (1896, p. 33):

> The rule for introspection, in the sphere of sensation, is as follows: *Be as attentive as possible to the object or process which gives rise to the sensation, and, when the object is removed or the process completed, recall the sensation by an act of memory as vividly and completely as you can.*

One asks what in this prescription of method is meant by the terms 'attention', 'process', 'act of memory', 'vivacity', etc.

However, the criticism raised later against the introspective method by Wittgenstein (1953) and philosophers inspired by him is far more serious. They maintain that immediate experience as presupposed by the method does not exist and consequently that it does not make sense to speak of an introspective method. As already noted, the idea of immediate experience raises the question of privacy and the related one of understanding what can be meant by something as given in consciousness. (See p. 74.) The difficulty of distinguishing perceiving, remembering, imagining and thinking from use of language makes it difficult to support the claim that the introspective method can yield reports which are not simply expressions of how various adult individuals use language.

Wundt and his contemporaries believed they could combine what they regarded as their 'method' with an experimental procedure. If the introspective method is just a way of obtaining a verbal report of some sort, their whole procedure would consist in an exploring of man's use of language under standardized conditions. The claim that an experimental procedure was being used would also lack support, because it would not be known in which respect conditions were standardized. Apparently the verbal reports obtained by Wundt and his contemporaries would only be of theoretical interest if they had been performed within a theoretical system which allowed one to deal with use of language. Because such a system was lacking, the investigations performed were of necessity deprived of meaning.

The question of whether or not introspection in some form can give new knowledge is an age-old one in philosophy. Thus it was central in Aristotle's account of how knowledge arose. (See O'Connor, 1964.) The difficulty of demonstrating that introspection represents an inner sense or direct observation and not simply a reflection in terms of a use of language already acquired, is emphasized in a critical review article by Landesman (1967, p. 193), who commented on the famous passage (quoted above p. 73) by Locke in the following way:

> According to Locke, consciousness provides us with our ideas of the various operations of the mind. No person can know what perception is unless he has observed a case of perception, and his own perceptions are the only ones he can observe. This theory is merely a special case of a fundamental psychological principle of traditional empiricism, which states that all ideas are abstracted from or compounded out of what is observed. Now the problem of how people do get ideas or concepts is very much up in the air and certainly cannot be solved without a great deal of psychological investigation. But this much can be said about the traditional theory: If introspection is best characterized not as inner sense or direct observation, but as thinking and judging about one's mental states, then it cannot be an original source of concepts. For thinking is an activity in which a person is already exercising the concepts he possesses; he cannot think about anything unless he already has an idea of it.

Actually, as early as 1868 Peirce (1960) had argued convincingly that introspection could not yield new knowledge. (On this point, see O'Connor, ibid.) In this article Peirce also argued that thinking could not be carried out without signs. This point may be regarded as a first step in the direction of the Wittgensteinian position on the idea of a private language.

The ego

The idea of consciousness rests on the presupposition that something existing within man is aware of events of various types. This 'something' is believed to be directly aware of, to have immediate experience of, the external world, other persons, the actions of the body, feelings, desires, impulses of the will, images and thoughts and also of experiences in the past in the form of memories. Obviously if it is difficult to conceive of immediate experience, it is also difficult to conceive of something which is having these experiences. In postulating a something of this type, named a self, an I, or an ego, we may easily be deceived by grammar (to use the Wittgensteinian expression). As was pointed out by Anscombe (1976), the fact that we express ourselves in the way that we say 'I see a stone', 'I hear a tone', 'I feel pain', etc. does not warrant the conclusion that there is an ego which sees, hears or feels. The expressions may simply indicate that when our body is in a certain relationship to the external world and certain conditions prevail within the body, we may say 'I see a stone', 'I hear a tone', 'I feel pain', etc. We never seem to be in a position to determine this 'something', or ego, within our body without referring to some relationship to the external world.

This difficulty is not overcome by reference to the fact that the adult human individual seems to be capable of structuring his perceiving, remembering, imagining, thinking and feeling in terms of the conception of an ego. There is no denying that such structuring is possible, and also that it may possibly be of central importance in understanding social relationships. However, as long as we do not know how this structuring is brought about, we are not allowed to conclude that the use of expressions such as those mentioned above ('I see a stone', 'I hear a tone', 'I feel pain', etc.) presupposes the existence of an ego. To say, as Descartes did, that the conception of the ego is innate or, as Husserl did, that there is a transcendental ego, or, as Hume did, that the ego is just a bundle of impressions, does not help us much towards an understanding of the nature of the activities engaged in by man. It seems reasonable to believe that the conception of an ego which structures the various activities develops as the human organism interacts with its environment, and the taking of a position on the question of this development solely on the basis of conceptions of an ego in the adult human being, may too easily lead to empty speculation.

The Wundtian system

In developing his framework for the study of psychology, Wundt (1874, 1896), the central figure in early psychology, assimilated various trends dominant in Western philosophical traditions. In the first place he took as his point of departure the belief in the inner man, which for centuries — as we have already noted — had been central in Western thinking. Wundt (1874, p. 7) expressed his adherence to this belief in the introductory pages of his book on physiological psychology: 'In der *Psychologie* schaut der Mensch sich gleichsam von *innen* an und sucht den Zusammenhang derjenigen Vorgänge zu erklären, welche ihm diese innere Beobachtung darbietet.'

Next he took over the belief of the British empiricists that consciousness was composed of mental elements in the form of sensations. To the element of sensation he added the element of feeling. Consciousness was then according to him constituted by two types of mental elements, sensations and feelings. These elements were believed to be compounded into *psychische Gebilde*. When the *psychische Gebilde* were made up of sensations, *Vorstellungen* were thought to arise and when they were made up of feelings, then moods, affects and acts of will were thought to arise. The term *Vorstellung* was said to be used in a way corresponding to the use of the word 'idea' in English.

Wundt's system was thus not strictly associational in the sense attributed to the British empiricists. Emphasis was placed on feeling and will, and according to the principle of creative synthesis, compounds of elements possessed characteristics which could not be regarded as the sum of the elements. (For a more detailed account of the points of difference between Wundt's system and that of British empiricism, see Pongratz, 1967.) However, there is no doubt that Wundt's thinking was deeply influenced by British empiricism, and Wundt would have clarified his position if he had related it to this philosophical tradition, in particular to Hume, who, more than one hundred years before him, had claimed that he had established an experimental science of man.

Apparently neither Wundt nor the other empirical psychologists who conceived of consciousness as being made up of elements, regarded the elements as theoretical postulates to be modified or rejected when found not to be useful in theory construction. The elements represented what was believed to be an ultimate reality.

Thirdly, Wundt took over from Cartesianism the belief in immediate experience. According to Wundt, psychology, on the one hand, and the physical sciences and physiology, on the other, rested on the same experience. In the latter sciences experience was said to be conceived of as abstracted from man as the experiencing subject. In contrast, in psychology no such abstraction was made, experience here being regarded as direct knowledge, in other words as being immediate. This bipartitioning of experience by Wundt probably arose as the result of an attempt to show that the new science which was to be established had a subject matter of its own, but that it could nevertheless be treated by the same methods (observation and experiment) as those used in the physical sciences and physiology. (On this point, see Pongratz, 1967.) Apparently Wundt did not attempt to explain how this bipartitioning of experience could be accomplished. The distinction attempted by Wundt reflected the positivist belief that scientific methods have an existence independent of subject matter.

Wundt's ideas concerning method and subject matter are well illustrated by the way he introduced the term 'apperception'. In his attempt to account for thinking he had recourse to the idea of apperception as used by Leibniz. (For an historical review of the idea of apperception, see Ulich, 1967.) According to this idea attention could be directed to specific aspects of consciousness. The aspect on which attention was concentrated was said to be apperceived. In introducing the idea of apperception Wundt likened consciousness to the visual field. On analogy with the distinction drawn in visual perceiving between a central and peripheral part of the field, it was held that attention could be focused on some central part of consciousness.

In Wundt's account it remains obscure what the basis for the analogy between the visual field and consciousness is. Attention seems to be postulated as some sort of force having an existence independent of any known domain of events. (A critical and more detailed review of Wundt's use of the term 'apperception' is given by Humphrey, 1963.)

It will be understood that an account of thinking centred around the idea of apperception can at best only have weak connections with reality, and it is hardly worth while going into it in any more detail. Yet it should be mentioned that Wundt (1907) argued that thinking was governed by use of language in such a way that it could not be investigated by experimental methods.

The early empirical study of thinking

As has been mentioned above, Wundt rejected the idea that thinking could be studied by experimental techniques. At the beginning of the twentieth century the position taken by Wundt was questioned by a group of psychologists at the University of Würzburg. These psychologists believed they could demonstrate that thinking could be fruitfuly investigated by experimental techniques. They also questioned the empiricist belief that images of various sorts were the vehicles for thinking, as had been maintained by Wundt. However, the psychologists of the Würzburg school, amongst others Külpe, Orth, Mayer, Marbe, Messer, Ach, Bühler and Selz, did not question the idea of the introspective method. Moreover it should be noted that, as was explicitly emphasized by Külpe (on this point, see Mandler and Mandler, 1964, pp. 208-217), the leader of the Würzburg school, it was believed that thinking could be carried out without the use of signs. This point makes it clear that the psychologists of this school regarded consciousness as some sort of ultimate entity. Questions concerning the relationship between the content of consciousness and the report to be given by the subject were not seriously dealt with, as will be understood. The Würzburgers opposed the idea that thinking was necessarily carried out by mental images of various sorts. They argued that thinking might take place by means of what they called *Bewusstseinslagen,* which by Mandler and Mandler (ibid) is translated by the term 'dispositions of consciousness'. They based this belief on the fact that, for example, when the subject was instructed to respond to a word by another word, images were not invariably found to be present. The thinking going on was explained by reference to the dispositions of consciousness. As will be understood, the psychologists of the Würzburg school were not able to state what was meant by 'dispositions of consciousness'. Messer (see Mandler and Mandler, ibid) identified them with thoughts.

The conclusions arrived at by the psychologists of the Würzburg school were strongly opposed by Wundt, Müller, and Titchener, and a heated debate arose. (For reviews of this debate, see Boring, 1950; Humphrey, 1963; Mandler and Mandler, 1964; Woodworth, 1938.)

The debate upon the question of the role of images in thinking was seriously affected by the confusion of epistemological and empirical questions. In this debate two different questions seem to have been confused.

The first question concerns the presence of imagery and the second the properties which must be attributed to the mental elements if they are to be regarded as mediators of thinking. It will be seen that even if imagery of some sort were invariably present when man was engaged in activities designated as thinking, no demonstration would have been made that thinking could be regarded as mediated by mental elements.

Concerning the first question, the question of the presence of imagery of some sort, we agree with Price (1953) that in some individuals imagery of some sort is probably present in a variety of situations involving thinking and in all individuals it is probably present at least in some situations.

The second question is of course the essential one regarding conceptions of thinking based on the idea of mental elements. As has already been noted, in order to meet the requirements of an explanation of the activity of thinking, one would have to presuppose the representation of the mental element in a pure form of some sort, and, as has been mentioned, it is difficult to understand what this can mean. The same would be true if we conceived of the element as a representation of sensory impressions of a type other than the one designated as sensations. Apparently, however one conceived of the sensory impression, it would have to be regarded as an abstraction.

Without denying that the question of the presence of imagery of some sort may be of some theoretical interest, it is difficult to see how this question is related to the fundamental question of how to evaluate the empiricist model of thinking The research of the Würzburg school may be said to illustrate the tendency in psychologists to begin empirical research before questions concerning the nature of the reality to be studied have been examined. Apparently Ryle (1953, pp. 195-196) was right when he stated that the psychologists engaged in the early empirical study of the activity of thinking did not know what they were looking for:

> My conclusion is that the experimental investigation of thinking has been, on the whole, unproductive, because the researchers have had confused or erroneous notions of what they were looking for. Their notions of what they were looking for were confused or erroneous partly because they were borrowed from the official philosophical doctrines of the day. They were the heirs of conceptual disorders. To get the conceptual disorders out of one's system what is needed is not hard experimental work but hard conceptual work.

Epistemological and empirical questions were still being confused when some of the Würzburg psychologists went on to study judgements. On instigating this study, Marbe (see Mandler and Mandler, ibid, pp. 145-146) conceived of a judgement in the following way: ' . . . to understand a judgement says the same as being able to experience certain other judgements.'

This conception of the judgement raises a number of questions. In the first place, what are the other judgements to which reference is made? This question leads us into the issue of universalia, which was not clarified by Marbe. Secondly, what does experiencing certain other types of judgements mean? This question leads into the Aristotelian theory of knowledge, which has been debated for centuries. (For an account of the Aristotelian theory, see O'Connor, 1964.) Thirdly, how can one possibly specify what is meant by 'being able to' with regard to this experiencing?

The tendency to believe that all problems meeting the psychologist can be solved by empirical research has persisted in psychology up to the present. It was carried to an extreme in the work of Titchener. For example, in his attempt to account for thinking and meaning he (see Mandler and Mandler, ibid, pp. 168-169) referred to the question of the nature of the general or the universal as a question concerning psychological fact. Peters and Mace (1967, p. 26) have found expression in Titchener's diary of the belief that the basic ideas of British empiricism could be tested empirically.

Passmore (1967, b), as I understand him, ascribed the tendency to regard all questions raised in attempts to establish a scientific psychology as answerable by empirical research, to a conception of philosophy predominant in the latter half of the nineteenth century (at the time when empirical psychology was established). According to this conception philosophy was regarded as the science of man. When philosophy is conceived of in this way, it may easily escape notice that a science of man must rest on presuppositions which require philosophical examination. Whatever the reason for this tendency it has had the fatal consequence that psychologists have neglected problems related to the choice of reference system.

Before leaving the work of the Würzburg school it should be mentioned that in this work the idea of a determining tendency (a set or an *Einstellung*) was introduced into psychology. The determining tendency was said to arise from the presentation of the goal to be reached by the subject confronted with a task in thinking. (On this point in the work of the Würzburg school, see Mandler and Mandler, ibid, extracts from Watt and Ach.) Apparently, in introducing the term 'determining tendency' the Würzburg psychologists overlooked the fact that in an experiment on thinking the subject must be instructed to reach a certain goal. The understanding of this instruction implies that the subject has a definite set, or a determining tendency. Thus, the determining tendency seems to be inseparable from the understanding of the goal to be reached. This means that one cannot speak of a determining tendency or set as some entity whose existence is independent of the task. The determining tendency or set must therefore be regarded as a defining characteristic of the task to be completed and not, as believed, as some force in consciousness.

The idea of the determining tendency or set, which is in line with Wundt's idea of attention discussed above, seems to have arisen in an attempt to explain how the mind could operate on mental elements. Rubin (1926) was correct in denying the existence of attention as long as it is regarded as a force in consciousness. But as was pointed out by Luria (1973) to deny the operation of different sets in psychological activities is tantamount to overlooking a fundamental point.

Psychoanalysis: a philosophy of the inner man

With its concentration on the inner man and its point of departure in the idea of consciousness, psychoanalysis must be regarded as a branch of Cartesian philosophy. As was mentioned above, the idea that unconscious and not conscious motivation determines man's actions, should not lead one to overlook the fact that the psychoanalytic determination of the unconscious is dependent upon conceptions of consciousness. As has been argued here, the various conceptions of consciousness are highly diffuse. This being so, the idea of the unconscious is also necessarily diffuse. For this reason it has proved extremely difficult to find empirical support for the psychoanalytic theory in which the inner man is equipped not only with an ego, but also with a superego and an id as well as with internal forces which determine what the effect of the various impressions reaching the organism from outside the body, as well as of the impulses coming from inside the body, will be.

In a detailed examination of psychoanalytic theory, Wisdom (1967, p. 190) argued that one has to distinguish between the concept of the unconscious and Freudian theory. I am unable to see how this distinction can be made, and as is evident from Wisdom's presentation of the theory, reference is repeatedly made in the latter theory to conceptions of consciousness:

> The developed form of Freud's theory of the unconscious may be summariz-
> ed in the following way: (1) There are networks of ideas — attitudes,
> thoughts, feelings, objects imagined inside a person, and so on — that he
> cannot realize he possesses, because of the influence of other such networks,
> which he also cannot realize he possesses as long as he relies only on free
> association. (This is ordinarily described as 'unconscious' conflict.) (2) These
> networks and their conflicts (a) influence the person's conscious ideas in all
> situations, reproducing the mutual relationships of the networks, however dif-
> ficult it may be to recognize them; and (b) in particular influence him at dif-
> ferent times, so that childhood networks and conflicts influence adult
> ideas. (3) These networks are related in accordance with a large group
> of theoretical hypotheses, such as that of the Oedipus complex.

Evidently the use of the verb 'to *realize*', as well as of the word 'idea' in the passage quoted, refers to conceptions of consciousness. The conclusion arrived at by Wisdom that the theory is testable would seem to be highly dubious. In view of the uncritical attitude to use of language in Freud and his followers and in view of the small progress made during the last fifty years in testing the theory, it seems far more reasonable to believe that it is based on ideas which make it untestable.

Attempts made by among others Habermas (1973), to elucidate the nature of scientific thinking by taking psychoanalytic theory as their point of departure may tend to confuse the issue rather than to clarify it.

CHAPTER 8

Psychology as the study of consciousness (continued)

Phenomenology

Phenomenology, which arose as a philosophical movement at the beginning of the twentieth century, represented a revival of Cartesianism and ideas about the inner man. Characteristically it developed in the countries where these ideas had the greatest influence, in Germany and France. However, there are many versions of phenomenology. (For a critical review of phenomenology, see Schmitt, 1967, b.) A characteristic of them all seems to be a belief in immediate experience and a belief in consciousness as having a separate existence independent of man's use of language. The main criticism raised against the ideas of consciousness in British empiricism as well as in early psychology is, therefore, relevant regarding phenomenology in its various versions.

The phenomenologists reacted to the empiricists' conceptions of elements. They emphasized the fact that parts formed structures, and in general they stressed the role played by the context, but phenomenologists reacted also to the positivists' conception of science as a task mainly consisting of relating facts to each other. The phenomenologists stressed the fact that the scientist had to carefully describe the events he wanted to study by making clear the presuppositions made when some type of event was said to be present. In agreement with McLeod (1964), many empirical psychologists would probably accept this antipositivist attitude without adhering to any one phenomenological system. Here I shall only be concerned with the question of whether or not one can say that the phenomenologists developed a specific method, the so-called phenomenological description, which they held was to supplant the introspective method.

When we turn to the thinker most articulate on the problem of method, Husserl, we find that he suggested and discussed a number of criteria and, in the light of this, then argued that he was in possession of a method. Schmitt (1967, b) examined the criteria suggested. Here I shall only be concerned with one aspect of this examination. Husserl wanted to etablish a comprehensive science of the a priori, and central in his thinking was, therefore, the assumption that the phenomena to be described in this science were non-empirical. Husserl argued that the claim to having a method was based on the claim that certain types of phenomenon were adequately described. Consequently, if the phenomena described cannot be regarded as non-empirical, the claim to method has little support. Apparently in order to decide on the question of whether the phenomena were non-empirical or not, the term 'empirical' must be elucidated. Having been influenced by Frege's Platonic ideas of logic as being independent of use of language Husserl failed to see this point and seems to have left the question of what can be meant by 'empirical' up in the air. This is the conclusion also arrived at by Schmitt (ibid, p. 148):

> It is undoubtedly a task for phenomenology to differentiate the different senses of 'empirical', that is, to describe the different kinds of intentional acts involved in what we call experience and the criteria of coherence belonging to each kind of act. Oddly enough, the phenomenologists so far have barely begun to undertake such an examination, and hence their conviction that statements about phenomena, as now defined, are nonempirical is not supported by adequate phenomenological analyses. This important shortcoming in the theory of the phenomenological method is all the more serious because there are good reasons for thinking that there is one perfectly good sense of the words 'experience' and 'empirical' in which statements about phenomena, as defined, *are* empirical.

Now as Hamlyn (1967, a) made clear in his critical article on empiricism, it is difficult to define the term 'empirical' without reference to use of language. Evidently Husserl failed to see that he could not argue consistently for his belief in a specific method unless he examined the relationship between use of language and consciousness. The failure to see this point is a fundamental weakness in all versions of phenomenology. Consequently it is difficult to see that the phenomenologists have presented convincing arguments for their claim that the phenomena they describe are non-empirical. At present it seems most reasonable simply to regard what is called the phenomenological method, just like what is called the introspective method, as an expression of the use made of language by specific individuals in specific situations.

As has been mentioned, Husserl seems to have been the thinker in the phenomenological movement most concerned with the problem of method, and he exerted a strong influence on many of the other phenomenologists. Inspired by the movement, empirical psychologists either did not see the necessity of elaborating the idea of a phenomenological method, or they may have believed that Husserl had argued convincingly on this point. The lack of concern for subject matter and method made phenomenologically oriented psychologists postulate wholes, structures, and meanings by diffuse reference to everyday use of language. In a previous work (Saugstad, 1965) I have shown that the so-called Gestalt laws of organization of structures, which have been regarded as central in the Gestalt movement, are probably empirically empty, or, as I would now say, most probably represent instances of a mis-use of language. Generally it must be said that adequate rules for specifying what is meant by parts and wholes as well as rules specifying the relationship between the parts making up the wholes are missing in phenomenology. In their attempts to determine what are to be regarded as structures, phenomenologically oriented psychologists have proceeded by way of vague analogy. (See for example the criticism made by Estes, 1954, of Kurt Lewin.)

By criticizing the earlier psychology as well as the contemporary behaviourism, and by insisting on more adequate descriptions, empirical psychologists such as Stumpf (1906), the psychologists of the Würzburg School, Katz (1930), Rubin (1921), Tranekjær Rasmussen (1956), the Berliner Gestaltists (for a review, see Woodworth and Shean, 1964), McLeod (1964), Merleau-Ponty (1945), and the so-called existential psychologists (for a review of this work, see MacIntyre, 1967; Needleman, 1967) have broadened the scope of psychology and have enriched it with empirical findings which may be essential in the further structuring of psychology.

While the phenomenologists' insistence on more adequate descriptions was a positive contribution, it should be noted that their belief in the whole as representing some ultimate reality probably led them to neglect the role of explanation in theory construction. Moreover it should be noted that when the Berliner Gestaltists advanced explanations, they tended to frame these in terms of underlying neurophysiological processes and thus actually replaced the earlier reductionism which they opposed with another type of reductionism.

The revival of conceptions of consciousness

Inspired by James, Selz, Bartlett and Piaget, American psychologists and linguists, headed by Bruner (Bruner et al., 1956; Bruner et al., 1966) Miller (Miller et al., 1960) and Chomsky (1957, 1965, 1966, 1972), revived the study of perceiving, remembering, imagining, thinking and use of language in terms of ideas about consciousness. This revival was not based on a careful examination of the difficulties met with in the old psychology of consciousness. The problem of how the research worker might communicate about consciousness without reference to use of language was left unexamined. The new approach, called the 'study of cognition', was influenced by information theory and later by the development of modern computers. This influence, at least in part, may explain why modern research workers have been able to leave questions concerning the nature of consciousness unexamined.

The term 'information' was taken over from a model developed by Shannon and Weaver (1949) for telephone engineering. Information was defined here in terms of reduction of uncertainty in situations where the total amount of information could be specified in terms of the number of questions that had to be asked in order to arrive at a correct answer (cp. the famous party game 'twenty questions'). This conception of information, as was demonstrated by Garner (1962), can be useful for determining more precisely the use of certain terms in situations which are relatively specifiable. However, to give a useful determination of the use of the term 'information' in terms of the models developed by telephone engineers is obviously problematic and today this is recognized, for example, by Norman (1969, p. 72):

> In the early 1950's, the mathematical theory of information played an important role in the thoughts, theories, and experiments of psychologists. The reasons are fairly obvious. Communication engineers had developed a formal structure for discussing the effects of channel capacity, noise, and transmission rate on the amount of information that any message could contain. Psychologists realized that the human could be viewed as an information processing device, reducing and transmitting the information contained in the environment through the sensory system and into some encoding in memory. Thus stated, the psychologists and engineers were studying similar problems. Limitations on memory capacity could be interpreted as limitations on our ability to receive information.
>
> The information concept ran into one serious problem in studies of memory: it didn't work. This is not to say that the basic concepts of information theory were not valuable, for they did provide useful new interpretations of psychological phenomena. The problem was that the way the communication engineer measured information just did not seem to apply to the human.

One must wonder how psychologists could fail for such a relatively long period of time to realize that the term 'information' was being used in a vague and diffuse manner. The reason is probably to be found in the fact that psychologists have tended to believe that theoretical terms could be operationally defined. This erroneous belief was discussed in Chapter 1 of this book.

Even if it has been accepted by now that a determination of the term 'information' in terms of the models developed by telephone engineering is at best highly inadequate when applied to man, psychol-

144

ogists still seem to believe that the term 'information' can be given a meaning independent of a reference to use of language. In the psychological approach called information processing — which may be regarded as a development of the earlier one based on information theory — the term 'information' has been equated with some inner process. Information was said to be processed, and it became fashionable to speak, for example, of perceptual processes, memory processes, imaginary processes, thought processes, and cognitive processes. The term 'process' replaced the older terms 'mental element', 'mental structure' or 'immediate experience'. While, as was mentioned in Chapter 4, the research workers of this orientation rightly emphasized the fact that the organism studied in psychology was an active one, the use of the term 'process' to denote an internal event of some sort had the unfortunate result that research workers lost hold of the fundamental idea that scientific psychology must be concerned with the interaction between an organism and its environment. The postulation of internal processes involves a substitution of explanation for description.

In the previous chapter I pointed out that in their approach to the study of problem solving, Newell and Simon (1972, p. 9) had left undefined all their central terms ('problem', 'symbol', 'information', etc.). Their use of the term 'process' may be regarded as representative of the use of the term in the study of cognition: 'The theory posits a set of processes or mechanisms that produce the behavior of the thinking human. Thus, the theory is reductionistic; it does not simply provide a set of relations or laws about behavior from which one can often conclude what behavior must be.'

With regard to the term 'process' it ought to be clear that it is not meaningful to speak of a process unless one is capable of stating an initial stage at which the process starts and a final stage at which it ends. As far as can be seen, research workers using the term have made no attempt to make this specification.

In line with the postulation of mental processes modern research workers have also postulated entities governing series of processes. Thus, Miller et al. (1960) introduced the idea of an image. As argued by Miller et al., an individual dealing with a complicated task may be said to be guided by plans for performing the task. It seems perfectly all right to state that an individual is performing a task according to some plan. However, in addition to a plan Miller et al. postulate an image as governing the internal processes of the individual. It is difficult to see what the difference is between a plan and an image. In Chapter 2 I discussed the use of the schema in Piaget. The use of the image in Miller et al. is based on the same presupposition. As mentioned in Chapter 2 the use of the term 'schema' seems to involve the confusion of statements in the first and third person. The idea of a schema was used by Kant (on this point, see Hamlyn, 1976, b) in connection with his account of concepts. It was later adopted by Selz (see Mandler and Mandler, 1964) and by Bartlett (1932).

As has been mentioned, the term 'process' seems to be a substitute for the terms 'immediate experience' and 'elements of consciousness'. When psychological activities are conceived of as the result of an interaction between an organism and its environment, it will be understood that they cannot then be explainable in terms of internal processes of various sorts. Characterizing the mental process along with the internal structure as a myth, Malcolm (1971, p. 387) pointed out how the idea of a process may have originated in attempts to explain various psychological concepts:

> The predicament is typical of the attempts of philosophers and psychologists to 'analyze' or 'explain' the concepts of mind, such as thinking, recognizing, perceiving, meaning, intending, remembering and problem solving. The feeling that we are dealing with hidden processes gives rise to theories and models. It fosters the desire (of which Dodwell speaks) 'to reach a deeper analysis of the phenomena'. We feel that when a person recognizes something, in addition to the various manifestations or characteristic accompaniments of recognition something must go on inside. This is the 'inner process' of recognition.

When it is borne in mind that fundamentally we are ignorant about psychological activities such as remembering, imagining and thinking, it will be understood that in theory construction it is of little usefulness to write programs for computers which simulate man's actual performance. While remarkable, the performance of electronic computers can, of course, be no better than the programs written for their performance. The idea of simulation is not at all clear. For example, what does it mean to simulate the activity of thinking? As noted in Chapters 3 and 4, thinking is closely related to the activities of perceiving, remembering and imagining, and as noted in Chapter 5, these four activities are closely related to use of language. This means that a clear conception of thinking requires an extensive theory relating all of these activities to each other. Apparently, it is hardly possible to understand thinking in man without accounting adequately for man's use of language. At present no single scientific discipline — nor all scientific disciplines combined — can give this account. Consequently, attempts at simulating thinking in man can only amount to guesses made more or less at random. If thinking in species other than man is to be simulated, it will be realized that in these species this activity must be conceived

146

of in terms of the total adjustment of the individuals of these species to their environments. Furthermore, the question of whether or not computers or variously constructed machines can think can only be answered by comparing the performance of these devices to the performance of individuals as biological organisms.

Moreover it must be clearly recognized that the performance of computers cannot be taken as evidence that a psychology based on ideas of consciousness is a sound endeavour, although this was argued by Neisser (1967, p. 237) in a defence of the modern study of cognition. Neisser used as evidence the fact that computers operated without the help of homunculi; consequently, even if the programs were written in terms of ideas of consciousness, this study did not make use of the idea of a homunculus. What is overlooked here is the fact that a psychology of consciousness only needs the idea of a homunculus in attempts to account for the relationship between a postulated content of consciousness and use of language. Of course, an endless variety of programs can be written for computers which do not involve problems concerning this relationship. This point was made clear above when the so-called introspective method was examined. Not until the nature of the introspective method has been shown to rest on a sound basis, can the modern study of cognition be said to be a sound scientific endeavour. Until psychologists have made clear how the terms they use to designate some postulated mental content are related to use of language, they will be condemned to continually repeating the errors committed by Wundt and his followers.

The return to the conception of psychology as the study of consciousness has led to a renewed concentration on the idea of attention or set. As might be expected, the term has not been introduced in the theoretical statements in a manner which makes its use less arbitrary than the use made of it in the early psychology of consciousness. Neisser (1967, p. 88) pointed out that most psychologists have tended to conceive of attention as a definite activity of some kind and as some sort of allocation of energy. This conception is in line with the Wundtian idea of attention as a force in consciousness. However, when Neisser continued by saying: 'It seems to me, therefore, that attention is not a mysterious concentration of psychic energy; it is simply an allotment of analyzing mechanisms to a limited region of the field', he seems to have returned to the idea of attention as some sort of force in consciousness.

Norman (1969, p. 2) made it clear that attention could not be separated from perceiving, remembering and learning. But then he argued that a unitary model for attention, perceiving, remembering and learning was required.

This whole statement about the relationship of attention, perception and learning is quite unsatisfactory to the psychologist. Naming something 'attention', something else 'perception', and yet something else 'learning', adds to our vocabulary, but not to our knowledge. The psychologist will not be satisfied until he can point to a specific process — that sequence of operations which performs transformations and makes decisions on sensory information — and identify this as a mechanism of attention. Then he tries to state the specific properties of each component of the overall process and show how they are related to other aspects of human abilities. The ultimate in specification is a model which describes in detail the operations which underlie attention, perception, learning and memory.

One may well ask how it is possible to develop a model for some entity which does not seem to be specifiable. Apparently, Norman, in line with a large number of modern psychologists, conceives of attention as some mechanism which can be specified without taking into consideration how man communicates about perceiving, learning and remembering. When this point is realized, it will be understood that attention represents a defining characteristic of psychological activities, and, therefore, that only *shifts* of attention can be the subject of empirical research.

Psycholinguistics

A revival of the old ideas of consciousness also took place within the modern study of grammar. In order to account for various grammatical principles advanced, Chomsky (1957, 1965, 1966, 1972) and followers (for a review of central parts of this work, see Miller and McNeill, 1970; Paivio, 1971; Brown, 1973) resorted to ideas of consciousness. A new branch of psychology, so-called psycholinguistics, originated. Here I shall be concerned only with conceptions of use of language in Chomsky, the central figure in this movement. (I shall turn to the study of use of language in terms of conceptions of behaviour below.) What is said of his conceptions will apply to much of the work in the psychology of language, also to work not based upon the so-called transformational grammars.

In his first published and widely influential work on grammar, Chomsky (1957) took as his point of departure the idea of grammaticality, i.e. language was treated from the point of view of what the adult individual would regard as a grammatical sentence. Problems of meaning were thus left aside. In this important respect the point of departure is in line with that of Chomsky's opponent, Skinner (1957). Chomsky (1965; 1972) later modified his position, but as will be clear below essentially he continued to treat use of language without concerning himself with the problem of meaning.

Leading linguists such as Hockett (1970) have disputed the claim made by Chomsky and followers to have constructed more precise and useful grammars than earlier ones. This dispute will not be considered here. However, attention should be called to the fact that if the new so-called transformational grammars really are more precise than the earlier ones, this may eventually contribute to a better understanding of various psychological activities.

Obviously an approach to the study of use of language which takes as its point of departure the idea of grammaticality will be seriously restricted. In the first place language is used in specific situations and no account of this use can be complete unless it is considered from this point of view. Chomsky and many other linguists may be said to have given an incomplete account because they have neglected the context in which language is used.

Secondly, it must be clear that any grammatical analysis presupposes familiarity with various grammatical categories. This familiarity again presupposes familiarity with concepts of different sorts. For example, the use of grammatical categories such as 'noun', 'verb', 'adjective', 'noun-phrase' and 'verb-phrase' presupposes an extensive familiarity with use of language. The linguist developing his frame of reference in terms of grammar, therefore, has to base his study on this familiarity and thereby has placed himself in a position which prevents him from understanding the use of language underlying his frame of reference.

The difficulty meeting Chomsky (and probably all thinkers approaching the study of use of language in terms of grammar) seems to be the following. Irregardless of whether meaning can be established without reference to use of language, it is, at least in essential respects, established in this way. If no frame of reference to account for meaning has been constructed, it does not seem possible to account for use of language by explicit or implicit reference to meaning. This may be tantamount to saying that use of language is use of language. The treatment of meaning in Chomsky and many linguists may actually be said to reflect naive conceptions regarding the nature of their study. In a more recent work Chomsky (1972, p. 116) outlined the task of the grammarian in the following way:

> To study a language, then, we must attempt to dissociate a variety of factors that interact with underlying competence to determine actual performance; the technical term 'competence' refers to the ability of the idealized speaker-hearer to associate sounds and meanings strictly in accordance with the rules of his language. The grammar of a language, as a model for idealized competence, establishes a certain relation between sound and meaning — between phonetic and semantic representations. We may say that the grammar of the language L generates a set of pairs (s, I), where s is the phonetic representation of a certain signal and I is the semantic inter-

pretation assigned to this signal by the rules of the language. To discover this grammar is the primary goal of the linguistic investigation of a particular language.

As has been mentioned, if meaning is primarily established by means of use of language it is difficult to see how the nature of language can in a fundamental sense be revealed by a grammar which pairs sound with meaning. Furthermore, it is not at all clear in this connection what is meant by the word 'sound'. Apparently the definition of a phoneme must ultimately rest on a reference to meaning. The linguists' studies of phoneme distributions in various languages have given information on new aspects of use of language, but this does not of course mean that the conception of the phoneme has been arrived at without reference to conceptions of meaning. Obviously, a conception of use of language as a system consisting only of phonemes would be a highly inadequate one.

To explain the nature of the various grammatical structures Chomsky resorted to conceptions of consciousness, but, like the earlier thinkers who had done so, he failed to account for the relationship between use of language and consciousness. In the quotation given above (p. 146), Malcolm (1971) argued that the internal structures referred to by Chomsky were myths. Indeed, one wonders how the claim that they are real might be substantiated.

Universal language

In line with some older linguists Chomsky (1972) argued that the various cultural languages have certain fundamental features in common. This suggestion seems to be a highly reasonable one, but it is not easy to formulate it in a useful manner. Evidently, if in some way use of language must be considered as necessary it must be universal, but the fact that use of language is necessary does not imply that all cultural languages have fundamental grammatical features in common. The structures of the various cultural languages might all be different with regard to phonemic and grammatical principles and still be based on certain common underlying rules. I am not saying that this is necessarily so, but that it may possibly be so. The point made here reveals the difficulty of finding criteria in terms of which use of language may be said to be universal. The only way to arrive at a satisfactory way of deciding that the various cultural languages have fundamental features in common is probably to compare them as systems of communication.

In discussing the problem of universal language, it is, as was emphasized by Hinde (1974), essential that man's total adjustment

150

to the external world is taken into account. This means that use of language must be considered within a context which includes a variety of psychological activities among which should be mentioned those of perceiving, imagining, remembering and thinking dealt with in Chapters 3, 4, 5 and 6.

Use of language and biology

In his attempts at basing use of language on Cartesian conceptions Chomsky (1972) also suggested that in some sense the capacity for forming sentences was innate. This idea of innateness apparently meets with the same difficulties as the Cartesian notion of innate ideas. (These difficulties were laid bare by Locke and Kant.) As was argued by Goodman (1967), it is difficult to understand what can be meant by the statement that the capacity for forming sentences is innate. However, instead of arguing that use of language is innate one might, as has been done by Lenneberg (1967), look for the biological bases for man's use of language. Lenneberg adduced evidence to the effect that use of language depends upon maturational factors and showed that this way of conceiving of use of language is fruitful for understanding how this use develops ontogenetically. Still, as pointed out by Malcolm (ibid), difficulties arise in accounting for this development. In Chapters 3, 4 and 5 it was argued that it is difficult to arrive at a clear basis for distinguishing between perceiving, remembering, imagining and thinking, on the one hand, and use of language, on the other. This being so the following question arises: In what sense can conceptions of biology be regarded as being independent of use of language? In this connection use of language must in some way be given logical priority over biology. Therefore, attempts to account for use of language in terms of biology may easily lead to an illegitimate extension of the use of the term 'biology'. Apparently unless we can specify the characteristics of the organism, it will not make sense to speak of biological adjustment, or of interaction between an organism and its environment. When account is taken of the extremely complicated interaction between the human organism and its environment which results in use of language, it will be understood that it is not easy to state what the biological bases for this use are. As long as a study of communication and use of language along biological lines is concerned with more limited aspects of communication between the child and its environment, such as smiling, crying, babbling, and the initial occurrence of speech, the study would seem to be a fruitful one, but as soon as meaning of a more complicated nature involving in some way use of morphemes is to be studied, it is difficult to see what is meant by 'organism' and what is meant by 'environment'. It must be clear that meaning is to be found neither in the organism nor in its environment. Therefore, when Lenneberg (ibid) began his treatment of meaning by assigning categories to the organism, he may have drawn dubious distinctions between the organism and its environment. Apparently, in order to treat use of language in a fruitful manner from the point of view of biology, it is essential to base this treatment on a theory of how meaning is established by use of language. If no fruitful theory of this nature can be established, no fruitful extension of the study of the biological foundations of man's use of language would seem to be possible.

Attempts to modify the Cartesian conception of consciousness

In developing his ideas of an empirical psychology Husserl's teacher, Brentano, suggested that perceiving and other activities of a psychological nature ought to be conceived of as acts. Unfortunately, probably because Brentano's thinking was so rooted in ideas of consciousness, he also came to conceive of the act as an entity within consciousness and thus failed to conceive of perceiving as an activity which arises as a result of an interaction between the organism and its environment. The passage in which he suggested the distinction between act and content is important and will be quoted [Brentano, 1874, p. 41]:

> Every presentation (Vorstellung) of sensation or imagination offers an example of the mental phenomenon; and here I understand by presentation not that which is presented, but the act of presentation. Thus, hearing a sound, seeing a colored object, sensing warm or cold, and the comparable states of imagination as well, are examples of what I mean; but thinking of a general concept, provided such a thing does actually occur, is equally so. Furthermore, every judgement, every recollection, every expectation, every inference, every conviction or opinion, every doubt, is a mental phenomenon. And again, every emotion, joy, sorrow, fear, hope, pride, despair, anger, love, hate, desire, choice, intention, astonishment, wonder, contempt, etc., is such a phenomenon.
>
> Examples of physical phenomena, on the other hand, are a color, a shape, a landscape, which I see; a musical chord, which I hear; heat, cold, odor, which I sense; as well as comparable images, which appear to me in my imagination.
>
> These examples may suffice as concrete illustrations of the distinction between the two classes.

As becomes clear from the quotation, and, as pointed out by Brentano himself in the paragraph preceding the one quoted here, he did not attempt to define what he meant by the terms 'act' and 'content', but restricted himself to the giving of examples. If he had made a serious attempt at definition he would probably have understood that his position was fraught with grave difficulties.

The distinction between an act and a content of perceiving was also adopted by Moore [1903] when, in opposition to the new-Hegelians, he argued for the existence of an external reality. For psychologists it is important to note that the idea of perceiving as being an act may be at the root of the behaviourist idea that perceiving, remembering, imagining, thinking and use of language can be conceived of as behaviour. The following passage from Watson's successor, Skinner (1964, p. 89), on perceiving is probably representative of behaviourist thinking: 'The heart of the behaviorist position on conscious experience may be summed up in this way: Seeing does not imply something seen.'

One wonders how man could have a conception of seeing if no content was provided by the activity of seeing. Fundamentally the activity of seeing and the activities indicated by other sensory verbs, such as to hear, to taste, to smell and to feel, cannot be conceived of as acts independent of some content. Of course, an individual who understands what is meant by seeing, hearing, feeling, etc. is capable of conceiving of these activities in another organism, but this is not the issue. The fundamental question to be answered by the believers in the distinction between an act and a content of perceiving is how man can conceive of seeing, hearing, feeling, etc. in another organism without basing this conception on conceptions of these activities as providing a content. Malcolm (1964) elaborated the distinction between statements in the first and third persons (between, for example, the sentences 'I see' and 'he sees' to which Wittgenstein, 1953, called attention) and argued that behaviourists overlook this fundamental distinction. To use the Wittgensteinian expression I would say that behaviourist thinkers on this point have been deceived by grammar. The fact that sensory verbs such as to see, to hear, to feel, etc., can be used as intransitive verbs has led them to believe that it is possible to conceive of seeing, hearing, feeling, etc. as acts independent of content.

I should like to emphasize the fact that this criticism represents no mere subtlety. The overlooking of the distinction between first person and third person utterances in all probability invalidates behaviourist attempts to deal with psychology in a fruitful manner.

A more fruitful attempt to break away from perceiving in terms of a content of consciousness was made by Marx [1845]. In some notes on materialism he suggested that perceiving and thinking ought to be conceived of in terms of man's practice, i.e. in terms of his activity in his efforts to deal with his environment. This view has later been developed by Soviet psychologists. (Cp. the collection of articles and abstracts of more extensive works edited by Kussmann, 1971; Kuss-mann and Kölling, 1971.)

Even if he was not able to break away from the Cartesian idea of consciousness Peirce insisted that consciousness must be regarded as a result of man's biological adjustment and that it should be conceived of in terms of an interaction between the organism and its environment. Thayer (1964, p. 440) has characterized Peirce's position in the following way:

> The resulting hypothesis, and the core of the theory, is that thought is one intervening phase of a single behavioral process mediating between a phase of sensory stimulation and a phase of purposeful resolution. As a process the occurrence, span, and termination of which will differ under differing stimulus conditions plus our humanly inherited equipment for response, the sequence of phases will exhibit variations in manifestation and in their grading off from one to another. Nonetheless, specific and describable operations occur within the phase of thought and afford classification and analysis of the 'fixation of belief' and of logic in a broad sense.

This suggestion by Peirce must be said to represent a decisive step in the direction of a more fruitful conception of perceiving and other psychological activities. Unfortunately, Peirce's ideas — like those of Marx — on the activities of perceiving and thinking remained unnoticed until the twentieth century.

Physiological reductionism

It is important to note that the belief that events of a psychological nature are explainable in terms of physiology, the so-called physiological reductionism, is related to the belief that perceiving and other activities are definable in terms of a conscious content. Believers in physiological reductionism overlook the fact that activities of a psychological nature are a result of an interaction between the organism and its environment. It is worth mentioning that in stressing this interaction Peirce objected to the belief in physiological reductionism in the early physiological psychologists. As has been emphasized, perceiving and other activities — whatever their nature may be — must be conceived of as a result of an interaction between an organism and its environment, and consequently must be described in terms of relationships between the organism and its environment. This means that reference to events or processes of a physiological nature cannot explain this interaction. It does not, for example, make sense to say that man or other animals see because they have a visual system. Seeing takes place when an organism which has a visual system interacts with an environment containing radiant energy. Similarly other types of perceiving or other types of activities take place not as a result solely of activity in the nervous system but, as has repeatedly been emphasized, as a result of an interaction between the organism and its environment.

While, on the one hand, it must be clear that psychological functioning cannot be reduced to a neurophysiological function or process or explained by reference to such a function or process, it should, on the other hand, be noted that it cannot be precluded that the best way of advancing psychology may be by attempting to redefine theoretical concepts in the light of psychological knowledge. An illustration of the fruitfulness of this approach may be found in the redefinition of a phase (a sleep phase) in the study of sleep by reference to the registration of eye movements and differences in EEG activity. Other illustrations may be found, but apparently it is not so easy as psychologists widely believe to find good illustrations of the fruitfulness of this approach. The reason may be that psychologists working on the borderline between physiology and psychology take too little care in examining the reality to be studied, the result being that there is a wide gap between physiology and what are regarded as theoretical statements in psychology. Research workers in physiological psychology or neurophysiology still tend to conceive of psychological functioning in terms of capacities (cp. Chapter 2).

CHAPTER 9

Behaviourism

The behaviourist tradition is closely allied to empiricism and positivism. It came into prominence at a time when empiricism and positivism were more or less dominant in the Anglo-Saxon world, and the central beliefs of these two philosophical movements were more or less uncritically adopted. This explains why behaviourism, as Taylor (1967) said, has been largely impervious to criticism. As soon as the central beliefs in empiricism and positivism are questioned, behaviourism is seen to rest on shaky foundations. Koch (1964) complained that behaviourism never was a serious intellectual endeavour, and apart from Tolman (1932) few psychologists have been preoccupied with questions related to the presuppositions on which the 'ism' may be said to rest. After sixty years of behaviourist dominance in psychology, reasoning on subject matter and method has hardly reached beyond the slogans of Watson, the founder of the movement.

Behaviourism arose as a reaction to the early psychology of consciousness and is usually characterized by contrasting it with this psychology. By characterizing it in this way one may easily come to overlook the fact that these two orientations in psychology have central beliefs in common. In the first place, psychologists of both orientations have believed in scientific methods of a general applicability and secondly they have believed that the subject matter of psychology was observable.

Before I proceed to discuss the idea that behaviour is observable, I shall call attention to the fact that behaviourists took over the belief of Titchener that empirical research in psychology could answer questions of a philosophical nature. In the last chapter I discussed this belief, which has been so widespread in psychology. As has been emphasized, it represents a serious obstacle to progress in scientific psychology because it prevents the development of a reference system. I shall focus attention on it by quoting the passage where Peters and Mace (1967, p. 26) criticized this belief in Titchener and the behaviourists:

156

The behaviorists, in their revolt against Titchener's introspectionism, had taken over quite uncritically Titchener's greatest error. Hegel had attempted to answer questions of empirical fact by a priori reasoning. Titchener made the opposite mistake, supposing that questions of philosophical analysis could be settled by observations made in a laboratory. His mistake is on record; he recalled that in 1888, when first reading James Mill's *Analysis of the Human Mind,* the conviction flashed upon him, 'you can test all this for yourself'. He thought he could test it by introspection. The *Analysis* of James Mill was an exercise in philosophical analysis which can be carried out in a soft armchair, perhaps more efficiently there than on a hard laboratory stool. The behaviorists also fell victim to the same error in confusing introspection and philosophical analysis, in failing to see that questions of analysis arise not only in regard to introspective reports but also in regard to behavioral concepts — stimulus, response, and behavior itself.

Watson [1919] claimed that behaviour possessed the property of being objective, and by this he meant that it was observable. Thirty-five years after Watson (1913) in his inaugural address to the American Psychological Association had launched behaviourism, Spence (1948, p. 174) reiterated the claim that behaviour was observable:

In other words, the events studied by the psychologist, Watson held, should consist in observations of the overt behaviour of *other* organisms, other persons than the observing scientist himself, and not in the observation of the scientist's own internal activities.

Tolman (1932) also emphasized that 'for the behaviourist all things are open and above board'. By ascribing to behaviour the property of being observable, psychologists believed that they could apply to their study scientific methods of a general applicability. It was, therefore, essential to the behaviourist who adopted a positivist orientation that behaviour could be ascribed the property of being observable, and this point seems to have been generally accepted among behaviourists. In Chapter 1 of this book I noted the difficulty attaching to the belief that scientific methods of a general applicability are available. Here I shall discuss the belief that behaviour is observable.

Before I proceed to discuss this belief, I would like to draw attention to the fact that there is little reason to object to the use of the term 'behaviour' as a designation for a variety of activities which may be indicated by verbs such as the following: 'to walk', 'to run', 'to jump', 'to climb', 'to smile', 'to weep', 'to laugh', 'to speak', 'to fish', 'to hunt', 'to work', 'to eat', 'to drink' and 'to mate'. One may also extend the term to sensory verbs, such as 'to see', 'to hear', 'to smell' and 'to feel', but it is not so obvious that the activities indicated by these verbs should be designated by the term 'behaviour'. Still less obvious is the extension of the use of the term 'behaviour' to verbs such as 'to remember', 'to imagine', 'to think' and to expressions indicating motivational and emotional states, such as: 'to be hungry', 'to be thirsty', 'to be angry', 'to be happy', 'to be afraid' and 'to be excited'.

As will be understood, the extension of the use of the term 'behaviour' to include all the types of activities mentioned above is not unproblematic. However, even if this extension were to be accepted, it must be clear that one has not determined a subject matter of a scientific study. In order to do so one would have to indicate methods which would allow one to study the activities indicated. Apparently, behaviourists came to believe that all types of behaviour could be accounted for by means of the stimulus—response paradigm. Stimuli and responses could be treated as events in the physical sciences.

The stimuli were held to be describable in physicalist terms, and the responses were said to refer to muscle contractions, to movements of parts of the organism, or to locomotion of the organism as a whole. These responses can be determined by reference to spatial and temporal coordinates and can thus be said to be determinable in an objective manner. To the extent that behaviour can be determined in this way it might be said to be observable. (On this point the reader is referred to my earlier work, Saugstad, 1965.)

The stimulus—response paradigm

The stimulus—response paradigm has dominated behaviourist thinking for more than fifty years. The paradigm, as introduced by Watson [1919], rests on the belief that it is possible to account for activities designated as psychological without presupposing properties of the organism of some sort. The term 'stimulus' was thus believed to be describable strictly in physicalist terms. This belief has repeatedly been subjected to trenchant criticism by thinkers such as Köhler (1929), Klüver (1933), Lashley (1930), Piaget (1950), Chomsky (1959), Koch (1954, 1964), Kaufman (1967) and Taylor (1967). This criticism reveals that up to the present no behaviourist has ever been capable of defining a stimulus. One can, therefore, understand that Koch (1964), in despair over the continued use of the term, characterized it as a form of scholasticism.

The use of the term 'stimulus' from the founding of the behaviourist school up to the present may be fairly adequately illustrated by a consideration of the use of it by the leading behaviourist theorists from the 1920's to the present. Watson [1919, pp. 10-11] introduced the stimulus—response paradigm in this way:

Use of the Term Stimulus. — We use the term *stimulus* in psychology as it is used in physiology. Only in psychology we have to extend somewhat the usage of the term. In the psychological laboratory, when we are dealing with relatively simple factors, such as the effect of ether waves of different lengths, the effect of sound waves, etc., and are attempting to isolate their effects upon the adjustments of men, we speak of stimuli. On the other hand, when the factors leading to reactions are more complex, as, for example, in the social world, we speak of *situations*. A situation is, of course, upon final analysis, resolvable into a complex group of stimuli. As examples of stimuli we may name such things as rays of light of different wave lengths; sound waves differing in amplitude, length, phase, and combination; gaseous particles given off in such small diameters that they affect the membrane of the nose; solutions which contain particles of matter of such size that the taste buds are thrown into action; solid objects which affect the skin and mucous membrane; radiant stimuli which call out temperature response; noxious stimuli, such as cutting, pricking, and those injuring tissue generally. Finally, movements of the muscles and activity in the glands themselves serve as stimuli by acting upon the afferent nerve endings in the moving muscles.

It must be emphasized here that only under the rarest experimental conditions can we stimulate the organism with a single stimulus. Life presents stimuli in confusing combinations. As you write you are stimulated by a complex system — perspiration pours from your brow, the pen has a tendency to slip from your grasp; the words you write are focussed upon your retinae; the chair offers stimulation, and finally the noises from the street constantly impinge upon your ear-drum. But far more important, delicate instruments would show that, though you are not speaking aloud, your vocal mechanisms — tongue, throat and laryngeal muscles — are in constant motion, moving in habitual trains; these laryngeal and throat movements serve largely as the stimuli for releasing the writing movements of the hands. The fact that you are here in the lecture room, facing your instructor and surrounded by your classmates, is another very important element. The world of stimulation is thus seen to be exceedingly complex. It is convenient to speak of a total mass of stimulation factors, which lead man to react as a whole, as a situation. Situations can be of the simplest kind or of the greatest complexity.

In introducing the stimulus—response paradigm Watson, as was seen, referred to the reflex reaction, but failed to see that this type of reaction cannot be accounted for without a reference to properties of the organism. Moreover he failed to see that specific mechanisms might underly the reflex reaction and thus that this reaction could not be regarded as a paradigm for the analysis of other types of reactions. Finally he failed to see that also in the psychophysical experiment — where attempts are made at an accurate description of the stimulation affecting the organism — the responses emitted are controlled by specific procedures. In experiments performed with human individuals control is achieved by verbal instructions and in experiments with individuals of other species by training procedures developed on analogy with the verbal instructions given the human individuals. (For a criticism of this point, reference is made to my previous work, Saugstad, 1965.) Apparently the introduction of the stimulus—response paradigm by Watson was based on the empiricist belief that the sensation was some sort of ultimate fact and on a general belief in determinism. The introduction of the paradigm thus represented no attempt at seriously thinking through the fundamental difficulties meeting a conception of psychology in terms of behaviour.

After Watson, i.e. from about 1930 to 1950, Hull became the leading figure in behaviourism. In Chapter 2 the use of the stimulus—response paradigm in his work was considered. I shall therefore proceed to discuss the use of the paradigm in Skinner (1938, 1957, 1969, 1974), the dominant figure in the movement from 1950 to the present.

Skinner modified the paradigm, but continued to use the term 'stimulus' more or less in the same way as his forerunners, i.e. by giving a vague reference to everyday use of language and operational procedures. Chomsky (1959, pp. 31-32) aptly characterized this use in his criticism of Skinner's (1957) book entitled *Verbal Behavior:*

> Consider first Skinner's use of the notions 'stimulus' and 'response'. In *Behavior of organisms* he commits himself to the narrow definitions of these terms. A part of the environment and a part of behavior are called stimulus (eliciting, discriminated, or reinforcing) and response, respectively, only if they are lawfully related; that is, if the 'dynamic laws' relating them show smooth and reproducible curves. Evidently stimuli and responses, so defined, have not been shown to figure very widely in ordinary human behavior. We can, in the face of presently available evidence, continue to maintain the lawfulness of the relation between stimulus and response only by depriving them of their objective character. A typical example of 'stimulus control' for Skinner would be the response to a piece of music with the utterance *Mozart* or to a painting with the response *Dutch*. These responses are asserted to be 'under the control of extremely subtle properties' of the physical object or event. Suppose instead of saying Dutch we had said *Clashes with the wallpaper, I thought you liked abstract work, Never saw it before, Tilted, Hanging too low, Beautiful, Hideous, Remember our camping trip last summer?* or whatever else might come into our minds when looking at a picture (in Skinnerian translation, whatever other responses exist in sufficient strength). Skinner could only say that each of these responses is under the control of some other stimulus property of the physical object. If we look at the red chair and say *red*, the response is under the control of the stimulus 'redness'; if we say *chair*, it is under the control of the collection of properties (for Skinner, the object) 'chairness', and similarly for any other response. This device is as simple as it is empty. Since properties are free for the asking (we have as many of them as we have nonsynonymous descriptive expressions in our language, whatever this means exactly), we can account for a wide class of responses in terms of Skinnerian functional analyses by identifying the 'controlling stimuli'. But the word 'stimulus' has lost all objectivity in this usage. Stimuli are no longer part of the outside physical world; they are driven back into the organism. We identify the stimulus when we hear the response. It is clear from such examples, which abound, that

160

the talk of 'stimulus control' simply disguises a complete retreat to mentalistic psychology. We cannot predict verbal behavior in terms of the stimuli in the speaker's environment, since we do not know what the current stimuli are until he responds. Furthermore, since we cannot control the property of a physical object to which an individual will respond, except in highly artificial cases, Skinner's claim that his system, as opposed to the traditional one, permits the practical control of verbal behavior is quite false.

Actually the behaviourists came to admit that they had to make reference to various sorts of properties ascribed to the organism but for reasons mentioned above they did not realize that this insight affected their conception of behaviour as the subject matter of psychology. Tolman (1932), who was no adherent of the stimulus—response paradigm, noted that behaviour could not be accounted for unless a purpose of some sort was presupposed. He distinguished between a molar or purposive, and a molecular behaviourism, and his conception of a molar or a goal-directed behaviourism as contrasted with the muscle twitches of Watson was widely accepted. Tolman (1936) further introduced the term 'intervening variable' to refer to internal mechanisms. It seems far-fetched to refer to the subject matter of a science by the term 'intervening variable' and it must probably be ascribed to the dominance of positivist thinking about reality that the use of this term has become so widespread. As was noted in the previous section, close to 30 years after the appearance of his first book Skinner (1964), too, arrived at the conclusion that behaviour could not be determined solely by reference to the observable: 'An adequate science of behaviour must consider events taking place within the skin of the organism, not as physiological indicators of behaviour, but as part of behaviour itself.'

After all, then, behaviourism was not only concerned with the observable. Behaviourists have attempted to handle this difficulty in various ways. Some, such as Osgood (1953), resorted to the postulation of stimuli which were located inside the organism and some declared that behaviour was mediated by verbal stimuli. Others resorted to the belief that behaviour could be reduced to an aspect of neurophysiology and equipped the nervous system with correlates to behaviour, and still others referred to dispositions to react. (For a review of these attempts see Woodworth and Shean, 1964; Taylor, 1967; Kaufman, 1967.) As has been mentioned, Koch (1964) referred to the continued use of the term 'stimulus' as a sort of scholasticism. Taylor (ibid, pp. 519-520) characterized the tendency to inflate the term 'behaviour' in the following way:

Difficulties of this kind have led to the invention of a host of secondary hypotheses, many of which have added as many difficulties as they solve and some of which seem incompatible with the goals of behaviorism once their

161

meaning is clarified (for example, responses defined by their result, drives by their goal, stimuli by their relations with others). At the same time molar behaviorism has not lived up to its promise. Its results have been relatively meager and very disparate; they have not converged toward any systematic conception of human behavior, as earlier theorists had hoped. Indeed, the number of theories grows unceasingly. The behaviorist school of thought is thus for the first time entering a period of doubt and uncertainty which accounts for the increased emphasis on centralist theory mentioned above, but which may have more farreaching effects.

Kaufman (1967, p. 271) arrived at a similar conclusion after having examined the position of the so-called philosophical behaviourists:

To summarize, philosophical behaviorists seem to be able to draw on unsuspected dialectical resources in meeting criticism. But in so doing they seem to purchase impregnability at the expense of those very features of the behaviorist outlook that attracted theorists to the position in the first place.

Behaviourism and meaning

Apparently use of the term 'behaviour' always implies a reference to properties of the organism. In order to meet this difficulty behaviourists have been forced to resort to an implicit reference to meaning in order to be capable of relating stimuli to responses. This implicit reference deprives behaviourist theory construction of rigour. Meaning is resorted to as a deus ex machina. In other words, the behaviourist's insistence that he observes behaviour results in a wiping out of the distinction between theoretical construct and observation. In order that the study of behaviour might be regarded as an objective study it would have to be supplied with a theory of meaning. Behaviourists have overlooked this point because they came to accept the empiricist belief that words and expressions can be ostensively defined and the belief related to this that empirical concepts in science can be aedquately defined in an operational manner. Because it is difficult to conceive of meaning as being independent of use of language, it is also difficult to conceive of behaviour as being independent of use of language. Therefore, the belief that behaviour can be ascribed logical priority over use of language meets with serious difficulties, and to treat use of language as a specific type of behaviour, so-called verbal behaviour, seems to be a practice resting on a very shaky basis.

The behaviourist stimulus—response paradigm forms a parallel to the analytic philosophy of Russell. (For a review of Russell's philosophy, see Edwards, Alston and Prior, 1967.)

In the next chapter I shall return to a central point in Russell's philosophy of language. Here I shall just point out that Russell believed that he could analyse complicated linguistic statements into sentences which derived their meaning from what he considered simple facts. The behaviourists believed that they could analyse complex reactions into stimulus—response relationships of a simple nature.

While Russell followed the empiricist tradition and presupposed that perceptual impressions of various sorts represented ultimate facts, Watson, as was noted above, believed that reflexes represented the ultimate facts and conceived of all stimulus—response relationships on analogy with reflexes. It is not surprising to note that Russell became the favourite philosopher of a number of behaviourist thinkers. The empiricist belief that meaning could be reduced to a reference to simple facts was taken over by the logical positivists, who formulated their verifiability principle of meaning in accordance with this belief. (For a review of their principle, see Ashby, 1967.) In retrospect one can understand that in the 1930's the logical positivists and the behaviourists embraced each other. Their conception of meaning as established by reference to simple facts had the same origin in empiricist and positivist philosophical traditions. These two philosophies also gave the behaviourists and logical positivists the same convictions with regard to issues in the philosophy of science.

Within the intellectual climate created by empiricism and positivism the Pavlovian approach to psychology naturally had to have great appeal. The Pavlovian design exemplifies the belief that meaning can be regarded as an association between simple facts.

Even if the reflex reaction is not solely determined by what may be considered a simple type of stimulation, but must be considered the effect of a complicated nervous activity, one can say that the reflex *approximates* an invariant stimulus—response relationship. (On the reflex as the result of a complicated nervous activity, see Bertalanffy, 1968; Kussmann and Kölling, 1971.)

The idea that complex activities are built up on reflexes or on relatively simple invariant stimulus—response relationships is intriguing. However, it loses much of its attraction when it is realized that this idea raises complicated questions of identity between the stimulus—response relationships on the complex level of adult human functioning and functioning at an earlier ontogenetic level of development. Of course, it is reasonable to believe that the stimulus—response relationships become more complex as the individual develops. On the other hand, the simpler the stimulus—response relationships are, the more difficult it is to make clear that these simpler relationships are identical to the more complicated activities. This is not a denial of the fact that a study of the effect of learning can contribute to clarifying what is involved in the more complicated activities in the adult organism. What I want to make clear is simply that

163

unless some reference system for dealing with the complicated activities on the adult level is worked out questions of identity cannot be answered.

The complexity of the problem of ascertaining identity between stimulus—response relationships may be illustrated by some simple examples which could be multiplied endlessly. Consider the response of bending one's middle finger prior to pressing a button. For the sake of simplicity let us consider only the movement involved in bending the finger. We can instruct an adult person to make the response of bending the finger in, say, a psychophysical situation when the hue of a light patch is varied, but we can also instruct him to make the response when the brightness of the light patch, or its form or size, is varied, or when the pitch of a tone is varied. We can even instruct him to make the response as an indication that he has solved a mathematical or a practical problem or when he feels in a certain mood, say, pleased or excited. In what sense can we say that the response is the same?

Similarly it can be shown that a seemingly endless variety of responses can be attached to what may be considered as a definite aspect of a situation. It is easy to see that in assigning identity to stimulus—response relationships of various types the behaviourist may come to presuppose what he is to investigate.

The difficulty involved in ascertaining identity between stimulus—response relationships is actually met with at the first stage of establishing stimulus—response relationships by means of Pavlovian conditioning. Here it has turned out that the so-called conditioned response is never identical to the so-called unconditioned response. The dog does not, for example, secrete the same amount of saliva in response to the sound of the buzzer as when presented with the food. Nor is the chemical composition of the saliva the same. (For a review of this issue, see Woodworth and Schlosberg, 1954.)

In retrospect it seems reasonable to state that behaviourist psychologists have in fact contributed to the understanding that psychology concerns interactions between the organism and its environment and not the study of inner events or intra-psychic entities. By insisting on the role played by learning, they have also shed important light on a variety of activities in man and animals. As has been argued, the weakness in the behaviourist approach is found in its unclear conceptions regarding the nature of the interactions between the organism and its environment.

Physicalism

As Malcolm (1964) made clear, the idea of physicalism is parallel to the idea of behaviourism. Physicalism rests on the presupposition that psychological statements are reducible to statements of a physicalist nature. Carnap [1931] seems to be chiefly responsible for the elaboration of this thesis, but adherents are also found among other logical positivists such as Hempel, Schlick and Neurath. (For further reference, see Ayer, 1959.) Carnap presented his thesis in the following introductory statement to the article entitled 'Psychology in physical language' (1959, p. 165):

> In what follows, we intend to explain and to establish the thesis that *every sentence of psychology may be formulated in physical language*. To express this in the material mode of speech: *all sentences of psychology describe physical occurrences, namely, the physical behavior of humans and other animals*. This is a sub-thesis of the general thesis of *physicalism* to the effect that *physical language is a universal language*, that is, a language into which every sentence may be translated.

Carnap concentrated on the following example: 'I assert the sentence P_1: "Mr. A is now excited." ' The example is elaborated in the following way (pp. 170, 171):

> There are two different ways in which sentence P_1 may be derived. We shall designate them as the 'rational' and the 'intuitive' methods. The *rational* method consists of inferring P_1 from some protocol sentence p_1 (or from several like it), more specifically, from a perception-sentence about the behavior of A, e.g. about his facial expressions, his gestures, etc., or about physical effects of A's behavior, e.g. about characteristics of his handwriting.
>
> In order to justify the conclusion, a major premise O is still required, namely the general sentence which asserts that when I perceive a person to have this facial expression and handwriting he (usually) turns out to be excited. (A sentence about the expressional or graphological signs of excitement.)
>
> The content of P_1 does not coincide with that of p_1 but goes beyond it. This is evident from the fact that to infer P_1 from p_1, O is required. The cited relationship between P_1 and p_1 may also be seen in the fact that under certain circumstances, the inference from p_1 to P_1 may go astray. It may happen that, though p_1 occurs in a protocol, I am obliged, on the grounds of further protocols, to retract the established system sentence P_1. I would then say something like, 'I made a mistake. The test has shown that A was not excited, even though his face had such and such an expression'.

(The quote has been slightly modified by the present writer since he has omitted statements from Carnap supposed by him to represent a parallel example of a statement of physical property). Apparently Carnap's conclusion cannot be accepted until the following question is answered: How can we know that the perception-sentence p_1 is related to the psychological statement, the sentence P_1? As is seen from the quotation, Carnap argued that we need a major premiss O which assures that 'when I perceive a person to have this facial expression and handwriting he (usually) turns out to be excited'.

Evidently the argument revolves around the interpretation to be given to the expression 'it turns out that a person is excited when he has this and this facial expression and this and this handwriting'. It is difficult to see that the expression 'turns out' can be given any other interpretation than the following: Taking into consideration the situation as a totality we can know that Mr. A is excited. This seems to be just another way of stating that we know what it means to be excited. This being granted, the only conclusion warranted is that when a person is excited, responses of certain types may be registered, but this does not allow us to conclude that excitement is definable in terms of physicalist statements.

Verbal behaviour

As will be clear from the preceding discussions, behaviourist theorists have ascribed logical priority to behaviour over use of language. In so doing they have failed to make clear how one could possibly communicate about behaviour without using language. The confusion arising from the failure to clarify this issue has had particularly unfortunate consequences for attempts at dealing with use of language. To the behaviourist use of language is simply a specific domain of behaviour referred to as 'verbal behaviour'.

Behaviourists have believed explicitly or implicitly that they could account for use of language in terms of some model for the acquisition of this use. Whereas in the early period, the 1930's and 40's, behaviourists were mainly preoccupied with the study of learning in species other than man, in the 1950's they became increasingly interested in the study of use of language. Osgood (1953, p. 727) ended his influential book *Method and Theory in Experimental Psychology* in the following manner:

> In terms of its central relevance to general psychological theory and its potential applicability to complex social problems, no other area of experimental psychology so greatly demands attention as language behavior — and in the past has received so little.

This emphasis on use of language represented a reorientation which has been fruitful for Western psychology. As has been noted, Soviet psychologists headed by Vygotsky (1962) had concentrated some 25 years earlier on the role played by use of language in human activities. The interest in use of language in behaviourism has resulted in a large number of studies in the 1950's, 60's and 70's. Here I shall only concentrate on certain fundamental points concerning the models used to explain the acquisition of use of language.

Behaviourist theorists took as their point of departure what they regarded as the fundamental principles of learning. Osgood (1953), Mowrer (1966) and Staats (1970) elaborated ideas on learning presented by Hull. Skinner (1957; 1969), on the other hand, approached this study in terms of his ideas of operant behaviour. In Chapter 3 the diffuse use of the term 'learning' in theorists in the Thorndike-Pavlov tradition was pointed out. Above I have also made it clear that the terms 'stimulus' and 'response' have been used in an arbitrary manner. The weaknesses resulting from the difficulties attaching to the terms mentioned came to affect the new field of study.

The difficulties met by Osgood, Mowrer and Staats come into sharp focus if we concentrate attention on Osgood's first exposition. Osgood conceived of use of language as mediating in some way between the stimulus and response which had earlier been connected. Meaning could be accounted for in terms of a hypothesis about this mediation (Osgood, ibid p. 412):

> As will be shown in the final chapter of this book, the major difficulty with most attempts to deal with 'the meaning of meaning' has been their failure to offer any convincing explanation of why a particular sign refers to a particular object and not to others. The mediation hypothesis offers an excellent and very convincing reason: the sign 'means' or 'refers to' a particular object because it elicits in the organism employing it part of the same behavior which the object itself elicits. In a very real sense — since it can be shown that most 'new' learning comes down to the association of new mediation processes with old stimulus patterns or new instrumental sequences with old mediation processes — this hypothesis places the problem of *meaning* directly at the core of learning theory.

Osgood rejected the early behaviourist view that the linguistic sign could be regarded as a substitute for the stimulus in the Pavlovian conditioning paradigm. He asserted that this paradigm had been adopted by Watson. In this connection mention should be made of the fact that the influential linguist Bloomfield (1933) had also applied this paradigm in a rather uncritical manner. Morris (1946) had realized the crudeness of this account of meaning. He attempted to improve upon the account by arguing that the organism acquired a disposition to react to a sign in the same way as it had previously reacted to the object in the original conditioning situation. Osgood pointed out that it was difficult to define the term 'disposition to react' in a satisfactory manner. He suggested that the term 'disposition' could be replaced by the term 'fragmentary reactions'. These fragmentary reactions were accounted for in terms of his mediation hypothesis, which was formulated in the following manner (Osgood, ibid, pp. 695-96):

Whereas Morris links sign and object through partial identity of object-

167

produced and disposition-*produced* behavior, we shall link sign and object through partial identity of the 'disposition' *itself* with the behavior elicited by the object. Words represent things because they produce some replica of the actual behavior toward these things. This is the crucial identification, the mechanism that ties signs to particular stimulus-objects and not to others.

Osgood (ibid, p. 697) illustrated his hypothesis by indicating how a child might acquire the meaning of the word 'hammer':

> The stimulus-object, a heavy thing having certain visual characteristics and certain tactual and proprioceptive effects, elicits in the young child, usually under instructions or imitation of some adult, a total pattern of behavior, including grasping and pounding movements. According to the mediation hypothesis, anticipatory portions of this behavior become short-circuited to the sign HAMMER. The process of reduction is especially important in the case of denotative signs — obviously, overt movements of the hands will interfere with other on-going instrumental behaviors and therefore tend to be extinguished. A young child, however, may actually be observed to clench his hand and move it up and down when asked for 'hammer'.

Difficulties of various sorts attach to this hypothesis, as has been made abundantly clear by Alston (1964). I shall point to the difficulties involved in treating behaviour as a domain of extra-linguistic events. In the first place, it is difficult to understand how one can communicate about the material object, in this case a hammer, without the use of language. Apparently Osgood has overlooked the fact that he must presuppose that the object, a hammer, is conceived of either as a particular or as a universal. The same will of course also hold true for the acoustic stimulation perceived as the sign by the child. If the object is conceived of as a particular, it becomes difficult to understand that the latter can be conceived of as a universal. On the other hand, if the latter is conceived of as a universal, it is difficult to see why the former should not be conceived of as universal. This means that no matter whether Osgood presupposes that the object is conceived of as a particular or as a universal, he must inevitably become entangled in fundamental difficulties. A further difficulty arises in accounting for the way the acoustic stimulation is connected with the object. It seems unreasonable to believe that the way the child has communicated previously would not affect this connection in a fundamental manner. For example, as suggested by Werner and Kaplan (1967), crying, smiling, babbling and gesturing probably influence the establishment of this connection. An attempt to deal with the acquisition of the meaning of words in children which does not take into acount how children are capable of communicating prior to this acquisition, can hardly amount to more than loose speculation.

In Skinner's (1957, 1969, 1974) approach to psychology, behaviour is regarded as an extra-linguistic domain of events and as being logically prior to use of language. Thus, the study of use of language is believed to form part of a general study of behaviour. In view of what has been said in the previous chapters, this idea will be seen to reflect a naive conception of the nature of use of language. The main reasons for this naiveté are apparently to be found in the fact that Skinner and his adherents never seem to have seriously questioned the central beliefs of British empiricism, and further in the fact that they have adopted a procedure of introducing their theoretical terms by merely pointing to the operations involved in their use. When the central terms in the Skinnerian approach are examined, serious limitations are revealed. I shall undertake an examination of Skinner's idea of verbal behaviour. The following passage from Skinner (1974, p. 94) epitomizes Skinner's beliefs concerning the establishment of meaning and use of language:

> There is no point in asking how a person can 'know the abstract entity called redness'. The contingencies explain the behaviour, and we need not be disturbed because it is impossible to discover the referent in any single instance. We need not, with William of Ockham and the Nominalists, deny that abstract entities exist and insist that such responses are merely words. What exist are the contingencies which bring behavior under the control of properties or of classes of objects defined by properties. (We can determine that a single response is under the control of one property by naming it. For example, if we show a person a pencil and say, 'What *color* is this?' he will then respond to the property specified as color — provided he has been subject to an appropriate history of reinforcement.)

Unfortunately, Skinner did not explain why there is no point in asking how a person can 'know the abstract entity called redness'. This question is not easy to answer. What Skinner and empiricist psychologists have overlooked is that if we cannot answer this question we are in no position to state how an individual who is not familiar with use of language will conceive of the utterance 'red'. We will be left vaguely guessing how the child acquires use of language.

In the passage quoted above, it was noted that meaning was believed to be establishable through contingencies of reinforcement. The idea of contingencies of reinforcement is not further elaborated in the book from which the quote is taken, and we must go back to an earlier work (Skinner, 1969, p. 7) to obtain more information:

> An adequate formulation of the interaction between an organism and its environment must always specify three things: (1) the occasion upon which the response occurs, (2) the response itself, and (3) the reinforcing consequences. The interrelationships among them are the 'contingencies of reinforcement'.

In his treatment of the terms 'environment' and 'organism' Skinner did not state how the environment and the organism can be distinguished from one another. An environment is, of course, always an environment for an organism which has specific properties. Unless definite aspects of the environment and specific properties of the organism have been specified, it makes no sense to speak of environment and organism. Instead of making these specifications, Skinner speaks loosely of responses and operants. Of course, in some way a response is related — as is implied by the word 'response' — to the environment. Therefore if a response is to be defined this relationship must be stated.

According to Skinner the environment can be described in terms of stimuli, and the stimuli in turn in terms of a physicalist description. This belief is expressed later in the book (pp. 78-79) as follows: 'An experimental analysis describes stimuli in the language of physics.' The same belief was expressed in his earlier work (Skinner, 1957, p. 1). As has been pointed out above, this physicalist description is not possible.

The use of the term 'response' in Skinner reflects his vague and diffuse ideas about behaviour. Concerning the latter term, Skinner made no attempt in his recent book, entitled *About Behaviorism,* to state what he meant by behaviour. Apparently he — along with the rest of behaviourists — believed that the term 'behaviour' had been satisfactorily defined by Watson. In connection with Skinner's use of the term 'behaviour' it should be emphasized that all through his work he has distinguished between a private world and a public one. Thus, a closer scrutiny of his theorizing reveals that he is entangled in ideas of consciousness.

An operant is said to represent a class 'of which a response is an instance or member'. (See for example Chapter 5 in his book *Contingencies of Reinforcement.)* The question which must be answered is how it is possible to define a class of responses without making this definition dependent upon use of language. If this question cannot be answered, behaviour cannot be ascribed logical priority over use of language. What are the criteria for specifying the various classes of operants? Apparently the belief of Skinner and his students that theoretical terms can be operationally defined has made them overlook the fundamental difficulty pointed out here.

The comments made here regarding the bases for Skinner's central theoretical terms clearly show that his approach is based on a more or less intuitive appeal to understanding of use of language in the normal adult individual, and that his claim that verbal behaviour has logical priority over use of language cannot be supported.

CHAPTER 10

Use of language and problems of meaning

The close relationship found to exist between the various psychological activities and use of language indicates that these activities and use of language must be conceived of as some sort of totality. This conclusion does not of course only mean that it is difficult to conceive of a study of the activities of perceiving, remembering, imagining and thinking, but also that it is difficult to conceive of a study of use of language in a more fundamental sense. In this chapter I shall consider difficulties attaching to the latter study.

Unless one makes some indefensibly simple presuppositions about the existence of domains of events of an extra-linguistic nature, it is difficult to imagine what might constitute the framework for a study of use of language. In the previous chapter the difficulty of conceiving of consciousness or of behaviour as constituting such frameworks was discussed. Furthermore it was made clear that linguistics as traditionally practised cannot be regarded as a study of use of language in a fundamental sense. The same is apparently true of biology. In a study of use of language based on biology we would not be capable of stating what is meant by the organism or by its environment. In this chapter I shall be concerned with attempts made by logicians to conceive of a framework for the study of use of language in terms of meaning.

On the face of it at least it seems reasonable to characterize use of language by saying that it is concerned with understanding or the establishment of meaning. Most thinkers preoccupied with problems raised by a study of use of language have probably more or less explicitly tended to conceive of the study in this way. Particularly in the latter half of the nineteenth century and the first half of the twentieth philosophers inspired by Stuart Mill attempted to approach the study of use of language more systematically in this way. As has been mentioned, it is difficult to imagine what might constitute the framework for a study of use of language, and for this reason it is perhaps not surprising that this endeavour seems more or less to have ended in what Ryle (1957, pp. 261-262) characterized as the postulation of a realm of Platonized meanings:

Thus, by the first decade of this century it was dawning upon philosophers and logicians that their business was not that of one science among others, e.g. that of psychology; and even that it was not an inductive, experimental or observational business of any sort. It was intimately concerned with, among other things, the fundamental concepts and principles of mathematics; and it seemed to have to do with a special domain which was not bespoken by any other discipline, namely the so-called third realm of logical objects or Meanings. At the same time, and in some degree affected by these influences, Moore consistently and Russell spasmodically were prosecuting their obviously philosophical and logical inquiries with a special *modus operandi*. They, and not they alone, were deliberately and explicitly trying to give analyses of concepts and propositions — asking: What does it really mean to say, for example, that this is good? or that that is true? or that centaurs do not exist? or that I see an inkpot? or What are the differences between the distinguishable senses of the verb 'to know' and the verb 'to be'? Moore's regular practice and Russell's frequent practice seemed to exemplify beautifully what, for example, Husserl and Meinong had declared in general terms to be the peculiar business of philosophy and logic, namely to explore the third realm of Meanings. Thus philosophy had acquired a right to live its own life, neither as a discredited pretender to the status of the science of mind, nor yet as a superannuated handmaiden of *démodé* theology. It was responsible for a special field of facts, facts of impressively Platonized kinds.

The tendency to conceive of meaning as a domain of events whose existence was independent of use of language was carried out to the extreme when a group of philosophers headed by Carnap declared that philosophy was to be regarded as the study of the language of science. In retrospect one can but wonder how one could think of separating empirical content in the various branches of sciences from the means of communicating about this content and, vice versa, how one could think of communicating about the means of communication in science without reference to empirical content. The belief that it is possible to speak of the language of science as if it were independent of empirical content is in line with the positivist belief that it is possible to state what the methods of science are without having to refer to subject matter. The idea of philosophy as a study of the language of science fundamentally influenced psychology. For some time it became fashionable also to speak of the language of psychology. (See for example Mandler and Kessen, 1959.) There is much to learn about empirical psychology by considering the various trends in Western philosophy, and I shall continue with a quote from Passmore (1967, p. 221), where he discusses the conception of philosophy as the study of the language of science:

The general thesis that philosophy is 'really about language' may well turn out to have the same fate as the thesis that philosophy is 'really about human nature'. It arose in much the same way. When, in the nineteenth century, the 'moral sciences' were gradually transformed into psychology and the social sciences, and even logic, in its more technical sense, was converted into a branch of mathematics, the philosopher seemed to be left with nothing to do. The distinction between 'language' and 'the world' has, in an important sense, replaced the older distinction between the inner world and the outer world. It provided the philosopher with an area in which to work — one that satisfied the traditional requirement of width of scope and at the same time left 'the world' to science. There was, it it true, some difficulty in explaining just how the philosopher's concern with language differed from the philologist's. But as long as philology was largely etymology, the distinction, although hard to pin down, at least had some justification. Now that philosophy has helped to create new forms of linguistics, however, the exact manner in which philosophy can be 'about language' without being a scientific discipline has become more and more obscure.

The Platonic conceptions of meaning discussed above, particularly those of Frege, Russell and Carnap, have exerted a strong influence on empirical psychology. This influence has contributed to the reinforcement of the positivist tendency to postulate domains of events for study without first ascertaining that it is possible to communicate about the events postulated. It has become habitual in empirical psychology to make obscure appeals to meaning. As a consequence of this appeal research workers who conceive of psychology in terms of consciousness have introduced terms such as 'mental element', 'internal structure', 'the unconscious', 'the ego', 'meanings' and 'intention' which, as I have argued, may merely be names for myths, and behaviourists have introduced terms such as 'stimulus' and 'response' and have thereby contributed to the upsurge of a new sort of scholasticism. In this and the next chapter we will have occasion to note the vague and diffuse use of the terms 'information' and 'process' in research workers operating within the framework of information and communication theory. On the whole I would say that theorists in psychology use appeals to meaning as a deus ex machina. In other words, whenever the theorist meets with difficulties in developing a coherent and consistent argument, he tends to make an obscure appeal to meaning.

The tendency to conceive of the existence of domains of events of an extra-linguistic nature has been criticized from various quarters. Thus Quine [1951, pp. 41-42] noted the tendency in a discussion of what he referred to as 'two dogmas of empiricism', the belief in the distinction between synthetic and analytic statements and in reductionism:

> The two dogmas are, indeed, at root identical. We lately reflected that in general the truth of statements does obviously depend both upon language and upon extralinguistic fact; and we noted that this obvious circumstance carries in its train, not logically but all too naturally, a feeling that the truth of a statement is somehow analyzable into a linguistic component and a factual

component. The factual component must, if we are empiricists, boil down to a range of confirmatory experiences. In the extreme case where the linguistic component is all that matters, a true statement is analytic. But I hope we are now impressed with how stubbornly the distinction between analytic and synthetic has resisted any staightforward drawing. I am impressed also, apart from prefabricated examples of black and white balls in an urn, with how baffling the problem has always been of arriving at any explicit theory of the empirical confirmation of a synthetic statement. My present suggestion is that it is nonsense, and the root of much nonsense, to speak of a linguistic component and a factual component in the truth of any individual statement. Taken collectively, science has its double dependence upon language and experience; but this duality is not significantly traceable into the statements of science taken one by one.

In the 1930's and 1940's Wittgenstein began questioning the tendency to postulate domains of events of an extra-linguistic nature and subjected the appeals made to meaning in attempts at handling problems in the study of use of language to a trenchant criticism. (For reviews of Wittgenstein's philosophy, see Malcolm, 1967; Pears, 1971.) Wittgenstein formed the slogan: 'Do not look for the meaning, look for the use'. This reorientation to the study of use of language seems to have led Wittgenstein to deny the possibility that use of language might be characterized in a fundamental sense by general statements. Apparently, if he was correct on this point, it is difficult to understand what can be meant by a scientific study of the psychological activities discussed in this book. Wittgenstein's later philosophy may therefore be said to represent a serious challenge to the theorist in psychology. Below I shall try to show that his conclusions on this point are not valid, and that they are probably the result of an error in his reasoning about use of language. Still, even if I should be correct in my criticism, there can be no denial of the fact that appeals to meaning as made by philosophers and psychologists are often of a highly dubious nature, and that attempts to characterize use of language meet with greater difficulties than believed by thinkers before him.

Apparently in order to characterize use of language we shall have to state what is communicated about when language is used. To the unreflective mind no problem may be seen to be involved. For example, let us suppose I am, as now, situated in a room. I might say that in this situation I could communicate about the shape and size of the room, its walls and furniture, etc. If I were situated in some landscape, I could communicate about the rocks, stones, trees and houses confronting me. On reflection it will be seen that matters are not so simple. The room, the walls, the furniture, the rocks, the stones and the houses must be perceived, imagined, remembered and thought of in order that I shall be capable of communicating about them. And how can we communicate about what we perceive, remember, imagine and think unless we use language? This question was discussed in the previous chapters.

Actually, attempts to say what is being communicated about when language is used have led philosophers into a number of highly intricate problems. It should be emphasized that these problems still await accepted solutions, and also that unless such solutions are found it will hardly be possible for there to be a fruitful scientific study of remembering, imagining and thinking or, perhaps, more generally, of psychology and the social sciences. Attention should also be paid to the fact that the problems involved tend to cluster in such a way that the position taken towards one of them affects the formulation of the others. In listing what seem to be some of the main problems, it is perhaps natural to begin with the problem of what constitutes a definition. In a sense it may be said that the whole discussion originated in the concern in Socrates and Plato for the problem of what constitutes a definition. (On this problem in Socrates and Plato, see Huby, 1964.) Moreover it is natural to place the point of departure in this problem because the way we conceive of definitions determines what we can accept as an adequate solution to a problem. At this point let me just emphasize that so far no accepted solution has been presented to this age-old problem. (For a critical review of the problem of what constitutes a definition, see Abelson, 1967.) Preoccupation with the problem of what constitutes a definition led Aristotle to consider the problem of what constitutes an individual thing. He postulated his famous essences and developed the theory of substance and attribute which so deeply affected later thinkers, for example, Descartes, Locke, Kant and Hegel. (For a review of Aristotle's philosophy, see O'Connor, 1964, and for a review of the problem of what constitutes an individual thing, see O'Connor, 1967.) Closely related to these two problems is the problem of accounting for the general or the universal, which since the days of Plato has been the repeated concern of philosophers. (For critical reviews of this problem, see Woozley, 1967.) In the discussions of the problems of definition, the individual and the universal conceptions of the material object have played a major role, and I shall consider certain ideas inherent in some of these conceptions.

In philosophers inspired by Stuart Mill, such as Frege, Russell and Carnap, the problem of stating what was being communicated about when language was used was formulated as being that of distinguishing between reference and meaning. (For a review of this problem, see Linsky, 1967, a.) Closely related to the problem of distinguishing between reference and meaning is the one of stating what is meant by 'a proposition' in logic. (On this problem, see Gale, 1967.)

Naturally, an examination of the problem of what is being communicated about when language is used also leads into a consideration of fundamental problems in linguistics, such as that of stating what constitutes the unit of language. This leads to questions concerning the nature of the phoneme, the morpheme and the sentence. (For a review of the modern use of these terms, see Lyons, 1971.) Also related to the question of what constitutes the unit of language is the problem of stating what is meant by 'a signal', 'a sign', and 'a symbol'. This problem, which is evidently fundamental to a scientific study of psychological functioning, is far from solved, even if theorists in psychology tend to proceed as if it had been. (For a review of this problem, see Alston, 1967, b.)

As has been mentioned, in his later philosophy Wittgenstein may be said to have effected a new orientation to these problems in the study of use of language. Of chief importance for the treatment of the problems listed above, is his pointing out that the idea of a private language is of a dubious nature. As was made clear in Chapter 5 of this book I believe it to be essential that the theorist in psychology does not entangle himself in notions of privacy and solipsism. However, in contradistinction to Wittgenstein I would insist that use of language concerns understanding and meaning and that it is reasonable to approach the problems from this angle. However, after having made this assertion, I must emphasize the fact that the words 'understanding' and 'meaning' have invariably been used in a confused manner by philosophers dealing with the problems mentioned above.

Understanding and statements in the first and third persons

In Chapter 8 attention was called to Malcolm's (1964) criticism of behaviourism. He argued that behaviourists had confused statements in the first and third persons. I believe this to be an acute and important observation. Confusion will arise if this distinction is not observed. I shall elaborate on this point to show that it does not make sense in discussions of problems concerning the nature of use of language to speak of understanding and meaning with regard to statements in the first person. In a fundamental sense understanding and meaning, I shall insist, can only meaningfully be applied to statements in the third person.

The point is perhaps most easily illustrated by an examination of statements about remembering. While situations can be described in which it makes sense to say that there is something which I do not remember, there are also situations in which it does not make sense to say that there is something that I do not remember. I would even claim that it is in the nature of remembering that I cannot say what I do not remember. Similarly situations can be described in which it does not make sense to say what I do not perceive, what I do not imagine or what I do not think. Only if what I do not see, what I do not imagine, or what I do not think is pointed out to me, or when the situation is such that my familiarity with it provides me with this understanding, can I say that there is something I do not perceive, something I do not imagine or something I do not think. In accordance with this line of reasoning I would claim that there are certain types of situations in which it does not make sense to speak of understanding or meaning because it is not possible to decide what is to be meant by *not understanding* or by saying that something *does not have meaning*. In other words unless we have criteria for deciding when understanding and meaning are present and how they are to be recognized we will not be able to discuss problems in use of language in a meaningful manner. This point seems to have been overlooked by philosophers who have discussed problems in use of language. To avoid unneccessary misunderstanding I should like to emphasize the fact that I am not saying that there are not situations in which the words 'understanding' and 'meaning' are applicable. I am merely pointing out the fact that these words are not applicable to all types of situations. Criteria for reaching a decision as to whether or not understanding and meaning are present are only available for statements in the third person.

It will be seen that if the line of reasoning outlined above is followed, the idea of a private language disappears. The procedure that must be followed precludes the possibility that man can have a private language and thus also the idea that knowledge can be of a solipsistic nature.

Before leaving the problem of distinguishing between statements in the first and third persons I should like to point out that what I have said here may probably be what behaviourists have wanted to say. That they have not been able to do so is clear from the fact that they have conceived of the study of psychology in terms of behaviour, stimuli and responses and have introduced the idea of verbal behaviour. Also I should like to point out that although he did draw attention to the difference between statements in the first and third persons Wittgenstein (1953) did not follow the course suggested here. In arguing against the idea of a private language he seems always to have taken statements in the first person as his point of departure. (On this point, see the quote previously given from Malcolm, 1966.)

From what has been said here about understanding, it follows that

177

the fundamental problems raised in the study of use of language cannot be avoided by a study of the acquisition of use of language in the child, as often seems to be believed by thinkers of an empiricist and behaviourist orientation. Unless one believes in the helpful intervention of divine powers, one will have to admit that it is difficult to understand what can be meant by understanding in the child. Of course I am not saying that the child has no under-standing, but as made clear during the discussion of Piaget in Chapter 2 it is difficult for an adult to grasp what understanding in a child involves and to make legitimate statements concerning how or what a child understands. Apparently, as was made clear by Lenneberg (1967, p. 275) we have to know a number of things before we can state in a fruitful manner what can be meant by the statement that use of language is learnt in the child:

> We cannot help but wonder how an infant at little over one year of age can ever learn to understand and produce this behavior. The number of articles and books that deal with the development of language goes up into the thousands. But only few authors have seen that there is a formidable and totally unsolved problem here. How does the child develop language? To say vaguely that it must be discrimination learning, secondary reinforce-ment, or stimulus generalization does not bring us any closer to a solution, because it is not at all clear *what* has to be discriminated or *what* is generalized from or to, nor is it clear *what* is being reinforced, when and how. Over-simplifications, and even representations that are blatantly contrary to observable facts regarding the nature of language, have often led to explanations for language learning that rest on nothing but fiction.

The problem of defining words and expressions

In earlier empiricist thinking as well as in the modern empiricist thinking of Russell and Carnap the idea that words and expressions can be defined in a fundamental sense in terms of some sort of ostensive definition, i.e. by pointing, gestures, or by placing an in-dividual in some definite situation, has played a major role. On the whole I believe this idea underlies much thinking about use of language and communication. In Chapter 5 of this book a quote from Hamlyn (1967, a) was given from an article where he laid bare the difficulties attaching to the ostensive definition. In his attempts at exploring the limits of use of language, Wittgenstein (1953) made it clear that words could not in a fundamental sense be defined ostensively. He made it clear that the ostensive definition was only useful when various presuppositions could be made concerning the definition to be presented. Wittgenstein (ibid, Sect. 29) illustrated his point by considering the possibility of defining various types of words, among them the number 'two' and words for colour:

> Perhaps you say: two can only be ostensively defined in *this* way: 'This

number is called "two" '. For the word 'number' here shews what place in language, in grammar, we assign to the word. But this means that the word 'number' must be explained before the ostensive definition can be understood. — The word 'number' in the definition does indeed shew this place; does shew the post at which we station the word. And we can prevent misunderstandings by saying: 'This *colour* is called so-and-so', 'This *length* is called so-and-so', and so on. That is to say: misunderstandings are sometimes averted in this way. But is there only *one* way of taking the word 'colour' or 'length'? — Well, they just need defining. — Defining, then, by means of other words! And what about the last definition in this chain? (Do not say: 'There isn't a "last" definition'. That is just as if you chose to say: 'There isn't a last house in this road; one can always build an additional one'.)

Whether the word 'number' is necessary in the ostensive definition depends on whether without it the other person takes the definition otherwise than I wish. And that will depend on the circumstances under which it is given, and on the person I give it to. And how he 'takes' the definition is seen in the use that he makes of the word defined.

As made clear by Wittgenstein in the section following the one quoted, no appeal to attention can help the individual who is to profit from the ostensive definition, to understand the meaning of the words to be defined. In Part 2 of this book I shall deal more systematically with problems attaching to the ostensive definition. At this point I shall just note that unless we resort to the idea of a private language, we seem to be incapable of accounting for how words and expressions derive their meaning. The examination seems to lead us to accept the view that use of language has definite limits, or as I would put it (for reasons to be given below): communication and use of language have definite limits.

To the biologically oriented thinker it should not be surprising that communication and use of language have definite limits. From biology he will know about a number of functions for which no adequate explanation can be given. Lenneberg (1967, p. 3) called attention to the tendency in Western thinking to conceive of use of language in rationalist terms. The belief that it is possible to give an adequate account of communication and use of language is probably a result of this tendency.

The difficulty of stating how words, expressions, and, as I shall show later, also sentences derive their meanings, suggests that communication or use of language is necessary in the sense that we cannot conceive of the state of affairs as being otherwise. At this point it should be noted that it does not follow from the examination undertaken above that use of language and not communication is necessary. Wittgenstein seems to have taken the position that use of language was necessary. Even if the private language thesis in the form that Wittgenstein apparently would have phrased it, i.e. that man cannot use language (or symbols) in a way that another individual could not possibly understand, is accepted, it does not follow that use of language and not communication of some sort must be regarded as necessary. As I have made clear above, I reject the idea of a private language. Still, I would like to stress that this rejection does not necessarily imply that use of language must be regarded as fundamental. It cannot be precluded that what may be referred to as certain characteristics of understanding (understanding involving perceiving, remembering, imagining and thinking) are necessary, and that use of language is based on these characteristics. In this connection attention should again be called to the fact that we cannot meaningfully speak of use of language unless we presuppose that the individuals communicating by means of language are capable of perceiving, remembering, imagining and thinking. To keep this possibility open I shall express matters by saying that communication and use of language are in some way necessary. This point is important because it allows one to suggest that use of language can be characterized in general terms, i.e. according to some general theory. Wittgenstein's position seems to have been that this was not possible. (On this point in Wittgenstein's philosophy, see Pears, 1971.)

It must be clear that when communication is discussed in connection with the problem of definition, the word 'language' seems to lose its meaning. The same seems to be true when we discuss problems at early ontogenetic stages in the child, and also when we compare communication in man with communication between individuals of other species. If — as is done in this book — the expression 'use of language' is used exclusively for communication between human individuals, one must take care to note that the extension of the expression to the types of situation referred to above may lead one to overlook the fact that use of language has a biological basis, and thus that it is most probably genetically determined and in all likelihood has features in common with communication in individuals of other species. This point should be stressed because Wittgenstein may have had a tendency to overlook the fact that use of language may have a biological basis. In spite of this, it must be underlined that Wittgenstein was correct in pointing to the difficulty of presupposing that communication or other sorts of activity underlie use of language. If this difficulty is not carefully noted, the theorist may easily come to make simplified statements, for example, of the type discussed in the previous chapter where the dubious view was put forward that consciousness or behaviour underlies use of language.

If no word, expression, or term can be defined in a fundamental sense in an ostensive manner, it follows that it is difficult to state what is meant by 'a definition'. As was made clear by Abelson (1967, p. 314) this difficulty should be emphasized because of the tendency to assume that the problem has been solved:

> The problems of definition are constantly recurring in philosophical discussion, although there is a widespread tendency to assume that they have been solved. Practically every book on logic has a section on definition in which rules are set down and exercises prescribed for applying the rules, as if the problems were all settled. And yet, paradoxically, no problems of knowledge are less settled than those of definition, and no subject is more in need of a fresh approach. Definition plays a crucial role in every field of inquiry, yet there are few if any philosophical questions about definition (what sort of thing it is, what standards it should satisfy, what kind of knowledge, if any, it conveys) on which logicians and philosophers agree. In view of the importance of the topic and the scope of the disagreement concerning it, an extensive re-examination is justified.

The problem of accounting for an individual thing

The problem of accounting for an individual thing has preoccupied philosophers since the days of Aristotle. According to O'Connor (1967) Aristotle's account of what constitutes an individual thing is obscure and probably inconsistent. To quote O'Connor (1964):

> For Plato, the ultimately real features of the universe were the forms. For Aristotle, they were the individual things that make up the world — people, animals, plants, stones, stars, and so on. The central concept of Aristotle's metaphysics (or theory of being) is substance, the concrete individual thing. His detailed account of substance is very difficult to understand. He treats it from several different points of view and seems at times to say inconsistent things about it. But the rough outlines of his doctrine can be discerned, and the rest of his philosophy develops naturally from his view of substance.
> In the CATEGORIES he talks about substance from the point of view of language and of logic. It is 'that which is neither predicable of a subject nor present in a subject; for instance, the individual man or horse'. The world is divided into (1) logical subjects of discourse that can be talked about, and (2) qualities and relations that can be affirmed or denied of logical subjects. Aristotle goes on to make a list (the Aristotelian 'categories') of nine types of predicate which can be attributed truly or falsely, to logical subjects. The doctrine is not a defensible one and owes a great deal to the accidental peculiarites of the Greek language. In other parts of his writings, chiefly in his PHYSICS and METAPHYSICS, we find a more understandable approach. It can be condensed briefly but not too misleadingly as follows. The concrete individual thing — man, horse, tree, stone, and the like — may be viewed by the philosopher from two different points of view. (1) He may look at it as a permanent static feature of the world with a fixed nature. A nature (or essence) is thought of by Aristotle as a core or kernel of properties of which three things can be said: (a) they are essential to a thing of that particular kind, so that anything which lacks them does not belong to that natural type; (b) they can be grasped by intellectual intuition (nous); (c) they can be expressed in language as a definition. (2)

We may also look at substances as centers of change. We then ask, simply, 'What happens when something changes?'

The examination of the ostensive definition undertaken above showed that it does not seem possible to define in a fundamental sense the meaning of any word or expression. According to this position it is not possible to define in a fundamental manner 'an individual of a specific kind' or 'a representative of some specific characteristic'. Apparently in order to account for the essences of some individual thing we would have to postulate domains of events of an extra-linguistic nature. The accounts given by Aristotle and by later thinkers, such as Descartes, Locke, Kant and Husserl, of what constitutes an individual thing, seem to represent attempts to pass beyond what I have referred to as limits of communication and use of language. In accordance with this line of reasoning it is to be expected that they are all inconsistent.

Wittgenstein seems to have placed himself in the same position as Aristotle on the question of the nature of the individual thing. While Aristotle came to make statements about the essences of things, Wittgenstein came to make statements about the essences of language in spite of the fact that he warned against it. In his reasoning about the word when it is used to name something, he seems to have presupposed that the word was used to make reference to an individual thing, which was not specified with regard to kind and, therefore, had to be understood within a wider linguistic context. In the section following the one quoted above he wrote:

So one might say: the ostensive definition explains the use — the meaning — of the word when the overall role of the word in language is clear. Thus if I know that someone means to explain a colour-word to me the ostensive definition 'That is called "sepia"' will help me to understand the word. — And you can say this, so long as you do not forget that all sorts of problems attach to the words 'to know' or 'to be clear'.

One has already to know (or be able to do) something in order to be capable of asking a thing's name. But what does one have to know?

Apparently it does not follow from the fact that words cannot be fundamentally defined in an ostensive manner that one should have to understand the overall role of the word in language. In a previous section, Sect. 26, Wittgenstein stated that meaning could be said to be preparatory to the use of the word. Again it is difficult to see that this follows. As long as we are incapable of stating what is needed in order to understand a word, it does not make sense to say what we need to understand.

The section following the one quoted from the *Philosophical Investigations* corroborates the impression that Wittgenstein, in examining the ostensive definition, made a serious error in his reasoning about use of language. Speaking about the king in chess he argued that it does not tell an individual how to use this piece in chess if one says that it is the king. Of course it does not. The statement 'This is the king' is only meaningful when it is understood to what kind the individual thing to which reference is being made belongs. Apparently Wittgenstein committed the error here of presupposing that reference could be made to an individual thing which was not specified either with regard to kind or as a representative of some characteristic.

The point here made has implications for the evaluation of Wittgenstein's ideas of language as a way of life and language as a game. Wittgenstein did not discuss the term 'language game' in greater detail. It is introduced by way of examples. It is therefore not easy to understand more exactly what is meant by the term. If he meant, as one may believe he did, that words would only derive their meanings when viewed in some cultural setting involving complicated interactions between various human individuals, I would claim that this is not necessarily so. There is no reason to believe that in order to understand that another individual wanted to communicate something to him by words such as 'rock', 'stone', 'tree', 'house', etc., an individual would not understand what was meant by these words without participating in some complicated interaction.

I would insist that words can make reference to definite modes of understanding which are biologically anchored, but which need not be anchored in some specific human culture.

The problem of the universal and conceptions of the material object

The conclusion arrived at with regard to the ostensive definition raises the question of whether or not one can make reference to something which is not a representative of some kind or some characteristic. Obviously one can make reference to a definite stone, or to a definite tree, to a definite colour, to a definite shape, or to a definite size. One can make reference to the colour, shape, or size of a definite stone, but it does not seem possible to make reference to some individual thing which is not the representative of some kind or some characteristic. Now kind and characteristic are general terms; they are what are called universals or universalia. Consequently the individual or the particular which does not represent some universal cannot be referred to. If this is so, it is not meaningful, although many philosophers do it, to ask how the universal may arise. The universal arises with the particular and the particular with the universal. An individual thing always seems to be an individual thing of a specific kind or a representative of some specific characteristic. In a critical review of the discussion of the universal, Woozley (1967, p. 194) pointed out that philosophers have disagreed not only on answers given to the questions asked, but also on exactly what the questions are:

> Indeed, Plato may be taken to be the father of the perennial topic of philosophy, for it is in his dialogues that we find the first arguments for universals and the first discussion of the difficulties they raise. Plato believed that the existence of universals was required not only ontologically, to explain the nature of the world which as sentient and reflective beings we experience, but also epistemologically, to explain the nature of our experience of it. He proposed a solution to his problem, but he also recognized the objections to his particular solution. Ever since, except for intervals of neglect, philosophers have been worrying about the nature and status of universals. No account has yet been propounded which has come near to receiving universal acceptance; this reflects not merely disagreement on the answers to be offered but also, and perhaps more importantly, disagreement on exactly what the questions are that we are, or should be, trying to answer.

If what is said above is correct, it is evident that the questions asked by the philosophers engaged in this issue are not well formulated. If communication presupposes that some reference is always made to a kind of some type, or to a characteristic of some sort, the universal is necessarily implied in any statement that can be made. Consequently it does not make sense to ask how the universal arises. A particular which was not a representative of some kind or characteristic could not be communicated about, and it seems difficult to imagine such a particular.

The idea of a particular in the sense of the philosophers referred to has probably arisen as a result of a consideration of the appearance of material objects. With regard to any material object a variety of reports can be given. If we take, for example, a definite stone, the following reports may be given: This is a stone, this is a material object, the colour is grey, the shape is square, the size is large, the surface is rough, it is heavy, it is located in front of me, it is moveable, it might give shelter, it might serve as a table, it has a pleasing appearance, etc. The fact that a number of successive reports can be given may induce one to believe that an invariable something exists which generates in man the various reports. It is not realized that this invariable something cannot be communicated about.

As was stated in Chapter 3, the material object represents a specific organization of sensory impressions. Thus the impressions of colour, shape, and size as well as the tactile and kinesthetic impressions fuse into a unit. Thus in visual perceiving, colour, shape, and size form part of the unit which we refer to as the material object. Still, we speak of the colour, shape and size as well as the other sensory impressions mentioned above as attributes of the material object.

184

The puzzling question arises: Of what are these attributes the attributes? Strictly speaking this way of expressing things is not adequate. The point made here is of some importance because, as was noted above, by this way of expressing matters one may be led to presuppose that there exists an invariant something which generates the various reports or ways of thinking in us. The point is also important because it indicates that statements made about the attributes of material objects may be ambiguous. The study of the so-called constancy of colour, shape and size of material objects is based on statements of this type. This study would, therefore, seem to involve an uncontrollable aspect. This is indicated by the fact that under different instructions different reports are given. (For a review of the study of the perceptual constancies, see Lian, in press; Fieandt and Moustgaard, 1977.)

Actually, Kant's [1781] *Ding an sich* seems to be just such an invariable something about which no communication can take place, and, of course, since it cannot be communicated about, it cannot be inferred either. Hegel [1807] rightly criticized the Kantian idea of a *Ding an sich*, but then proceeded to suggest the equally fanciful idea of *reines Sein* ('pure being').

In an exposition of Hegel's philosophy Findlay (1964, p. 331) introduced the term this way:

> The Logic begins with the notion of pure being, the notion of something as being merely 'there', while nothing more is said of it or predicated of it. It corresponds on the plane of thought to the dumb confrontations of sense-acquaintance, in which *something* stands indubitably before us, but something which as yet is we know not what. Modern logic may find no place in its schedules for such a direct acknowledgement of being, but it is a fault of that logic, not of Hegel's treatment. Hegel holds that we must begin our study of categories with this simple notion, since, of all notions, it is the most abstract; everything whatever, when emptied of determinate content, or not as yet given it, becomes the abstraction of a mere *ens,* of which no more is predicable. As used in ordinary thought, this simple notion of entity is of course quite innocuous; it is a mere preliminary to further characterization. But the metaphysical understanding 'fixes' the notion in an unwarrantable manner in order to provoke dialectical comment.

Prima facie one may tend to agree with Findlay that the idea of pure being is a reasonable one. It seems to have a basis in a description of the external world as it appears to us. However, when the idea is further examined, it becomes difficult to understand that it can have a basis. I shall examine the belief underlying the idea of pure being. Let us consider some scenery confronting us — which also seems to have been the point of departure taken by Hegel [1807]. Suppose scenery containing, for example, an area covered by grass, a rock, a square, grey stone, a tree, some bushes and some pebbles is visually present to us. The question arises: Is it reasonable to believe that at any moment in time this scene appears to us as a something merely there, as some sort of unspecified totality? Apparently, as we change our point of fixation by moving our eyes, the ground, the grass, the rock, the stone, the tree, etc. become present in a successive fashion. Still, one might argue that at some definite moment in time the objects and their perceptual attributes may appear as simultaneously present. What is said here about perceiving by means of the modality of vision seems to be relevant for perceiving by means of the other modalities as well.

This seems to lead to the following question: How could we possibly find out that the objects and their attributes were present in this way, and thus that the scenery was present as some sort of totality? The question does not seem to be answerable because we have no means of communicating about this simultaneous presence, or this sort of totality. The same seems to hold true for a belief in the existence of an unspecifiable entity of the type 'pure being'.

Of course, along with Hegel one might postulate the existence of an abstract entity. However, in postulating this type of entity, we have not made clear how we might communicate about it. This last point seems to have been overlooked by Hegel and Hegelian-inspired thinkers. Evidently, if it is not possible to communicate about the entity of pure being, it does not make sense to place the idea of it, as was done by Hegel, in opposition to anything else. In other words the idea cannot be used in a dialectical argument.

Hegel was probably led astray by a belief in consciousness as some sort of creator of sensory impressions, memories, images, thoughts, feelings and impulses to action. This led him to his brand of idealism. Berkeley [1710], and inspired by him Hume and other empiricist thinkers, had previously been led astray by the same type of belief, namely the belief in a consciousness of some sort as the creator of our sensory impressions. Evidently both versions of idealism are based on the same presupposition concerning the nature of sensory impressions. The belief that sensory impressions are the result solely of some capacity in the organism and not a result of an interaction between the organism and its environment, must be considered as unwarranted. As was made clear by Moore [1903] in his criticism of idealism, the belief that perceiving does not bring man into direct contact with the external world is unwarranted. (On this point, see Hirst's, 1967, b, critical article on the nature of perceiving.)

Hegel and the new Hegelians such as Bradley [1893] seem to have confused statements in the first and third persons. As emphasized, we do not seem to be in a position to determine what can

186

be meant by understanding with regard to to statements in the first person. This state of affairs has been obscured by the introduction of the idea of immediate experience and the related one of a private language.

In connection with the point about Hegelian idealism made above, it should be noted that both Husserl's phenomenology and modern existentialism also seem to be rooted in a belief that conscious experience can have some sort of unspecifiable existence. Apparently all of these philosophies rest on dubious beliefs concerning consciousness. They cannot be regarded as representing coherent and consistent systems, until it has been demonstrated that the problem of communication can be adequately handled.

In connection with the point made above, mention should also be made of the fact that the rejection of the use of the word 'understanding' in reports based on statements in the first person, leads to a rejection of distinctions between an inner and outer man, between appearance and reality, between the subjective and the objective, and between private and public. The term 'inter-subjective agreement', as used by the logical positivists in their attempts to account for scientific procedures, must, of course, also be abandoned.

In developing his theory of signs Peirce seems to have been led astray by the Hegelian idea of pure being. In his letter to Lady Welby in 1904 he wrote (Peirce, 1958, pp. 221-222):

Firstness is the mode of being of that which is such as it is, positively and without reference to anything else.

Secondness is the mode of being of that which is such as it is, with respect to a second but regardless of any third.

Thirdness is the mode of being of that which is such as it is, in bringing a second and third into relation to each other. I call these three ideas the cenopythagorean categories.

The typical ideas of firstness are qualities of feeling, or mere appearances. The scarlet of your royal liveries, the quality itself, independently of its being perceived or remembered, is an example, by which I do not mean that you are to imagine that you *do not* perceive or remember it, but that you are to drop out of account that which may be attached to it in perceiving or in remembering, but which does not belong to the quality. For example, when you remember it, your idea is said to be *dim* and when it is before your eyes, it is *vivid*. But dimness or vividness do not belong to your idea of the quality. They *might* no doubt, if considered simply as a feeling; but when you think of vividness you do not consider it from that point of view. You think of it as a degree of disturbance of your consciousness. The quality of red is not thought of as belonging to you, or as attached to liveries. It is simply a peculiar positive possibility regardless of anything else. If you ask a mineralogist what hardness is, he will say that it is what one predicates of a body that one cannot scratch with a knife. But a simple person will think of hardness as a simple positive possibility the *realization* of which causes a body to be like a flint. That idea of hardness is an idea of Firstness. The unanalyzed total impression made by any manifold not thought of as

187

actual fact, but simply as a quality, as simple positive possibility of appearance, is an idea of Firstness. Notice the *naïveté* of Firstness. The cenopythagorean categories are doubtless another attempt to characterize what Hegel sought to characterize as his three stages of thought. They also correspond to the three categories of each of the four triads of Kant's table. But the fact that these different attempts were independent of one another (the resemblance of these Categories to Hegel's stages was not remarked for many years after the list had been under study, owing to my antipathy to Hegel) only goes to show that there really are three such elements. The idea of the present instant, which, whether it exists or not, is naturally thought of as a point of time in which no thought can take place or any detail be separated, is an idea of Firstness.

The criticism made of the Hegelian idea of pure being is also relevant in connection with the idea of firstness in Peirce. One wonders what can be meant by a something which is at it is without reference to anything else. Peirce is equally obscure when he goes on to suggest that one is to drop out of account that which may be attached to it in perceiving or in remembering. His further statement concerning 'red' as a mere possibility seems to be another way of suggesting something as being independent of perceiving and remembering.

Of greater interest than Peirce's idea of firstness is his attempt at making a distinction between an index ('a sign which refers to the object that it denotes by virtue of being really affected by that object') and a symbol ('a sign which is constituted a sign merely or mainly by the fact that it is used and understood as such'). As was pointed out by Alston (1967, b) this distinction may be useful. Nevertheless it must be noted that it does not allow us to decide whether words should be regarded as indexes or symbols. Peirce (see Alston, ibid) seems to have regarded them as indexes or partly as indexes and partly as symbols.

The nature of a symbol

Since we do not understand how words derive their meaning through use of language, it is not meaningful to say that words are symbols.

A definition of the symbol which is frequently advanced goes as follows: 'A symbol is something which stands for something other than itself.' The definition seems to be meaningful to the extent that one can understand what is meant by the expression 'to stand for itself'. Apparently it is presupposed in the definition that objects or events can be conceived of as existing without reference to use of language. If this presupposition is rejected, and instead it is presupposed that all objects and events form part of use of language, it will be clear that the definition is not a fundamental one, because it presupposes that the individual who is to profit from it is familiar with use of language. Usually in order to understand what is meant by a symbol, an individual must be familiar with a complicated linguistic and cultural frame of reference.

Peirce suggested that a general science of signs which included the study of use of language should be established. (For an account of this point in Peirce, see Murphey, 1967). Although unaffected by Pierce's work in this field, Saussure made the same suggestion. (For an account of this point in Saussure, see Mounin, 1968.) The idea of a general science of signs has had a profound influence on conceptions of use of language in thinkers in the twentieth century. Unfortunately it is not clear either in Peirce or in Saussure how they conceived of the relationship between signs of a non-verbal nature and signs used in language. Apparently they both believed that signs of a non-verbal type could be accounted for without referring to use of language. Without, of course, denying that man can communicate by means of facial expressions, gestures, pointing, variously accepted signals, and by ceremonies and rituals, I would contend that it remains obscure what is meant by a study of non-verbal signs as long as the relationship between these signs and use of language has not been stated.

In connection with Peirce's idea of a general science of signs, mention should be also made of the fact that he gave birth to the idea of a threefold division of the study of signs. Elaborating on these aspects Morris (1946) designated them later by the terms 'syntactics', 'semantics' and 'pragmatics' (on this point, see Kretzman, 1967). According to Kalish (1967) syntactics is described as the way symbols are related to other symbols, semantics as the way symbols are related to things other than symbols by relations such as referring, denoting, meaning and connoting, and pragmatics as the way symbols are related to things other than symbols by relations such as using, uttering, responding to and noticing.

As will be understood, this division is rather superficial. As was noted above, it is not at all clear what can be meant by 'a sign' or 'a symbol'. As in the discussion above, one may ask how one can conceive of a sign or symbol without referring to what is communicated about by means of the sign or symbol. Unless this question is satisfactorily answered, it is not clear what is meant by a relation between a symbol and a thing communicated about, by relations such as referring, denoting, meaning and connoting, and by relations such as using, uttering, responding and noticing. Evidently this threefold classification — like that of the idea of a science of signs — may too easily lead one to base arguments on the postulation of the existence of domains of events of an extra-linguistic nature.

CHAPTER 11

Use of language and problems of meaning (continued)

Reference and meaning

Closely related to the beliefs concerning the individual thing and the universal discussed in the previous chapter is the belief that fundamentally communication about the external world (and also communication about all other topics) can be conceived of as involving reference and meaning. According to the latter belief, in order that an individual shall be capable of understanding use of language, he must be capable of understanding what is being made reference to and what is predicated about that to which reference is made. For example, when in a definite situation the word 'stone' is uttered, in order to understand the meaning of the word an individual must understand what is being made reference to as well as what is predicated. Philosophers have long been preoccupied with the distinction between reference and meaning and have used a variety of expressions to indicate the distinction. Strawson (1959, p. 139) presented the following list of pairs of verbs which could be used to express the distinction:

Referring to something and describing it
naming something and characterizing it
indicating something and ascribing something to it
designating something and predicating something of it
mentioning something and saying something about it.

Apparently in order to be understandable any act of communication must have a reference to a something which is of a certain kind. Therefore, no fundamental distinction between reference and meaning may be said to be possible. Any attempt to extend logic by presupposing, as for example Frege, Russell and Carnap did, that a distinction can be made between reference and meaning, will be of limited fruitfulness. (For a critical review of the positions of these and other thinkers on this distinction, see Linsky, 1967, a.)

Strawson (ibid) also pointed out that the belief that a fundamental distinction could be drawn between reference and meaning was rejected by Ramsey. In a discussion concerning the proposition in logic, Ramsey [1932, p. 116] wrote:

> Both the disputed theories make an important assumption which, to my mind, has only to be questioned to be doubted. They assume a fundamental antithesis between subject and predicate, that if a proposition consists of two terms copulated, these two terms must be functioning in different ways, one as subject, the other as predicate. Thus in 'Socrates is wise', Socrates is the subject, wisdom the predicate. But suppose we turn the proposition round and say 'Wisdom is a characteristic of Socrates', then wisdom, formerly the predicate, is now the subject. Now it seems to me as clear as anything can be in philosophy that the two sentences 'Socrates is wise', 'Wisdom is a characteristic of Socrates' assert the same fact and express the same proposition. They are not, of course, the same sentence, but they have the same meaning, just as two sentences in two different languages can have the same meaning. Which sentence we use is a matter either of literary style, or of the point of view from which we approach the fact. If the centre of our interest is Socrates we say 'Socrates is wise', if we are discussing wisdom we may say 'Wisdom is a characteristic of Socrates'; but whichever we say we mean the same thing. Now of one of these sentences 'Socrates' is the subject, of the other 'wisdom'; and so which of the two is subject, which predicate, depends upon what particular sentence we use to express our proposition, and has nothing to do with the logical nature of Socrates or wisdom, but is a matter entirely for grammarians. In the same way, with a sufficiently elastic language any proposition can be so expressed that any of its terms is the subject. Hence there is no essential distinction between the subject of a proposition and its predicate, and no fundamental classification of objects can be based upon such a distinction.

The belief that the distinction between reference and meaning is a fundamental one apparently derives from the idea that words, linguistic expressions and sentences are names for material objects and for the attributes of material objects, and consequently can be defined ostensively. According to this belief the material object, in this case the stone, may be pointed to while the words 'The stone is grey' are uttered. This pointing, it is believed, makes clear what is being referred to and the person who has learnt the meaning of the words 'stone', 'grey' and 'is' will understand the sentence. However, when it is realized that no term can be defined fundamentally in an ostensive manner, it is seen that there can be no reference without a meaning and no meaning without a reference. Fundamentally reference and meaning cannot be separated. As has been made clear above, reference to something in the external world presupposes that indication is made of the kind to which the something to which reference is made belongs. The word 'stone' can only be understood when it is clear to the individuals participating in communication about it that that which is being communicated about is an instance of the kind of stone. Similarly in order that a person shall understand the word 'grey' in the sentence given

191

above he will have to understand the kind specified by the word.

Going back to Scholastic philosophers Mill [1843, p. 19] argued that words and expressions could be divided into two different types: The non-connotative or denotative and the connotative. The former type referred to something without attributing meaning and the latter both referred to something and attributed meaning:

> A non-connotative term is one which signifies a subject only, or an attribute only. A connotative term is one which denotes a subject, and implies an attribute. By a subject is here meant anything which possesses attributes. Thus John, or London, or England, are names which signify a subject only. Whiteness, length, virtue, signify an attribute only. None of these names, therefore, are connotative. But *white, long, virtuous,* are connotative. The word white denotes all white things, as snow, paper, the foam of the sea, etc., and implies, or in the language of the schoolmen, *connotes,* the attribute *whiteness.* The word white is not predicated of the attribute, but of the subjects, snow, etc. but when we predicate it of them, we convey the meaning that the attribute whiteness belongs to them. The same may be said of the other words above cited. Virtuous, for example, is the name of a class, which includes Socrates, Howard, the Man of Ross, and an undefinable number of other individuals, past, present and to come. These individuals, collectively and severally, can alone be said with propriety to be denoted by the word: of them alone can it properly be said to be a name. But it is a name applied to all of them in consequence of an attribute which they are supposed to possess in common, the attribute which has received the name of virtue. It is applied to all beings that are considered to possess this attribute; and to none which are not so considered.

Central in Mill's conception of use of language is, as is seen from the quote, that words are names for things. His reasoning seems to be based on the following presupposition: On the one hand, there are the material objects and their attributes, and, on the other, the words constituting language. The words are attached to the material objects and their attributes in the same way as we learn the name of individuals we meet. (Cp. Hume's conception of an association p. 79.) As I have emphasized before, in order that an individual shall learn the use of a word he must understand that it refers to something which is an instance of a kind. This means that no word or expression has a simple relationship to any material object or any particular attribute of the material objects.

Ryle (1957, p. 243) emphasized the fact that a sentence is not a list of names and further that it is difficult to see what kind of names words belonging to grammatical categories such as adjectives, adverbs and prepositions are. He characterized the logicians' idea as a howler and listed philosophers who up to the present have been inspired by the above-mentioned idea that words are names for things:

> Before going any further, I want to make you at least suspect that this initially congenial equation of words and descriptive phrases with names is

from the outset a monstrous howler — if, like some of Mill's successors, though unlike Mill himself, we do systematically construe 'name' on the model of 'proper name'. The assumption of the truth of this equation has been responsible for a large number of radical absurdities in philosophy in general and the philosophy of logic in particular. It was a fetter round the ankles of Meinong, from which he never freed himself. It was a fetter round the ankles of Frege, Moore and Russell, who all, sooner or later, saw that without some big emendations, the assumption led inevitably to fatal impasses. It was, as he himself says in his new book, a fetter round the ankles of Wittgenstein in the *Tractatus,* though in that same book he had found not only the need but the way to cut himself partially loose from it.

Alston (1967, a, p. 234) has pointed out that the referential theory of meaning seems to stem from concentration on the proper name:

> The referential theory is, on the surface, the simplest, and it dominates most thinking about meaning. It usually stems from concentration on the proper name as the typical unit of meaning. With a proper name everything seems to be simple. Here is the name 'John'; there is the man named. All the factors are out in the open, there is nothing mysterious about it (until we ask what makes the word 'John' the name of this man). It is tempting to generalize this account and hold that for any word to have a meaning is for it to name, designate, or refer to something other than itself.

Apparently Mill was correct in believing that the proper name is used mainly for referring to persons and things; however, in this respect the proper name is hardly representative of other words.

Furthermore it should be noted that the proper name also indicates kind or class. Thus different words are used to indicate names for men, animals, geographical places, boats, etc. Therefore, it is not entirely correct to say that proper names do not indicate kind, but it does seem correct to say that the chief function of the proper name is to refer to something. This also seems to be the conclusion arrived at by Searle (1976) in a critical article on proper names (p. 491):

> But the essential fact to keep in mind when dealing with these problems is that we have the institution of proper names to perform the speech act of reference. The existence of these expressions derives from our need to separate the referring from the describing functions of language. But reference never occurs in complete isolation from description, for without some description, reference would be altogether impossible.

Frege and Russell apparently missed the point made by Mill about proper names. Wittgenstein (1953), too, seems to have been confused on this point. (See for example Sect. 43 of *The Philosophical Investigations.)* (For reviews of the literature on the issue, reference is made to the above-mentioned articles by Ryle, 1957; Searle, 1967; Linsky, 1967, a.)

Frege [1892], one of the logicians influenced by Mill, suggested that words, expressions and also sentences had a meaning as well as a referential function, a reference *(ein Sinn und eine Bedeutung)*. Frege did not make clear how one single definite word, expression or sentence could allow one to distinguish both a reference and a meaning. Frege seems to have considered the use of language without due regard for the context in which linguistic expressions have to be understood. Thus the well-known example 'The Morning Star is the Evening Star' can only be understood in terms of a complicated context which contains the information that the Morning Star and the Evening Star are both names for the same planet, namely Venus. Without overcoming the inherent difficulties Carnap (1947) elaborated the Fregian distinction between reference and meaning into the distinction between extensionality and intentionality.

In his attempt to develop an extensional logic Frege also made a distinction between the reference and the thought or proposition of a sentence. The reference was the truth-value of the sentence and the thought or proposition was the meaning of the sentence. When this distinction is viewed in terms of acquisition of use of language, it is difficult to see how it can be a fundamental one. When an individual at an early stage of language development is to acquire the meaning of simple sentences such as the following: 'This is a stone', the sentence can hardly be meaningful unless it is true. Therefore truth-value and meaning are hardly separable in a fundamental sense and indeed it would be unreasonable to believe that language and logic were not intimately interwoven.

The idea of an ideal language

In a series of lectures given in 1915 and entitled *The Philosophy of Logical Atomism,* Russell (1956, pp. 197-198) made an attempt to determine meaning, not for single words and expressions, but for certain sentences in an ostensive manner. His taking as the point of departure the sentence and not single words or expressions is of importance. We shall therefore examine his attempt to construct the ideal language. Here we shall only deal with Russell's early version of an ideal language. (As regards the later versions of Russell's philosophy of language the reader is referred to the review article on Russell's philosophy by Edwards, Alston and Prior, 1967.) We shall show here that the idea of an ideal language meets with the same difficulties as attempts at defining words or single expressions in an ostensive manner.

The ideal language, the logically perfect language, was to be characterized by a complete correspondence between the individual words and the objects communicated about:

In a logically perfect language the words in a proposition would correspond one by one with the components of the corresponding fact, with the exception of such words as 'or', 'not', 'if', then', which have a different function. In a logically perfect language, there will be one word and no more for every simple object, and everything that is not simple will be expressed by a combination of words, by a combination derived, of course, from the words for the simple things that enter in, one word for each simple component. A language of that sort will be completely analytic, and will show at a glance the logical structure of the facts asserted or denied.

Sentences which corresponded to the simplest facts were called atomic propositions. It is easy to see that Russell's atomic proposition meets with the same difficulty as that involved in defining words ostensively:

The simplest imaginable facts are those which consist in the possession of a quality by some particular thing. Such facts, say, as 'This is white'. They have to be taken in a very sophisticated sense. I do not want you to think about the piece of chalk I am holding, but of what you see when you look at the chalk. If one says, 'This is white' it will do for about as simple a fact as you can get hold of. The next simplest would be those in which you have a relation between two facts, such as: 'This is to the left of that'. Next you come to those where you have a triadic relation between three particulars. (An instance which Royce gives is 'A gives B to C'.) So you get relations which require as their minimum three terms, those we call triadic relations and those which require four terms, which we call tetradic, and so on. There you have a whole infinite hierarchy of facts — facts in which you have a thing and a quality, two things and a relation, three things and a relation, four things and a relation, and so on. That whole hierarchy constitutes what I call *atomic* facts, and they are the simplest sort of fact. You can distinguish among them some simpler than others, because the ones containing a quality are simpler than those in which you have, say, a pentadic relation, and so on. The whole lot of them, taken together, are as facts go very simple, and are what I call atomic facts. The propositions expressing them are what I call *atomic propositions*.

As was made clear above, the sentence 'This is white' may be subjected to a number of interpretations by an individual not familiar with the English language. It may, for example, be interpreted in the following nine ways:

1. There is something which has a certain location in space (in front of me, to the left of me, to the right of me, as the case may be).
2. There is a material object.
3. There is something which is small.
4. There is something which is elongated.
5. There is something which is round (or square as the case may be).
6. There is something which is light in weight.

7. There is something made of chalk.
8. There is something to write with.
9. There is something white.

Actually Russell's example of an atomic proposition entangled him without his noticing it in complicated problems of colour perception. In the situation to which he referred, the piece of chalk is perceived as having a definite location in space and is perceived simultaneously with a number of other material objects. The situation is thus not one found in the classical studies of colour vision, and more than one dimension for the description of the colour (white) must be introduced. (Cp. the accounts of these problems given by Judd, 1951; Lie, 1970.)

As can be seen from the quote, Russell conceived of a fact as a particular. Apparently, he did not realize that he could not communicate about the particular without specifying it as being representative of some kind or characteristic. This idea of the particular was thus unclear, and seems to have remained so also in his later philosophy. (On this point, see O'Connor, 1964.)

Above mention was made of the tendency in logicians at the end of the nineteenth and the beginning of the twentieth century to regard meaning as some sort of entity underlying words or sentences. The logicians' preoccupation with the idea of a proposition led them to presuppose some logical entity underlying ordinary sentences. (Cp. the review article on the problem of what can be meant by a proposition by Gale, 1967.) Russell's attempt at distinguishing between the sentence 'This is white' and what he regarded as the fact that the chalk is white, is in line with this tendency.

In connection with the idea of an ideal language it should be mentioned that, as Alston (1964, p. 71) made clear, the verifiability theory of the logical positivists is the same theory as that underlying *The Philosophy of Logical Atomism:*

> In fact, logical atomism and the verifiability theory are virtually the same theory stated in different ways. They sound different because the verifiability theory looks down from the nonobservation sentences, asking how they can be verified while logical atomism looks up from the observation sentences, asking what else can be explained in their terms. It is, however, the same topography whichever perspective we take.

(For a critical review of the verifiability principle see also Ashby, 1967.) Actually Russell's idea of an ideal language, the logical positivists' verifiability principle and the behaviorists' stimulus—response theory may all be traced back to Hume's theory of meaning presented in 1739 (cp. MacNabb, 1967).

Russell's ideas on use of language have had a profound influence on empirical psychologists. He strongly influenced behaviourist thinkers and more recently he has influenced theorists within communication theory. (On this point, see Watzlawick et al., 1967.) It should be clear from the examination of Russell's idea of an ideal language that this idea gives no adequate basis for defining the terms 'information' and 'process' in information and communication theory. In view of the discussion undertaken previously in this chapter one must wonder what may possibly constitute the basis for the use of these terms.

Concepts, classes, resemblance and dimensions

In Chapter 6 I pointed out that attempts made by philosophers and psychologists to conceive of concepts in a fruitful manner had been unsuccessful. From the conclusion arrived at in the examination of the nature of definitions and of the individual thing it follows that we are not capable of stating in an adequate manner what the basis for our use of concepts is. This conclusion may explain why the attempts to conceive of concepts made by philosophers and psychologists have been so unfruitful.

Apparently, the use of the term 'class' is closely related to the use of the term 'concept'. What was said above about the basis for the use of the term 'concept' seems to apply also to the basis for the use of the term 'class'. Concerning the use of the term 'class' I should like to draw attention to the following point. If, as argued, we are not able to distinguish between the particular and the universal, it seems to follow that in a fundamental sense a class can only have one member. For this reason the use of the term 'class' in discussions of the nature of the use of language may be misleading. I would agree with Russell that it is hardly meaningful to argue, as Frege did, for the inclusion of the class itself within some definite class, but I must disagree with him on the point that a class can have different members. (For a review of this problem in Russell's philosophy, see Edwards, Alston, and Prior, 1967.)

In view of what has been said here about concepts and classes I wish to question Wittgenstein's idea of a family relationship. Wittgenstein (1953) suggested that what games might have in common might more appropriately be described as family resemblances than as common attributes or characteristics. The fact that we are not able to state what the basis for the use of the terms 'concept' and 'class' is, does not imply that this use does not involve some common fundamental characteristic. If we cannot make a distinction between the particular and the universal, it seems reasonable to regard instances of a statement to the effect that something belongs to some definite class as identical. For example, when we say about football: This is a game, and when we say about chess: This is a game, we make two identical statements.

It follows from the argument presented above that 'resemblance' and 'similarity' are empty terms unless specification is made of the respect in which impressions resemble each other. Two impressions can always resemble each other in more than one respect. Therefore indication must be made of the kind of which the instances are representative. Both empiricist philosophers and empirical psychologists have frequently overlooked the problem arising in connection with appealing to resemblance (or what apparently amounts to the same, dissimilarity) as an explanatory concept. The problem of handling resemblance or dissimilarity is, as was noted in Chapter 4, a basic one in accounting for learning.

The problem of structuring impressions according to scalable dimensions is closely related to that of stating what is meant by resemblance. Before a scalable dimension can be worked out, it is necessary to make clear the kind of which the impressions represent instances. This seems to raise a fundamental problem in measurement in psychology. (Cp. what was said about problems of measurement in psychology in Chapter 4.)

Language conceived of as a system or as a structure

The view discussed above of communication or use of language as being in some way necessary, raises the problem of what can be meant by saying that language represents some sort of system or structure. One of the first thinkers to stress the fact that language might be conceived of as a system was Saussure [1906-11], who is frequently regarded as the founder of modern linguistics. Saussure rightly stressed what has since been corroborated, that in some way the sounds (he did not use the term 'phoneme', which is of later origin) used in the various cultural languages were determined by their reciprocal relationships. The same applied to grammatical rules of various types. This is revealed when different cultural languages are compared with each other. (For a modern treatment of these problems in linguistics, see Lyons, 1971.) There is no reason to doubt that in order to understand the use of the phonemes and morphemes of a given language one must in some way take into consideration use of language as some sort of totality. However, from the previous discussion it will be clear that as long as linguists or other theorists in use of language are unable to state what is being communicated about when language is used, it is difficult to conceive of language as some sort of system or as some sort of structure.

The fundamental difficulties met with by Saussure in his attempt to conceive of language as some sort of system or structure have not been eliminated by thinkers in the modern movement called structuralism. (For a review of this movement, see Fages, 1967.) Moreover it should be noted that these difficulties also inhere in the approach to psychology in terms of so-called general system theory. In the latter approach emphasis is placed on the interaction of elements within a system. (For an account of this approach to psychology and other fields of science, see Bertalanffy, 1968.) Unless it is made clear how communication can be carried out in ways which are fundamentally independent of man's use of language, it remains obscure what can be meant by the term 'structure' in structuralism and by the term 'system' in general system theory.

Apparently when linguists and research workers in other branches of science argue that languages should be regarded as systems or as structures of various sorts, they overlook the fact that use of language is not arbitrarily related to material objects and their attributes or to man's feelings or motivational states. The fundamental weakness in Saussure's thinking about use of language is expressed in what he referred to in his lectures as 'the first principle'. This principle stated that the signs used in the various cultural languages were arbitrary. Saussure correctly pointed out that different cultural languages would use different words for designating what may be regarded as the same concept; for example, in French one uses the word *cheval* and in German the word *Pferd* to designate what in English is designated by the word 'horse'. Furthermore he correctly pointed out that words and expressions in different cultural languages often do not correspond to each other; for example, the French word *louer* would mean both to pay rent and to receive rent for a room whereas in German the two words *mieten* and *vermieten* would be used to express the two types of relationships. Finally, he correctly pointed out that the grammatical rules of the different languages did not always correspond to each other. From observations of relationships of this sort he concluded that the signs used in language were arbitrary.

It will be understood that what Saussure demonstrated was that an arbitrariness was involved in the choice of articulatory signs used in the different cultural languages, but he did not, of course, demonstrate that the relationships between the signs used and the events (whatever their nature) communicated about were arbitrary. The unfortunate effect of Saussure's mistake was that linguists have tended to conceive of language as some sort of abstract entity. This conception, as was noted in the previous chapter, has been expressed in modern treatments of grammar, as for example in Chomsky.

The tendency in Saussure to conceive of language as some sort of abstract entity also received expression in his famous distinction between the two terms *langue* and *parole*. The former was supposed to refer to use of language as some sort of total social organization and the latter to use of language in the individual. The introduction of the distinction seems to reflect the idea of language and culture as superstructures of some sort erected above man's social activities. In a previous section I noted that the word 'language' and the expression 'use of language' tended to lose meaning when used in discussions of various fundamental problems in the study of use of language, and furthermore that they could not easily be applied to activities of children at early ontogenetic stages, or to communication between individuals of species other than man. At this point it should be noted that the word 'language' also tends to lose its meaning when used about some sort of total cultural activity. The same is true of the use of the words 'social' and 'culture'. In speaking of language as being social or as being culturally determined, care must be taken that the biological aspects are not overlooked, and, vice versa, when language is spoken of as being biological, care must similarly be taken that the social and cultural aspects are not overlooked. Of course, there can be no fundamental distinction between the use of the terms 'biological' and 'cultural' or between the use of the terms 'biological' and 'social'. Probably the use of the word 'language' should be discouraged, because it may so easily lead the theorist to conceive of language as some sort of abstract entity. Moreover, as was mentioned in Chapter 3, the use of the term 'language' may lead one to neglect the fact that use of language is always made within a certain context. For this reason the expression 'use of language' is probably preferable.

It follows from the discussion presented above that, given the present state of knowledge, it is hardly possible to state what might preferably be regarded as the fundamental unit in use of language. Depending upon the type of questions asked, linguists regard the phoneme, the morpheme or the sentence as this unit. In order to clarify the problem of what might most fruitfully be regarded as the basic unit in use of language, it seems to be essential, as has been made clear above, that the problem should be dealt with in a way which allows one to distinguish between statements in the first and third persons. In Part 2 of this book I shall suggest a way of dealing with use of language which makes it possible to observe this distinction.

Communication and use of language

As has previously been mentioned, there can be no doubt that man can communicate by means of facial expressions, gestures, pointing, various signals, ceremonies and rituals. In the discussion of Peirce's treatment of signs, mention was made of the fact that he and Saussure had suggested that a general science of signs should be established. I pointed out that neither of these thinkers made clear the relationship between the use of signs of a non-verbal nature and use of language. However, their idea of a general science of signs has led to the widespread belief that communication can be conceived of without reference to use of language. This belief has been strengthened by the behaviourist belief that a domain of events designated as behaviour can be regarded as existing without necessary reference to use of language. It has become customary to speak of communication without specifying the rules used for this communication. It must be clear that unless such rules have been specified, communication can only be given a meaning through the intuitive appeal to understanding.

More recently an approach to the study of psychology in terms of communication — frequently designated as communication theory — has been outlined (Watzlawick et al., 1967). As was mentioned in Chapter 2, this approach represents an important innovation because it emphasizes the necessity of studying psychological activities in terms of social interactions. Unfortunately, the use of the term 'communication' is diffuse. Theorists embracing this approach took as their point of departure the idea of a general science of signs in which non-verbal signs could be conceived of without reference to rules for their use. Furthermore, they adopted the threefold division of the study of signs suggested by Peirce and Morris. Concentration was centred on pragmatics. From what has been said above and previously in this chapter the uncritical acceptance of the idea of a general science of signs and the idea of a threefold division of the use of these signs which followed precludes a consistent and, I believe, fruitful use of the term 'communication'.

After having accepted the two ideas referred to above, the theorists who adopted the communication approach seem to have proceeded by conceiving of interaction between individuals in behaviouristic terms. This step in the procedure inevitably entangled them in the problems regarding behaviourism discussed in Chapter 9. Research workers using this approach tend more or less to identify communication with behaviour. Thus, they state as their first axiom, or principle, that behaviour always involves communication. It will be apparent that this is not so. We can speak of behaviour even if the individual behaving is not noticed by other individuals. If a person who is alone can be said to be behaving, behaviour and communication must be different in important respects.

The axiom that behaviour always involves communication must obviously be modified. If it is modified in such a way that it is said that behaviour involving interaction between individuals always involves communication, the axiom is still of a dubious nature. It is important to note that it is not reasonable to identify social interaction with communication. In many instances it is not possible to state what is being communicated when two individuals interact. Let us look at the following example: Does a newborn baby sucking at its mother's breast communicate something by this activity? We know that when the so-called rooting reflex is elicited the baby will turn its head so that it has a good chance of getting the nipple oi its mother's breast in its mouth, and further we know that the presence of a nipple in the mouth of the baby will elicit the sucking reflex. To say in this instance that the baby communicates something to its mother seems to be far-fetched. To take another example, when two human individuals mate, they interact in a way which, like the sucking of the baby, can only be accounted for in terms of theories concerning biological evolution. Again it seems far-fetched to say that these individuals are communicating. I am not, of course, saying that communication in various forms may not be going on along with the activity of mating, but that is beside the point. These examples, which can be multiplied, show that not all social interaction should be regarded as communication. Unless we can state what is being communicated, by what means and according to which rules, it is hardly advisable to speak of communication.

To round off this criticism I want to emphasize again that the study of psychology in terms of interactions as suggested by theorists in communication is a step in the right direction. The well-known double-bind theory is probably correct in suggesting that an important source of conflict in human individuals may be found in the fact that an individual is reacted to by another individual (or individuals) in an inconsistent manner. But as long as the rules for communication by non-verbal signs have not been specified, it is probably fruitless to attempt to account for the origin of these conflicts in terms of communication.

Part 2
The theory

CHAPTER 12

Introduction

In Chapter 2, where I introduced the problems to be dealt with in this book, I pointed out that empirical psychologists had shown little concern for questions pertaining to the nature of the subject matter of their science. Under the impact of the positivist thinking which has dominated the scientific climate of the West from the nineteenth century to the present psychologists have tended to conceive of the events to be studied as facts existing independently of and without a necessary connection with definite contexts. This tendency has been strengthened by the belief that language, as ordinarily used, could provide a reference system for empirical psychology. As a consequence of this tendency the theoretical approaches available can only make possible vague and diffuse reference to the events postulated for study. Moreover the events postulated for study frequently seem to be fictitious. In order to improve on this state of affairs I suggested that reference systems based on more coherent and consistent arguments would have to be developed. In Chapter 1 I also expressed the belief that theory construction in science was primarily concerned with the question of developing reference systems for identifying types of events which might fruitfully be made the subject of empirical study.

In Part 1 of this book I showed how a reliance on language, as ordinarily used, has led empirical psychologists to make theoretical statements which on further examination prove to be highly incoherent and inconsistent. I also made clear that current views on psychology as the study of consciousness as well as of behaviour rested on certain simplified notions concerning the nature of use of language. This point, I maintained, becomes evident when it is realized that no theoretical term in psychology can be fruitfully defined by ostensive definitions or by reference to operational procedure. Modern psychology will then be seen to rest on a use of ordinary language which does not allow the theorist to make theoretical statements of a precise and consistent nature.

In Part 1 of this book a number of theoretical concepts on which psychologists of the various schools and research interests have based their approaches were examined. This examination revealed that the concepts were used in a vague and diffuse manner. Attention was devoted to the concepts which must be considered central in psychology, such as capacity, perceiving, remembering, imagining, thinking, learning, development, mental element, mental structure, sensation, Gestalt, process, processing, experience, act, ability, intelligence, concept, problem, association, consciousness, intentionality, meanings, the unconscious, ego, attention (set), information, simulation, grammar, behaviour, verbal behaviour, verbal mediation, operant, stimulus and response. In Chapters 10 and 11 I pointed out that concepts taken over from logicians were used in an equally vague and diffuse manner. Examination was made of the following concepts: meaning, individual, particular, universal, reference, denotation, connotation, class, sign, symbol, syntactics, semantics, pragmatics, linguistic structure, system and communication. I tried to present a general argument to the effect that as long as theoretical concepts are introduced without connection with a reference system, they will necessarily have to be vague and diffuse.

As was made clear in Part 1, conceptions of consciousness or of behaviour do not represent useful reference systems. In Chapters 7, 8, 10 and 11 arguments were presented which showed that linguistics, biology, physiology and logic do not provide such systems. Reference systems based on notions of transmission of information of various sorts were found to be spurious because no precise determination could be made of the nature of information or of the postulated processes underlying the reception and use of this information. It was further demonstrated that conceptions about learning and ontogenetic development, as advanced by many psychologists, did not remove the difficulties met with in developing a useful reference system.

In an attempt to develop a scientific reference system the first question to be asked appears to be the following one: What are the events to be studied? The argument must be so developed that this question can be given a satisfactory answer. It is satisfactorily answered when procedures can be described which allow the research worker to identify events of various sorts which can fruitfully be subjected to an empirical study.

To answer this question I shall not begin — as seems to be usual in empirical psychology — by pointing to a few situations of a type containing the events to be studied, then proceeding to state operational procedures for the further identification of the events. Instead I shall begin by considering what may possibly constitute a domain containing the events to be studied. Then, in accordance with the remarks given in the introductory chapter (A View on the Nature of Theory Construction) I shall attempt in various ways to specify this domain of events so that events suitable for an empirical study can be identified. It will be clear that the events to be identified, even if they are regarded as in some way representing reality, are dependent upon the procedure adopted and thus not to be regarded as ultimate in the sense that their nature is independent of the procedure followed to identify them.

In line with the remarks on theory construction in science referred to above, I can also indicate the procedure to be followed by making an attempt to state the presuppositions made when something is regarded as a type of event. In stating presuppositions, or, as previously expressed, in specifying the domain of events I shall take care to avoid the difficulties discussed in Part 1 of this book.

In Part 1 I argued that it was difficult to understand what can be meant by a domain of events of an extra-linguistic nature. Various difficulties attaching to a belief in domains of such a nature were discussed, and in the treatment of the ostensive definition in Chapter 11 it was emphasized that it did not seem possible to define ostensively what was communicated about when language was used. This conclusion concerning the possibility of postulating domains of events of an extra-linguistic nature, as well as the difficulties attaching to the ostensive definition, seem to force the theorist to conceive of use of language as the domain containing the events which constitute the subject matter of a study of psychology. In accordance, then, with these considerations I shall postulate use of language as the domain containing the events to be studied.

The examinations undertaken in Part 1 were based on considerations of language as used by normal adults mastering any one cultural language. As I have argued, the possibility of taking as the point of departure communication in children at various stages in their ontogenetic development, or in individuals of other species, must be excluded. It should be noted that use of language should be conceived of as spoken language. As insisted by linguists, all other uses of language must be regarded as derived from this use of language. (See for example Lyons, 1971.) Accordingly the theorist must take care to take as his point of departure a conception of use of language which does not exclude any aspect of spoken language. Thus he must not start out with notions that use of language might take place by signs of a nature different from those used in spoken language. The signs of spoken language, it should be noted, are sounds produced in the articulatory organs by the interplay of definite groups of muscles. They are perceived auditorily, and related to the events communicated about in specific ways. Nor must the theorist start out with notions that the rules underlying the use of the signs could be different from what they actually are. It will be seen that if the nature of language as actually spoken is not carefully observed, the theorist may come to prejudge fundamental theoretical issues.

The remark made above does not of course preclude the possibility that the research worker may attempt to communicate something in other ways than by means of the spoken language. It means that if he is doing this he must note what presuppositions are made and then carefully consider these presuppositions in terms of what is known to characterize spoken language.

The difficulty of conceiving of domains of an extra-linguistic nature apparently excludes the possibility of studying use of language in terms of some framework which is not dependent upon use of language. As was made clear in Part 1 neither psychology, linguistics, biology, physiology, nor any other branch of science can reasonably be said to provide such a framework.

Having arrived at the conclusion that use of language contains the events to be studied in psychology, I shall have to specify this domain in such a way that identification can be made of what may constitute types of events suitable for study. This raises the question of whether or not use of language can be characterized in a general manner.

As was made clear in Chapters 10 and 11 and as has been repeated above, we are not in possession of theories which allow us to state what the events communicated about when language is used are. However, as emphasized, this conclusion does not necessarily preclude the possibility of characterizing use of language in a general manner. This problem was discussed in connection with the ostensive definition. It will be remembered that the conclusion arrived at in Chapter 5 was not that the activities of perceiving, remembering, imagining and thinking are identical to use of language, but only that it is difficult to see how a distinction can be made between the four activities and use of language. I regard a belief in identicalness on this point as unreasonable. This seems to open the possibility that use of language may be characterized in a general manner.

Language is used in many ways. It is used to communicate about man's relationships with the external world and with other individuals. It is used to express wishes and desires as well as feelings and emotions. Still, language may be said to have the fundamental characteristic that in some way it is used to transmit information. Consequently I should like to begin by characterizing use of language by saying that it is fundamentally used for transmitting information. This characterization does not of course preclude the possibility that it is also used for thinking. To avoid misunderstandings I should also like to call attention to the fact that so far I have not specified the meaning of 'information'.

In order to characterize use of language further, I shall consider the various types of situations in which human individuals communicate with each other. Apparently, whether they communicate about the external world, social relations, desires, wishes, or feelings and emotions, it must be presupposed that the individuals participating in communication are in some way capable of perceiving, remembering, imagining and thinking. (If desires, wishes, feelings and emotions are ascribed logical priority over communication as means of transmission of information we shall have postulated — as indicated in the previous chapter — a domain of extra-linguistic events.) As was made clear in Chapters 5 and 6, serious problems are raised if one conceives of these activities as being independent of use of language, but this conclusion does not imply that use of language must be ascribed logical priority over the four activities mentioned. Asking the reader to bear in mind that use of language presupposes the activities of perceiving, remembering, imagining and thinking, I shall characterize use of language by saying that fundamentally it concerns understanding of some sort.

Having specified use of language by saying that it involves understanding of some sort, I shall proceed to specify understanding further so as to avoid the confusion of statements in the first and the third persons. As argued in Chapter 10, this confusion would entangle me in ideas of a private language and solipsism. In order to avoid this confusion I shall say that *understanding refers to one individual who is to understand what another individual is attempting to communicate to him.* I shall regard this specification as a fundamental methodological principle. I should like to emphasize the fact that unless great care is taken to adhere to this principle, confusion will arise.

The characterizations of use of language made above may be said to specify certain conditions under which the events to be studied in psychology may be said to occur. It will be noted that the specification of the conditions so far undertaken does not allow me to identify these events. To arrive at this identification I shall further have to state requirements that must be met in order that one can say that an individual has understood what another individual has communicated to him. When these requirements have been stated, it is believed to be possible to identify various types of events which may be fruitfully subjected to an empirical study. I shall then have developed a reference system which allows the research worker to deal with various types of events. In line with the remarks made in the introductory chapter on theory construction in science, I would contend that I have developed a reference system which is of such a nature that a domain believed to contain the events to be studied has been so specified that it is possible to identify these events in a way that allows the research worker to subject them to a study, or to put it in another way, I would claim that I have arrived at a reference system which allows one to state the presuppositions made when something is regarded as an event.

In the attempt to state the requirements to be met in order that one can say that understanding, as here specified, has taken place, it is essential that these requirements are formulated so generally that no type of event is excluded which may constitute empirical evidence with regard to the theoretical statements made. This point was discussed in the remarks on theory construction referred to above. As I emphasized in the introductory chapter to this book, explanations must not be sought for in the postulation of events which are excluded by the requirements stated. The requirements arrived at according to the procedure outlined here may be regarded as empirical laws stating relationships between the organism and its environment which make understanding possible. Since the requirements stated are concerned with understanding relative to communication by means of use of language, they may be regarded as fundamental principles of communication. I shall show that it is possible in terms of these empirical laws or fundamental principles to formulate research problems which can be fruitfully investigated. In line with the remarks on theory construction in science referred to, the laws or principles formulated will determine what is to count as knowledge, and they will also form part of explanations given of events of various types.

In my attempts to state the requirements to be met in order that one can say that understanding has taken place, I shall make the presupposition that the individual who is to understand what another individual attempts to communicate to him is not familiar with the cultural language of the latter. This presupposition is made to avoid statements concerning understanding being restricted only to understanding in individuals familiar with some definite cultural language. By making this presupposition I shall hope to arrive at statements applicable to individuals without the necessity of reference to the particular cultural language with which they are familiar. From the discussion in Chapter 5 it will be understood that it would not be meaningful to presuppose that the individual is not familiar with any cultural language.

In connection with the latter point I also want to underline that in order to arrive at the greatest possible degree of generality

I have tried to develop the reference system by considering types of situations which are so simple that they could be used in communication with individuals of species other than man. The situations are of a type similar to those that have been used for discrimination studies in animals other than man.

In connection with the placement of the point of departure here in the understanding of use of language it should be noted that understanding a language is not identical to speaking a language. We know that in certain respects there is a difference between the capacity for understanding a language as spoken and the capacity for speaking a language. This is, for example, manifested in the difference in command of vocabulary as determined in terms of understanding and in terms of speaking. It is also manifested in findings in research on aphasia. Here it has been frequently found that the capacity for understanding and speaking can be affected differently by brain damage of various sorts. It should, therefore, be noted that if principles derived from a consideration of understanding are applied to the activity of speaking various presuppositions will have to be made. I shall return to this point in Chapter 12.

It will be understood that a reference system, as outlined here, only represents a primary stage towards the development of a more complete theory of psychology. In the initial phase it will probably be wise to restrict attention to situations in which there is a fairly high degree of certainty that communication can take place. While there can be no doubt that understanding takes place when language is used for communication, it is doubtful whether understanding takes place in all situations where individuals make contact with each other by means of sounds and signs used in language. Situations in which one cannot be fairly certain that understanding has taken place should accordingly not be considered. Also it would probably not be wise to consider situations in which it is difficult to reach agreement on what is being communicated. One can only turn to situations of this type when the development of the reference system has been elaborated in greater detail.

Apparently the approach for arriving at statements of requirements for understanding outlined here has similarities to the Kantian way of approaching the question of what might be meant by knowledge and it may help to clarify the present approach if we contrast it with the Kantian one. Kant [1781] asked for the conditions under which we can have experience. The difference between the approaches is that the present one has its point of departure in a characterization of language as actually used, while Kant, following the tradition of Descartes, took as his point of departure conceptions of consciousness. (In Chapter 4 of Part 1 of the present book difficulties in determining the use of the term 'experience' without considering the relationship between experience and use of language were noted.) Furthermore Kant based his approach on a distinction between perceiving and reasoning. As a consequence, his conclusions, while still highly provocative, are disputable and perhaps not very useful for research. (For reviews of this issue, see Warnock, 1964; Walsh, 1967; Hamlyn, 1967, b.)

Apparently the understanding involved in use of language is the result of an extremely complicated interaction between the organism and its environment, and a variety of conditions must be met in order that this interaction shall take place. The presupposition made here that the individual who is to understand what is being communicated is familiar with language, involves a number of conditions with regard to development of the activities of perceiving, remembering, imagining and thinking. It should be noted that the presupposition that the individual understands that another individual wants to communicate something to him, involves complicated conditions concerning attention and social interaction. This being the state of affairs, it is hardly possible to arrive at a conception of a prioris. Instead of aiming at conclusive arguments I have attempted to state what may be regarded as highly general laws of understanding. These laws should not be evaluated only in terms of their reasonableness, but in terms also of their usefulness in empirical research.

CHAPTER 13

A fundamental principle of understanding

In the previous chapter I argued that in order to characterize use of language it is essential to characterize understanding in an individual who understands that something is being communicated to him by means of language. As I have mentioned, I shall presuppose that the individual (to be referred to as the second individual) who is to understand what is communicated to him is familiar with use of language, but not with the cultural language of the individual (to be referred to as the first individual) who is attempting to communicate something. Furthermore I shall presuppose that the second individual understands that the first individual wants to communicate something. For an understanding of the reasoning which follows it is essential, as emphasized in the previous chapter, that the reader does not confuse statements relevant to the second individual with statements relevant to the first and vice versa. The situations of the two individuals are not identical.

In line with what was said in the previous chapter, I shall attempt to formulate some fundamental requirements to be met in order that understanding, as dealt with here, can be said to take place.

As has been emphasized, understanding must ultimately be determined by reference to statements in the third person, i.e. I shall have to ask what requirements must be made in order that it can be concluded that an individual has understood what another individual has attempted to communicate to him. However, when the point of departure is placed in the conception of use of language as fundamentally involving social interaction, it is not meaningful to begin the examination by making presuppositions only concerning the second individual. Accordingly I shall begin by making a presupposition underlying use of language in both individuals. I shall presuppose that communication and use of language involve a selectivity in the sense that communication can be about more than one thing.

As was suggested in the previous chapter, I shall concentrate examination on relatively simple situations in which the individuals are confronted by material objects in the external world, either by some particular individual material object, or by some scenery or landscape, but I shall emphasize that this concentration does not mean that the conclusions arrived at are not valid for all types of situations where communication by means of use of language takes place.

Communication seen as the interaction of the human organism with its environment

I shall begin the examination by supposing that the two individuals are situated in front of a specific stone. In this situation it will be realized that the second individual (the individual who is to understand what the first individual communicates) may interpret an utterance by the first individual in more than one way. For example, he might give the following interpretations:

1. Some material object is present.
2. Some material object designable as a stone is present.
3. Some colour is present (say, a brownish colour if the stone should happen to have a brownish colour).
4. Some shape is present (say, round if the stone should happen to have a round shape).
5. Some size is present.
6. Some surface texture is present.
7. Something movable is present (if the stone should happen to be movable).
8. Something having a certain weight is present.
9. Something is present which may be thrown (if the stone has an appropriate weight).
10. Something is present which can be used for support (if the stone has an appropriate shape and size for this use).
11. Something is present which can be used as a building block.
12. Something is present which has an aesthetic quality.

Further the second individual may interpret the first individual as indicating spatial location of the stone (say, that it is in front of him, to the left or right, as the case might be). The second individual might even give the interpretation: Here is some point in space.

It will be noted that in the situation described above, the first individual, the individual attempting to communicate something, has no way of ascertaining that the second individual understands what he is attempting to communicate. Whether he attempts to do so by pointing, gestures, or by placing the second individual in some specific position in relation to the stone, he cannot ascertain that the second individual is interpreting him in the way he wants him to do.

If the second individual interprets him correctly, this is because he understands use of language, and apparently we are not in a position to say what is meant by understanding use of language. As I shall make clear in a later section of this chapter, this understanding is not, as believed by empiricist and behaviourist thinkers, explainable in terms of differential learning. Evidently we are unable to say how the individual who is to understand what is being communicated is capable of doing so. This point is of course of vital significance.

On reflection it will be realized that it is not possible to imagine a situation which is of such a nature that the first individual could ascertain that the second individual has interpreted him in some definite way — in the way the word, the expression, or the sentence was to be understood. No situation can be found which guarantees unequivocal communication when the presuppositions made at the beginning of this chapter are met. Even the most barren landscape, say, one completely covered by sand, dust or snow, does not allow of unequivocal communication. Faced with such a landscape the second individual might understand the pointing, the gestures, or the utterance of the first individual in more than one way. He might, for example, interpret the first individual as meaning:

1. Sand, dust or snow is present.
2. The landscape has a certain formation (is flat or rounded as the case might be).
3. This formation has some definite location in space.
4. Some definite location in space is meant.
5. Some definite colour (say, white, red or grey) is present.

In most landscapes or sceneries there would usually be more than one material object present, and this would imply that relationships of various sorts could be indicated; for example, that one material object was above, below, to the right or left of another object, or near or far away from it.

Above we have mainly considered visually presented situations. If we excluded the visual sense and concentrated on the auditory sense, it will be seen that we would still not be able to construct a situation so that the requirement of unequivocal communication was met. A sound is usually localizable in space, consists of more than one pitch, has a certain loudness, and usually characteristics pertaining to the temporal aspect (being continuous, reverberating, rythmic, of short duration, etc.).

If we proceeded to exclude both vision and audition, and olfactory and thermal impressions, tactile impressions having more than one characteristic would still be left.

It is important to note that in any situation we can imagine for the normal adult human being, sensory impressions from more than one sensory modality are always present.

The examination undertaken above has involved communication between adult human individuals. One might possibly believe that what is taken here to be a characteristic of all situations in which communication by means of use of language can take place, does not apply to situations where the participants are an adult and a child at an early ontogenetic stage. One might believe that at an early ontogenetic stage a situation might be found in which the child could only give one interpretation. Actually it is difficult to find support for this belief, which has apparently played a central role in empiricism from Locke to the present. While it must be admitted that the number of interpretations which can be given in a situation of the type examined above will be reduced as one descends the ontogenetic scale, it is not reasonable to believe that a stage will be reached at which only one interpretation can be given. At any stage of ontogenetic development where the child is capable of identifying a sign of some sort, it is apparently capable of interpreting the sign in more than one way. For one thing, at that stage the child is capable of reacting discriminately to stimulation from the various senses. Furthermore at such a stage it can in all probability react to a variety of material objects in the external world and to various attributes of these objects as well as to social relations of various sorts. It must be born in mind that in order to participate in communication the child must be capable of identifying some sort of sign. Whether this sign consists in vocalization of some sort, in pointing, or gesturing, the child must have developed so that it can react in a variety of ways before identification of the sign can take place. As was made clear by Brown (1958), the identification of specific sounds or of sound patterns making up words is evidently the result of complicated activity on the part of the individual perceiving. On the whole the identification of any sign that can be used in communication must be regarded as the result of complicated activity, and it is unreasonable to believe that at a stage of the ontogenetic development where the child is capable of identifying the sign, it is not also capable of reacting to the situation in more than one way. Thus the argument that at some early stage of ontogenetic development the individual would only be capable of interpreting the sign in one way, is hardly tenable.

In connection with the point discussed above, it should be noted that the argument presented by theorists such as Vygotsky (1962) and Luria (1961) that the activity of perceiving is in a fundamental sense structured by the verbal teaching carried out by adults, is not easy to support. As we have seen, the activity of perceiving must have reached a relatively high degree of development before the child is capable of identifying the verbal sign. At this stage of development the perceptual world of the child is probably already structured in a way similar to that of the adult.

It must be realized that if no situation can be found in which the second individual (the individual who is to understand what is being communicated) may only give one interpretation, the ostensive definition cannot be fundamental. No way of pointing or making gestures nor any type of arrangement of the situation can guarantee that the individual who is to understand will do so in an unequivocal manner. As was made clear in Chapter 10, this does not mean that the ostensive definition cannot be useful, but it must be noted that this definition is not, as has been believed by empiricists from Locke to Russell and Carnap, fundamental in the sense that in terms of it one can account adequately for the establishment of meaning.

It will be clear that what is said here about the ostensive definition is also relevant to the operational definition. As I mentioned in Chapter 2, operational definitions are essential for the advancement of the construction of psychological theory, but they must not be considered as fundamental. It is not possible to infer the precise meaning of a theoretical term from the operations performed by the research worker. A theoretical term must be introduced by the use of language as well as by reference to specifically devised procedures. By relating words and expressions actually used in language to specific research procedures the meaning of these words and expressions may be modified so as to allow of a more precise as well as a more general use, but if it is not realized that theoretical terms have a basis in use of language, they will be left hanging in the air.

In Chapter 5 of Part 1 it was pointed out that it was difficult to compare psychological activities in different species. For this reason the belief that situations can be found in which only one reaction can be made on the part of the individual cannot be supported simply by reference to reactions in species other than man. However, it should be noted that the present way of characterizing situations in which communication can take place will also apply to situations in which man can communicate something to individuals of any or all the mammalian species, i.e. in which he can get an individual to understand something. The conclusion arrived at seems therefore to cover a very broad range of situations.

The physiological reflex

In the previous examination attention has been restricted to situations in which communication by some sort of sign could take place. For this reason physiological reflexes and instinctive reactions have not been considered. Apparently the reflexes and possibly instinctive reactions of various sorts represent borderline examples of situations involving communication. One might say that the stimulation eliciting the response of a reflex represents a sign used in a specific kind of communication. A stroke on a contracted tendon, the placing of some material object in the oral cavity, or a puff of air to the eye, to take a few examples, might be said to transmit some specific information to the organism and thus to represent some sort of sign used in communication. The response of the reflex, one might argue, is invariably elicited when certain specified conditions are present. However, as is well documented, certain induced attitudes in the individual may change the reaction. Consequently the situation in which this type of response is elicited can only be said to approximate a situation in which only one reaction can be given.

Secondly it must be noted that the stimulation eliciting the responses of the reflexes or of instinctive reactions is of such a nature that it could not easily be used as a sign for communication in a greater variety of situations. The fact that in a Pavlovian setup a so-called conditional or conditioned stimulus, say, the sound of a buzzer, will elicit a response similar to the response of the reflex, is no argument to the contrary. The fact that the conditioned stimulus can elicit a response similar to the response of the physiological reflex does not mean that the organism reacts to the two types of stimulation in the same way. It should be noted that the point made here is not whether the two types of stimulation elicit according to the Pavlovian procedure what seems to be a similar response, but whether the two stimulations do so before the procedure is started. It is not reasonable to believe that this is the case; for example, we would not expect that before the procedure reaction to a buzzer or the presentation of a light would be similar to the reaction to, say, the placing of food in the mouth.

Of course, even if the signal introduced as the conditioned stimulus cannot be used as a sign for communication in a greater variety of situations, the Pavlovian theory might still be fruitfully elaborated to account for the development of psychological activities. However, for various reasons one may doubt that this could be the case. In Chapter 3 of Part 1, I pointed out that the theory suffers from the fundamental weakness that the relationship between the activities of perceiving, remembering, imagining, thinking and use of language has not been worked out. At this point Pavlov seems to have unreflectively taken an empiricist position.

Understanding involves specifying

The conclusion arrived at above concerning the situation in which communication can take place would seem to have the following important implication: If it cannot be ascertained that the individual who is to understand what is communicated cannot interpret the utterance (or the type of sign used) in only one way, it is difficult to see how the object of understanding can be something which is not specified in some definite way. In the situation considered above, understanding would either have to involve a kind of some sort, i.e. that some specific type of material object was involved, say a stone, a rock or a tree, or that some specific attribute of a material object was involved, say, some definite colour, shape or size. In other words, in the situation in which communication can take place, it does not seem possible for the individual to understand a something which is not specified in some definite way. Even if the presupposition were made that the individual who is to understand what is being communicated understands that that which is communicated about is located in a certain position in space, the individual cannot understand what is meant by something which is not specified in some definite way.

The belief that understanding of something which is not specified can take place is actually a belief in the existence of something about which man cannot communicate. This belief is probably at the root of the idea of a private language as well as of the idea that knowledge is ultimately of a solipsistic nature.

It will be seen that the position taken here, as was made clear in Chapter 10, leads to rejection of the formulation of the question of universalia as conceived of by philosophers from Plato to the present. A particular cannot be regarded as existing unless it is in some way specified, i.e. unless some universal is indicated, the particular and the universal being inseparable. This was the point emphasized in Chapter 10 when the problem of conceiving of the material object was treated. There the belief in an invariant something which generated in man various types of reports, was rejected and along with it Kant's idea of *Das Ding an sich,* Hegel's idea of pure being and Peirce's simple existence. Also it will be seen that both Aristotle's idea of the individual and the idea of introspection in Locke and the early psychologists are based on a belief that understanding of something which is not in some way specified can take place. Further it will be seen, as was also emphasized in the chapter referred to, that a distinction between **reference** and meaning in logicians such as Mill, Frege, Russell and Carnap is not meaningful because one cannot refer to a something which is **not** specified, and this specification would imply meaning. As I pointed out in the same chapter, the position taken that existence must be limited to something which is in some way specified, should not be confused with an idealist position. From what has been said, it does not at all follow that man does *not* make direct contact with the external world in the activity of perceiving, and thus it does not follow that the belief in the independent existence of the external world must be rejected.

Requirements of understanding

Having examined the situation in which communication takes place, I shall attempt to formulate what seem to be certain fundamental requirements to be met in order that understanding can be said to take place. First it will be noted that because the second individual, as has been supposed, is not familiar with the cultural language of the first individual, it is not conceivable that he would be capable of understanding what this individual attempts to communicate, unless what is being communicated about is represented in the situation. Secondly, because an attempt at communicating something can be interpreted in more than one way, the second individual would have to understand what kind of material object (stone, rock, tree, etc.) or what attribute (colour, shape, size, etc.) is being communicated about. Because both the first and the second requirement must be met, we shall have to state as a fundamental requirement of understanding that the individual must understand that reference is being made to some specific kind or attribute represented in the situation. To illustrate this requirement by referring to concrete examples, I should like to point out that in order that the second individual shall understand that communication concerns some definite stone, he must understand that the kind 'stone' is represented, or, if he is to understand that the attribute 'colour' is being communicated about, he must understand that the attribute 'colour' is represented, or further, if he is to understand that the attribute 'shape' is being communicated about, he must understand that the attribute 'shape' is represented, etc. Because it is difficult to conceive of a situation in which this requirement of communication would not have to be met, I would say that in general the understanding of use of language requires that the individual who is to understand what is communicated, must understand that reference is being made to some specific kind or attribute represented. As made clear above, this requirement must also be met in situations involving communication by means of gestures. So it must be said to be a general requirement of understanding in situations involving communication.

If it is accepted that understanding presupposes that some kind or attribute is represented, it follows that it is not possible to distinguish between kind and representation of the kind or between attribute and representation of the attribute. I would claim that it is always some specific kind or attribute represented which is understood. Evidently it is not possible to conceive of kind or attribute as originating in the way that events of a similar nature are classed together, because we are not in a position to know what is meant by 'a similar nature'. Apparently the appeal to similarity is just another way of saying that words, expressions or sentences can be ostensively defined. This belief in the ostensive definition has already been rejected.

In the description of the external world which has been indicated above, I have referred to kind of material object (stone, rock, sand, mountain, tree, bush, grass, water, snow, ice, house, chair, car, etc.) and to attributes of material objects (colour, shape, size, texture, weight, etc.). Both kind and attribute may be said to indicate a certain type of information about the external world. I shall refer to these types of information by the term 'category' and shall speak either of the representation of some definite category or I shall say that a category is represented, the two expressions being regarded **as equivalent.**

Returning to the example treated above, I shall express myself by saying that representation is of the category 'stone', the category 'tree', the category 'colour', the category 'shape', the category 'size', etc., or that the category 'stone', 'tree', 'colour', 'shape' 'size', etc. is represented. In accordance with this way of expressing myself, I wish to formulate the requirement of communication arrived at in the above examination in the following way:

In order that an individual shall understand what another individual is communicating, he shall have to understand that communication concerns the representation of some definite category.

It is believed that this formulation holds true for understanding by means of use of language as well as for all conceivable types of communication in which human individuals can participate, and I shall refer to it as *the fundamental principle of understanding.*

It will be understood that the word 'representation' is not used in the Cartesian sense of some entity in consciousness. I shall have to speak of the representation of some definite category, because otherwise the category might be conceived of as some abstract entity constructed by man in contemplating individuals of various sorts.

In line with what was said above, it is not possible to conceive of the representation of some definite category and the category itself independently. Any category conceived of must be a category represented and any representation must be a representation of some definite category. This means that *it is not conceivable that two or more categories could have the same representation*. This is another way of saying that we cannot conceive of something which is not specified. Obviously it does not make sense to say that that which represents, for example, the category 'stone' is the same as that which represents the categories 'colour', 'shape' or 'size'. This point seems to be essential for the development of a scientific study of psychological functioning.

In connection with the point made above, it should be noted that the expression 'the attributes of the material objects' may be misleading. (Cp. Chapter 10.) This expression may lead us to believe that there is a something making up some definite type of material object which also has some specific attribute; for example, in the way that there is a something which makes up some specific stone and that this something has the attribute of, say, greyness, squareness or largeness. According to the examination conducted above, this belief must be rejected. Sentences such as the following 'The stone is grey', 'The stone is square' or 'The stone is large' must not be interpreted in the way that there is a something which is a stone and which is respectively grey, square or large. It must be interpreted in the way that the category 'stone' is represented and the category 'grey', 'square' or 'large' is represented. In Chapter 14 of this part of the book I shall return to this fundamental point.

The aim of this chapter being to examine how man communicates about the external world, I shall have to introduce as categories other perceptual characteristics. I shall regard, for example, tone, pitch, loudness melody, smell taste and tactile impressions as categories represented. Further I shall regard movements and still further indications of spatial relationships as categories represented. For example, I shall speak of the representation of the category 'in front', the representation of the category 'behind', the representation of the categories 'to the right' and 'to the left', of the representation of the categories 'here' and 'there' and of the representation of the categories 'above', 'below', 'under', etc. In this way a more or less complete description of the external world by means of the term 'representation of some category' will be possible.

I have used the term 'representation of category' to refer to what may be regarded as a type of information, as this is indicated by use of language. In general what can be regarded as a type of information will be designated here by this term. Consequently what is to be regarded as the representation of some definite category is to be determined by appeal to familiarity with use of language. In a rough sort of way I believe it possible to make this determination not only with regard to descriptions of the external world, but also with regard to use of language in all domains of human activity.

The use of the term 'representation of some definite category' with regard to indication of spatial relations may seem a little queer. One might ask: What is represented? In Chapter 3 of Part I of this book I argued that the perceiving of spatial relationships and the identifying of material objects were inseparable, and that the spatial relationships might be regarded as attributes of the material objects in the same way as colour, shape and size. Therefore, the representation of spatial relations of various sorts may be said to transmit types of information of a nature similar to that of the attributes of the material objects.

It must be noted that the term 'representation of some definite category' does not correspond to the term 'member of some definite class'. According to the position taken here a category is always represented in the same way and consequently cannot have different members. Thus the representation of the category 'stone' is the same whether the stones are grey or brown, square or round, small or large, and the representation of the category 'colour' is the same whether the specimen of colour is red, green or blue. The understanding that some definite category is represented may be characterized as a mode of understanding.

The representation of the category as a logical necessity

The understanding that some definite category is represented may be said to represent that which limits use of language. When no definite category is represented, there can be no understanding and communication cannot take place. Another way of stating what has been said above is to say that we cannot conceive of the representations of the various categories as being otherwise; in other words the representation of some definite category is necessary or essential. Whatever representation of category is chosen, it can be shown that that which makes the representation of the category specific cannot be accounted for.

I shall illustrate this point by the representation of the category 'colour'. Different specimens of chromatic colours, say a red, a green, and a blue, have in common that they may be said to be visual impressions, but they are not adequately characterized in this way. To characterize the specimens as colour we shall also have to say that they are not shapes and not sizes, shapes and sizes also being visual impressions. Evidently it is not meaningful to ask: What makes the specimen a colour and not a shape or a size? That specimens of red, green and blue are colours and not shapes and sizes we have to accept without further inquiry. Similarly we have to accept that geometrical shapes, such as balls, cubes and solids represent the category 'shape' and not 'colour' or 'size'.

It will be seen that if we examine representation of the category 'visual impressions' we shall arrive at the same conclusion. We can say that visual impressions have in common that they are sensory impressions, but so are auditory, tactile, gustatory, olfactory, kinesthetic and proprioceptive impressions. So again we have to say what something is not, and not what it is.

Taking as another example the representation of the category 'stone', it will be seen that it is not possible to characterize adequately what makes a representation of the category a stone. We can say that it is a material object having hardness, but so have a number of other material objects, such as metals, trunks, ice, coal, etc. If we say that it has some *definite* hardness, we are just referring to what is specific without making clear in what this specificity consists. At this point it must be noted that it is just by accepting this specificity that the physicist can begin specifying more exactly the nature of the hardness of a stone. The physicist has to begin his study by accepting the category represented. In other words the physicist takes as his point of departure use of language.

Finally let us consider man-made objects, for example, a chair. Again we may characterize it by means of other categories. We might say that it is used for sitting, but so are stones, trunks, sofas, stools, etc. So once again we have to say what it is not, and we are not capable of saying what it is. The same would hold true if we characterized it as a piece of furniture. Again we have to say what it is not, and not what it is.

To conclude this examination I shall claim that any definition of the representation of some specific category must be a dictionary definition. It is not possible to define such representations in terms of Aristotelean essences or the like. However, categories represented must be regarded as necessary and not as arbitrary.

It will be seen that what is called 'a concept' is a representation of some definite category; for example, the representation of the category 'stone', 'man' or 'horse'. It follows from what has been said, that a concept cannot be adequately defined. It can be characterized in language, but this characterization cannot definitely tell us how categories are represented. This characterization can only give us information about how we use language. In the empirical study of concept formation this fundamental point has been missed. As was noted in Chapter 6, psychologists have believed that they could construct situations in which it was experimentally shown how some definite concept was acquired by individuals having specifiable characteristics. Studies of the types undertaken by psychologists in the field of study called 'concept formation' cannot tell us how the representations of definite categories originate, nor can they tell us in general terms how language is used. They just give the trivial information that, in a situation of a particular type, a given type of individual will use language in some particular way. In Chapter 4 of Part 1 it was shown that the study of concept formation seemed to be in a state of confusion. The above reasoning may explain why this is the case.

In the situations examined, man has been considered in a position where he faces the external world. In these situations we have found that understanding, as specified here, must in some way be regarded as necessary. If we take a realist position on the question of the external world, in other words, if we believe the existence of the external world is independent of man's existence, it is reasonable to believe that in some fundamental way understanding reflects man's biological adjustment to the external world. (For critical reviews of issues involved in realism, see Hirst, 1967, c; Ramsperger, 1967; Robischon, 1967.) Understanding may then be seen to reflect relations between the human organism and its environment. That these relations are necessary would mean that man is in some way informed about the relations but not directly about the properties of the organism; nor about the aspects of the environment involved. I propose that the representations of the categories reflect fundamental relations between man and his environment.

One may ask why the belief in use of language as contingent and not in some way necessary has been so deeply rooted in Western thinking. It may be of some help in thinking about psychological functioning to reflect on this question. I want to draw attention to the fact that one main reason why thinkers in the past have tended to believe that use of language is contingent is probably to be found in the way the external world appears to us. In the first place, the appearance of the external world seems to be unaffected by our thinking and speaking about it. Furthermore when we communicate about it, we seem to be capable of concentrating on some definite material object or on some definite attribute of some material object without this causing a change in the way other objects or other attributes appear to us. Thus, while I think or speak of the hardness of some definite stone, the appearance of its colour, shape or size does not seem to be affected. This may give the impression that use of language is contingent and not necessary.

The emphasis that in some way understanding is necessary must not lead one to overlook the fact that understanding must also be regarded in some way as arbitrary. This point was discussed in connection with the work of Saussure in Chapter 11.

The learning of words by differential learning

Related to the belief that the equivocality of the situation in which communication takes place is a result of learning, is the belief that it is possible to account for the learning of words, expressions or terms by some principle of differential learning. In Chapter 4 I discussed difficulties attaching to the term 'learning', and in Chapter 9 I pointed out that the behaviourists' attempts to account for the acquistion of use of language were defective. These accounts were based on the principle of association by contiguity combined with the principle of reinforcement. (The term 'association' was examined in Chapter 4.) Below I shall show that it is not possible to account for the acquisition of the use of words by differential learning.

Let us consider the example frequently examined, i.e. learning the use of the word 'red'. The choice of example (the word 'red') is of no consequence here; the same argument might be employed for the learning of any word used for describing the external world. It is contended that the word is learnt by an individual when he is placed in a situation where the word 'red' is presented in temporal contiguity with some red object.

Bearing in mind the considerations presented above, it will be clear that the word 'red' when uttered while a red object is present may refer to characteristics of the situation other than the fact that the object has a red colour. It might, as has been mentioned, refer to the fact that the object occupied a certain location in space, to the fact that it had a certain size or shape, etc. The word might also refer to the fact that the object was an object of a certain type (e.g. an apple) or simply to the fact that the object was a material object.

It can be seen that a repetition of the procedure would not change the situation; the word 'red' might again refer to characteristics of the situation other than that the object was red.

The question arises: Could the situation be changed so that the word 'red' would refer solely to the characteristic of red colour? We shall consider the various possibilities.

Instead of one object, two identical objects might be presented.

Evidently in this case no matter whether the two objects were presented simultaneously or successively, the word 'red' might refer to characteristics other than that of the red colour. The same would also hold true if the two objects differed in all characteristics other than that of colour. In this case, if the two objects were presented simultaneously the word 'red' might refer to a number of different relationships between the two objects. It might, for example, refer to the distance between them or to the fact that the two objects were both material objects.

If the two objects were presented successively, but still in the same spatial location, one might possibly eliminate the possibility that the word referred to spatial relationships, but the other possibilities would be left. By presenting the objects successively, one would also have to presuppose that the individual learning the use of the word 'red' was capable of remembering the object previously presented in such a manner that he was capable of deciding that the previously presented object differed from the object being present in all characteristics other than that of red colour. Furthermore — and this is essential — the individual would have to know that the word only applied to a characteristic in respect of which the two objects were identical. This seems to be tantamount to saying that the individual understands that the category 'red' is represented, or, in other words, that the individual understands use of language, but this understanding is not explainable by reference to the procedure followed. So what the behaviourists, in line with Hume and the British empiricists, actually can say on the basis of their procedure, is the following: When an individual understands use of language, in a certain type of situation he will use language in a particular way. Apparently thinkers in the empiricist tradition overlook the difference between the understanding that some definite category is represented and the way references can be made to that representation.

Finally, in connection with this discussion of the problem of differential learning, it should be noted that a situation is rarely found in man's environment where two material objects differ in all characteristics apart from one. Thus, when two apples, two fishes, or two plants differ in size, shape and texture, they will most probably also differ with regard to the chromatic aspect. If illumination or the location relevant to the object is changed, change will usually also take place in the relevant characterictic. As long as the word 'red' may be interpreted to refer to characteristics other than the chromatic one, it will be seen that no techniques of reinforcement would bring about the differential learning of the word 'red'.

In the above discussion we have not considered the problem

arising in connection with the perceiving of the sound pattern of the *word* 'red' on the part of the individual learning the use of the word. If we assume, for the sake of argument, that acquisition of use of language can be accounted for in terms of stimuli and responses and the principle of contiguity combined with the principle of reinforcement, it must be presupposed that when the word 'red' is successively presented (for example by two articulations of the word), what is presented must be perceived as identical. Thus the pitch pattern, the duration and the impression of loudness must all be identical. Otherwise the empiricist explanation must also be extended so as to account for how the individual learns that the word 'red' when presented on different occasions represents the same sign. Regarding this complicated problem the reader is referred to the discussion by Brown (1958). Apparently the empiricist account of the learning of terms by some principle of differential learning is simplicistic. In Chapter 9 a quote was given from Lenneberg, where he made clear that the account by behaviourists of acquisition of use of language presupposed that answers had already been given to a variety of questions which have been dealt with neither by behaviourists nor by thinkers of other orientations.

One reason for the overlooking of the difficulties met with in attempts to account for the acquisition of use of language is probably to be found in the fact that we may easily come to conceive of this in terms of the acquisition of a second language. For example, an individual who has English as his mother tongue tends to consider this in terms of his learning of a second language, e.g. French. By considering the problem of acquisition of use of language in this manner, one may easily overlook the fact that one may come to discuss it in terms of the knowledge about use of language already gained in the acquisition of the first language (the mother tongue). (In this connection it should be noted that it is beside the point that the acquisition of the second language may have features in common with the acquisition of the first. This is an empirical question which should not be confused with the epistemological one dealt with here.) Wittgenstein (1953) seems to have been well aware of the tendency mentioned here. He began his *Philosophical Investigations* with a quotation from Augustine's *Confessions* where the acquisition of use of language is reflected upon. Later on in the *Investigations* Wittgenstein (Sect. 32) characterized Augustine's account in the following way:

> And now, I think, we can say: Augustine describes the learning of human language as if the child came into a strange country and did not understand the language, only not this one. Or again: as if the child could already *think,* only not yet speak. And 'think' would here mean something like 'talk to itself'.

This way of characterizing Augustine's account of acquisition of use of language would also apply to the beliefs of modern thinkers and research workers, such as Russell, Carnap, Quine, Skinner, Osgood and Staats.

Direction of attention

At the beginning of this chapter I characterized the type of situation in which communication between human individuals can take place by saying that the individual who is to understand what another individual is attempting to communicate to him can interpret the other individual in more than one way.

On reflection it will be understood that use of language presupposes that the individuals engaged in communication are capable of selecting the same category represented. If they did not have this capacity the individual who is to understand (the second individual) would not be capable of correcting interpretations which were not in agreement with what was communicated by the first individual. Furthermore the first individual would not be capable of ascertaining that the second individual had understood him correctly. It must be clear that unless this capacity is presupposed both for the first and the second individual use of language could not function socially. By overlooking this point one may easily become entangled in the idea of a private language. I have stressed the importance of determining understanding in the second individual, but this must not lead one to overlook the fact that use of langauge contains statements in both the first and third persons.

It follows from the examination undertaken in this chapter that we are not in a position to account for the capacity for selecting some specific category represented. If we attempt to account for the selection of some definite category represented by the individual wanting to communicate something we may easily become entangled in ideas of consciousness. (The attempt to give this account may possibly have led Descartes to make his mind—body distinction. See the quote given from Descartes' *Principles* in Chapter 4.) Furthermore it should be noted that this reference to capacity does not imply that some sort of voluntary control is necessarily involved.

However, in order to refer to the fact that some selection is involved in all types of reports given we need a term. I would suggest the term 'direction of attention'. In the two chapters on psychology as the study of consciousness I discussed the term 'attention'. The idea of attention as a force in consciousness was rejected. It must be noted that the term 'direction of attention' is used by me in a descriptive manner and not as an explanatory concept referring to some sort of mental mechanism. This form of attending should not be regarded as an activity. Perceiving, remembering, imagining and thinking involve directions of attention. It will be understood that all reports of categories represented involve in each case a definite direction of attention; thus the direction of attention is inseparable from the report of (and also the reaction to) some given category represented. *Direction of attention must be regarded as a defining characteristic of all psychological reports (and reactions) studied.*

The fact that direction of attention is regarded as a defining characteristic excludes the possibility of using the term in an explanatory manner. Explanations can be given in terms only of shifts of direction of attention. Thus it is possible to study empirically shifts in direction of attention. However, great care must be taken that shifts in direction of attention are not confused with a study of attention taken in a fundamental sense, as has been frequently done by psychological workers. (Cp. the discussion in Chapters 7 and 8.)

In the examination undertaken in Chapter 10 of Hegel's idea of pure being I emphasized the fact that communication cannot be of situations perceived as some sort of totality. We always have to report on some definite kind or attribute. This means that the term 'direction of attention' must also include the reports of a perceptual nature. As the reader will remember, in Chapters 3 and 4 I rejected the possibility of making a fundamental distinction between the activities of perceiving, remembering, imagining and thinking. I have stressed here that use of the term 'direction of attention' must include perceptual reports because some thinkers have tended to restrict use of the term 'attention' so that it does not cover perceptual reports. In Chapter 3 it was noted that Hebb insisted that attention or set was involved in all reactions in mammals. The position taken here is in line with that of Hebb, but while Hebb apparently considered attention as an empirical phenomenon I shall regard direction of attention as a defining characteristic.

In Chapter 9 difficulties attaching to the conception of behaviour as the subject matter of psychology were discussed. At this point I shall just call attention to the fact that if my characterization of the situation in which communication can take place is correct, it does not seem possible to define a stimulus unless reference is made to properties of the organism as well as to a response. The fact that more than one interpretation can be given by the individual who is to understand that something is being communicated to him, thus seems to preclude the possibility that a stimulus can be defined in physical terms. This again apparently implies that behaviourism cannot be regarded as a consistent philosophical doctrine. It should be noted that the situations in which activities of individuals of other mammalian species can be investigated must also be characterized as situations in which more than one type of reaction can be given by the animal. A reaction on the part of the organism must be conceived of as a selective reaction.

CHAPTER 14

A theory of communication and use of language

In this chapter I shall present a theory of communication and use of language based on the application of the principle of understanding developed and discussed in the two previous chapters. After having presented the theory I shall indicate some of its implications for the scientific study of psychology.

The principle developed is a principle of understanding, and, as was emphasized in the introduction to this part of the book, the activity of communicating something and the activity of understanding what is being communicated differ in important respects. Nevertheless it is reasonable to believe that the two activities may have a common basis in the sense that the activity of communicating is based on the activity of understanding. I shall make the presupposition that the two activities have this common basis, and accordingly I shall presuppose that the individual communicating something does so in accordance with what I have called the fundamental principle of understanding.

As will be remembered, the principle is based on the belief that understanding of something cannot take place if the 'something' is not in some way specified. I expressed this conclusion by saying that an individual, in order to understand what is being communicated to him, must understand that reference is being made to the representation of some definite category, the representation and the category being inseparable.

If the activity of the individual previously referred to as the first individual, the individual communicating something, is also based on the understanding that some definite category is represented, it follows that communication takes place in the way that references are made to representations of definite categories. *The unit of communication in language and in general for all types of communication between individuals is then reference to some definite category represented.*

In what follows I shall indicate what may be a fundamental structure of use of language, but I shall make no attempt to deal with use of language in all its complicated aspects. As I have done

232

in the two previous chapters, I shall concentrate on language as used in communication about material objects in the external world.

If one accepts the presupposition that in using language man proceeds in the way that he makes reference to the representation of definite categories, it seems reasonable to believe that principally the words and expressions of language are used to make reference to representations of this type. I shall presuppose that this is the case and that nouns, adjectives, verbs, adverbs, prepositions and pronouns are so used. Even articles and the so-called connectives may be regarded as having the function of being used for the making of references of the type indicated. According to this position the word, or better, the morpheme, is closest to the linguistic unit. In this book I shall consider the use of a few nouns, adjectives, adverbs and prepositions used in communication about the external world.

In the exposition which follows note should be taken of the fact that in the two previous chapters I made the presupposition that the individual (referred to as the second individual) who is to under-stand what is being communicated was not familiar with the language of the individual (referred to as the first individual) attempting to commmunicate something. In this chapter I shall have to presuppose that they are both familiar with the actual language used. However, attention should be called to the fact that it is still essential that the reader does not confuse statements made relevant to the individual who is to understand what is being communicated with statements made relevant to the individual attempting to communicate some-thing.

Direction of attention and use of language

Throughout this book I have emphasized the close relationship be-tween the activities of perceiving, remembering, imagining and think-ing, on the one hand, and use of language on the other. Before I proceed to show how use of language may be regarded as being based on references to categories represented, it is essential that attention be called to a presupposition made in the previous chapter.

As will be remembered, in developing the fundamental principle of understanding, I presupposed that the second individual (the in-dividual who is to understand what is being communicated) was familiar with language, but not with the cultural language of the first individual (the individual wanting to communicate something). As was made clear in Chapter 3 of Part 1, it is difficult to understand what can be meant by an individual who is not in some way familiar with language, language and culture being closely related. For this reason I had to presuppose that the second individual was familiar with language. However, I shall have to examine more closely what is meant when it is said that an individual is familiar with use of language.

In Chapter 13 of this part of the book I argued that the understanding that some definite category was represented involved some sort of selective mechanism on the part of the individual. I referred to this selective mechanism by the term 'direction of attention'. This argument was based on the presupposition that the individual who was to understand that something was being communicated to him, was familiar with use of language. Evidently use of language is not conceivable without some direction of attention. As was made clear in Chapter 13, both the individual attempting to communicate something and the individual who is to understand what is being communicated must understand that in some definite situation they may select any one of a number of categories represented. Thus looking at a view, the individual wanting to communicate something must in some way understand that he can make reference to the representation of the category 'stone', the representation of the category 'tree', the representation of the category 'colour', etc. Similarly the individual who is to understand that something is being communicated to him must understand that communication can be of the representations of the categories 'stone', 'tree', 'colour', etc. In other words, when I speak of the 'representation of categories' I have presupposed same fundamental aspect of use of language, namely the capacity in the individual for selecting for reference some definite category represented. When in Chapter 13 of this book I said that the understanding that some definite category was represented reflected a necessary relationship between a 'something' in the external world and a 'something' in the organism, I based this statement on a reference to a fundamental aspect of use of language. In other words, I cannot account for the selectivity involved in use of language by reference to my theory. In terms of my familiarity with use of language I can suppose that an individual can select for reference some definite category represented, and I can also suppose that an individual will understand which category represented is selected for reference, but I cannot account for this selectivity.

The point made above may easily be missed, probably because it is so easy to confuse the fact that an understanding of what is being communicated is dependent upon the particular context in which communication takes place, with an account of the selectivity involved. While it must be emphasized that no use of language can be adequately understood unless the context in which language is used is taken into consideration, it should be clear from the discussion in the two previous chapters that use of language cannot be adequately accounted for by reference to the context.

Even if no adequate account can be given of how the individual familiar with language selects for communication the representation of some definite category, it is reasonable to believe that this capacity for selecting is somehow connected with his learning to use language in concrete types of situations. Therefore, to clarify questions concerning use of language, it is frequently of help to consider concrete situations where language is used in a specific manner, or to consider situations in which children might learn to use language in a specific manner. This was probably one reason why Wittgenstein (1953) formed the slogan: 'Do not look for the meaning, but for the use.' In Chapter 8 I pointed out that the placing of the point of departure for a study of language in the idea of grammaticality as done by Chomsky seriously restricts perspective on use of language. As was emphasized earlier, a weakness in the approaches to the study of use of language developed by linguists is the tendency *not* to relate the utterances examined to use of language in concrete situations. I shall insist that the understanding of any utterance remains incomplete until the context is carefully considered. In this connection it should be noted that the fact that grammatically correct sentences can be translated from one cultural language into another does not mean that they have meanings which are not dependent upon definite contexts. Thus, for example, the sentence 'The man loves the woman' can be translated into a variety of cultural languages, but this does not mean that it can be properly understood without a reference to some context. It is worth considering in what context a grammatically correct sentence, such as the one mentioned, can be used.

The nature of the reference

According to the position taken, the representation of categories reflects relationships between the external world and the organism which are in some way invariant or necessary. However, the words or expressions used to refer to them are not invariant. Thus, as discussed in Chapter 11 of Part 1, the various cultural languages use different words to make the reference. For example, as has been mentioned, the representation of the category 'horse' can be referred to by the English word 'horse', by the French *cheval,* or the German *Pferd.* The representation may also be indicated by pointing or gestures. This latter point must not be understood in the way that I am saying that words or expressions can be fundamentally defined in an ostensive manner. In contrast to the situation depicted in Chapter 13 of this part of the book, I am speaking here of human individuals familiar with use of language. I shall use the expression 'way of reference' to express the fact that the reference to some category represented can be made by different words or by pointing or gestures.

In accordance with the fundamental principle of understanding, the limits for use of language are set by the categories represented. This means in the first place that communication cannot take place unless reference is actually made to the representation of some definite category, and secondly a representation is not modified by the way the reference is made to it. These two points are essential for an understanding of how communication proceeds and should be considered more carefully.

With regard to the first point, it will be realized that unless some category is represented, no understanding can take place. A determination of whether or not reference is actually being made to the representation of definite categories is often difficult to make. As was noted in Part 1 of this book, philosophers such as Hume, Frege, Russell and Carnap attempted to develop rules of a relatively simple nature for this determination. As will be understood from the position taken here, it is in the very nature of use of language that no such simple rules can be made. When material objects are perceptually present, a determination can relatively easily be made with regard to whether or not some category is represented. Thus, when some definite stone is visually present, a determination can be made with regard to whether or not reference is actually being made to, say, the representation of the category 'stone'. However, when reference is made to some stone by the activities of remembering, imagining and thinking, this determination is more difficult to make. (This does not, of course, mean that in such instances the category cannot have a representation.) Furthermore the representations of categories are obviously dependent upon each other; for example, the representation of the category indicated by the word 'over' is dependent upon the representation of the material objects (rocks, stones, trees, branches, pebbles, houses, etc.). This means that a determination of whether or not reference is actually being made to the category represented in this instance must also include a determination of whether other categories are also represented. A determination of highly abstract representations of categories, such as justice, equality, democracy, freedom, beauty, etc., is apparently not easy to make. A result of this difficulty in determining whether reference is actually being made to the representation of some definite category, is, of course, that words can be used in a way which does not qualify as use of language. Referring to what was said about operational definitions in Chapter 10 of Part 1, it must be noted that the fact that no *simple* rules are available for this determination does not mean that no rules are available. As was emphasized, reference to operations is an indispensable means in the elucidation of psychological concepts. The point made here is that no matter whether communication is of imagined or thought of stones, of democracies, beauty, science, unicorns or ghosts, communication presupposes that reference is actually made to the representation of some definite category.

In connection with this point, it should be noted that it follows that negations must be thought of as introduced after understanding has taken place that some definite category is represented. Thus the utterance 'No stone is present' presupposes the understanding that communication is of the representation of the category 'stone'. Unless this understanding is present, the negation cannot be introduced. Similarly the statement 'No ghost is present' presupposes the understanding — whatever its nature — that the category 'ghost' is represented.

Furthermore in connection with the point made above, it must be clear that statements involving so-called propositional verbs, such as 'to judge' and 'to believe', must be conceived of in the way that representation is of some definite category which is the subject of the judgement, the thought or the belief. The propositional verb cannot be thought of as influencing the representation of the category. For example, the statement 'I believe that a stone is present' must be conceived of in the way that understanding is of the fact that representation is of the category 'stone' and that the perceptual presence of this representation is the subject of my belief. Similarly the statement 'I believe that ghosts exist' must be conceived of in the way that understanding is of the fact that the category 'ghost' is represented and this representation is the subject of my belief. In other words, the statement is meaningful only if understanding is possible of the representation of the category 'ghost'. The use of the verb 'believe' in contrast to the use of verbs such as 'to know' or 'to see' or 'to attest', does not make the statement meaningful if understanding is not possible of the representation of the category 'ghost'. This conclusion is in line with the position taken on the use of the so-called propositional verbs that a false judgement, thought or belief can have no object (cp. Gale, 1967).

With regard to the second point, it should be noted that confusion arises if care is not taken to distinguish between the understanding that some category is represented and the way the reference to the representation is made. While the understanding is regarded as being in some way invariant, the way the reference is made is not. Consequently the way the reference is made can be modified, but what was called the mode of understanding cannot be modified. As has been mentioned above, the way the reference is made to a stone can be modified in the way that an individual either utters the word 'stone' or points to the stone, but this does not affect the understanding that the category 'stone' is represented. As is well known, different individuals can use different words to make reference to the representation of the same category and the same verbal sign to make reference to the representation of different categories.

To illustrate how confusion arises when the point made above is overlooked, an example from Russell, one of the analytic philosophers mentioned above, may be considered. Russell (1956) believed that he might subject the following sort of utterance to a logical analysis: 'The square circle does not exist'. The use of the word 'square' here is a result of overlooking the fact that the word 'circle' makes reference to some definite category represented. The representation of this category excludes the representation of the category 'square'. Therefore, the statement does not qualify as use of language. Another significant example of the type of confusion that arises when the point above is overlooked is found in the illustration made by Gestalt psychologists of the statement that the whole is more than the sum of its parts. Here they point, for example, to the fact that a triangle is not identical to the three lines circumscribing it. Of course, the representation of the category 'triangle' is different from the representation of the category 'line'. Therefore, this example does not qualify as use of language. Elsewhere I (Saugstad, 1965) have suggested that a number of the central theoretical statements made in Gestalt psychology may not qualify as use of language.

In connection with the two points dealt with above, attention should be called to the fact that the position taken here on use of language implies a rejection of the belief that logic must be ascribed priority over use of language. No statement can be considered as true or false unless it reflects the understanding that some definite category is represented. As suggested in Chapter 11 of Part 1, the question of the truth or falsity of a statement cannot be considered without reference to its meaning. For example, unless it is understood what is meant by the representation of the category 'stone', it is not possible to ascertain whether a given statement containing a reference to that representation is true or false. The position taken by Russell, as indicated by the example given above, may be regarded as an illustration of the confusion which arises when logic is ascribed priority over use of language. This confusion, I suspect, has permeated not only the philosophy of

Russell, but also that of Frege, Husserl and Carnap.

It must be noted that words and expressions, when used to make reference to the representations of categories, are not used to make references to an individual, or to a particular. Therefore, these references must not be confused with the use of proper names. The word 'stone' is used for the representation of the cartegory 'stone' irrespective of where in space this representation is located and irrespective of whether the stone is large or small, grey or brown, square or round. Similarly the word 'grey' is used for the representation of the category 'grey' irrespective of its location in space and irrespective of the shade or nuance of grey. The reference, one might say, is to a mode of understanding and not to an individual or a particular.

In accordance with this line of reasoning, I shall reject Mill's division of words into the denotative and the connotative as well as the distinctions made by Frege, Russell and Carnap between 'reference' and 'meaning', as discussed in Chapter 11 of Part 1.

Reference to the representation of single categories

As I have stated above, the unit of communication is considered to be the reference to the representation of definite categories. If, as indicated, words are used principally to make reference to the representation of categories, it is reasonable to believe that single words or expressions referring to one single category might represent an adequate use of language. For example, in certain contexts, the utterance of the word 'stone' meaning that the category 'stone' is represented, or the utterance of the word 'grey', meaning that the category 'grey' is represented, ought to be considered as adequate use of language. If this is so, the word, or better, the morpheme, probably comes closest to the linguistic unit. I shall examine the question of whether or not the use of single words or expressions can be said to represent an adequate use of language.

Apparently it is not difficult to find situations where the utterance of the single word 'stone' would be perfectly adequate. Let us suppose that two individuals see some material object at a distance and wonder whether it is a stone or a stump and one of the individuals moves up to the object to examine it, and having examined it, utters the word 'stone'. This would represent a perfectly adequate use of language. If it is objected that this is only so because that utterance is made in a particular context, I would answer that understanding of use of language always presupposes some definite context. Take, for example, the utterance 'The stone is grey'. It is a grammatically correct sentence, but it is not completely understood unless it is considered in an appropriate context. If two individuals were out for a walk and they had not talked about the colour of stones and this had never been the subject of a discussion between them, the utterance by one of the individuals of 'The stone is grey' would probably make the other individual suspect either that the former was alluding to some previous incident of some sort or that he was insane. This example illustrates the fact that grammaticality without reference to some definite context is never sufficient for making a complete analysis of use of language.

To take another example, it is not difficult to find some context in which the utterance of the single word 'grey' might be perfectly adequate. Suppose for some reason two individuals were looking for some grey surface to use as camouflage. On discovering such a surface one of them might utter the word 'grey'. Again I would insist that the utterance would represent an adequate use of language.

To take a third, more dramatic example: Two individuals are fleeing from a wild bear and one of the individuals sees the bear behind the other individual and utters the word 'Behind'. Again I would claim that the utterance *may* represent a perfectly adequate use of language.

The examples given above could be multiplied endlessly. There can be no doubt that in a variety of situations utterances of single words or expressions represent a perfectly adequate use of language. If this use is regarded as fundamental, it is possible to relate use of language to understanding and to develop a simple theory of use of language. It should be noted that this theory can explain how use of language develops ontogenetically and how it has developed culturally more easily than a theory based upon the sentence as the linguistic unit.

As has been mentioned above, it is difficult to see that the position taken here can be invalidated by an argument to the effect that single words or expressions are understandable only in specific types of contexts. I would say that it represents a misunderstanding of use of language to believe that use of language can be adequately understood without taking into account the context in which language is used. In order to argue forcefully for the position that the grammatical sentence is the fundamental unit of use of language, the theorist must be capable of showing that sentences can be adequately understood without reference to some sort of context. An argument of this type would have to be based on an account of how the individual using language is capable of selecting one aspect of reality for communication. As was made clear above, at present it does not seem possible to give an adequate account of this capacity. Much of the modern work in linguistics seems to be based on simple-minded notions regarding the role played by the context.

The emphasis placed here on the role of context in use of language is inspired by Wittgenstein's (1953) later philosophy, where use of language is regarded as originating in man's way of life and where the examination of use of language is concentrated on the so-called language game. However, apparently the present position contrasts with that of Wittgenstein with regard to the nature of the reference made by words. As was previously pointed out, Wittgenstein seems to have been unwilling to accept that use of language was based on what I have called definite modes of understanding. (Cp. the discussion in Chapter 11, Part 1.)

As will be clear from what has been said above, I do not find it unreasonable to assume that a word used to make reference to some category represented should be regarded as representing what Wittgenstein called 'a move in language'. Under certain conditions utterances of this type will be incomplete, but, as I have argued, this is not always the case. One might say that language games may be more or less complicated and that those made up of single words and expressions will represent relatively simple ones.

The relationship between the references: the sentence

Having dealt with the question of whether references to the representations of single categories would be understandable, I shall now turn to the question of the relationship between references. According to the position taken, communication proceeds in the way that references are made to categories represented. When more than one reference is made, the references have to be made in a succesive fashion. The question arises: How are the references to the categories represented related to each other?

In the previous chapter I argued that, if it was accepted that understanding of something could not take place if the 'something' was not in some way specified, each category would have to have its specific representation. This means that two different categories cannot have one representation in common, and no single category can have two different representations. *Accordingly it is not possible to represent the representation of two different categories by means of a third category.*

It follows from the reasoning above that the understanding that the representations of two different categories are related to each other is of a different nature from the understanding that some definite category is represented. In the previous chapter I argued that the latter form of understanding reflected necessary relationships between a 'something' in the external world and a 'something' in the organism. In contrast relationships of the former type seem to be of a contingent nature, i.e. they can be conceived of as being otherwise. For example, a stone may be brown, grey, red or white, round or square, small or large, etc. The relationship between the reference to the representation of the category 'stone' and, say, the representation of the category 'brown' would, therefore, be contingent.

Unless we resort to the device of postulating a something which is not specified, as has apparently been done by logicians and linguists up to the present, we shall have to answer the question of how two or more references to categories represented can be related to each other. The question is a puzzling one. Before I attempt to answer this question I shall point out that the idea of language as a system may easily lead one astray when one attempts to answer the question.

In Chapter 11 I made it clear that this idea was highly inadequate. I argued that use of language reflects necessary relationships between man and the external world. It is not, I maintain, possible to conceive (as done by Saussure and probably most linguists), on the one hand of language as a phonological and grammatical system, and on the other of an external world to which the system is applied. Use of language, I would say, is so closely related to man's physical and social environment that it is not possible fundamentally to conceive of the one without the other. According to this position it is only possible to speak of use of language as constituting a system when a variety of presuppositions are made concerning man's relationship to his physical and social environment. Therefore, a conception of the phoneme or the sentence as existing outside this relationship may lead to statements which have little relevance to reality.

To return to the question of the relationship between references to the representations of categories, I would insist that what can be regarded as an adequate use of language must be determined by a consideration of how the external world appears to man. As has been emphasized, this determination does not contain an explanation of this use of language. I shall illustrate this point. Let us suppose the following two references are made: (1) to the representation of the category 'stone' and (2) to the representation of the category 'grey'. Apparently these two references can only be related to each other if this relationship reflects a relationship in the external world as it appears to us. To express the fact that communication is of this relationship, some linguistic convention must be invented. This linguistic convention, I suggest, is the grammatical sentence. Accordingly the grammatical sentence is an arbitrary or conventional means of relating two references to each other. The grammatical sentence will thus be seen to be highly useful, but it is not indispensable. It would be possible to communicate by making two or more references and have the individuals who are to understand guess what the relationship between them is. Whether or not the sentence may be said to represent some form of cultural refinement according to this view is not easy to say. However, one can go so far as to say that it would be difficult to state what might constitute support for the view that the capacity for forming sentences is innate.

Apparently when two references are related to each other in a sentence, neither reference is more important than the other — it is the *relationship* between the references which is essential. For example, in the sentence 'The stone is grey' the reference to the representation of the category 'grey' is just as important as the reference to the category 'stone'. Similarly in the following sentences: 'The stone is square', 'The tree is green', 'The stone is here', 'The tree is here'. (Cp. the position taken by Ramsey on the nature of the proposition referred to in Chapter 11, p. 191.) However, as will be understood, two references can be related to each other in such a way that one of the references is the most important one, the other being in some way subordinate.

For example, instead of saying 'The stone is here' I *may* say 'Here where the stone is'. Apparently I have the same two references in either case, but whereas in the former utterance they are related to each other in a sentence, the reference to the representation of the category 'stone' in the latter utterance is subordinate. Similarly I may say 'The stone is grey' or 'The stone which is grey' or simply 'The grey stone'. In the last two utterances the reference to the representation of the category 'grey' seems to be subordinate to the representation of the category 'stone'. How can these two different types of relationship be explained?

I think it is possible to explain the difference by a consideration of the appearance of the external world. I shall illustrate this by an example. Let us suppose two individuals are looking for a stone of some definite type. Upon discovering one which may be regarded as appropriate, one of the individuals may make the utterance 'stone'. As was made clear in the previous section, I shall insist that this may be regarded as adequate use of language. However, whether it is adequate use of language depends upon the situation — the context. Let us suppose the two individuals are confronted by more than one stone; in such a case the utterance 'stone' might not represent an adequate use of language. To indicate which stone was meant, the individual would have to indicate where the category 'stone' which he had in mind was represented. He might say 'Grey stone' or 'The stone which is grey', or he might even say

'Grey, square, large stone, on top of the rock, to the left of the tree.' In this case the references to the representations of the categories other than that of 'stone' would apparently serve the purpose of directing the attention of the individual who is to understand what is communicated, so that this individual can understand where the particular representation of the category 'stone' can be found. That this type of relationship between references is arbitrary, can be seen from the fact that in many situations it is of no importance which one of a variety of references is made. For example, in the above utterance one may either refer to the representation of the category 'grey' by saying, 'Grey stone' or to the representation of the category 'square' by saying 'Square stone'.

Whether the relationship expressed by a grammatical sentence or the other type of relationship between the references is involved is determined by a consideration of the context in which language is used.

According to the theory of communication and use of language developed here language is used in the sense that references are successively made to categories represented. These references may be related to each other by means of the grammatical sentence, or, as has been made clear, they may be related to each other in other ways. Therefore, there is no reason to believe, as linguists adhering to the so-called transformational grammar believe, that one sentence is to be regarded as the transformation of another sentence. For example, there is no reason to believe that the sentence 'The house is being built by the man' must be a transformation of the sentence 'The man is building the house'. In the former sentence communication is probably concentrated on the house — and in the latter on the man.

I have argued that the morpheme which refers to some definite category comes closest to being the unit for use of language, not the sentence or the phoneme. With regard to the phoneme it will be seen that it does not represent an objection in principle to the position that a description of what is regarded as a word in terms of acoustics and muscular innervation in the production varies from individual to individual and from instance to instance within an individual. The understanding that reference is made to some definite category represented is dependent upon the context. If the context makes clear what reference is being made, it may be of no consequence that the word is produced in different ways. As has been emphasized above, the reference to the representation of some definite category can be made in different ways. A word is used to make reference to a relationship of a particular kind; therefore it is neither definable only in terms of acoustics nor merely in terms of innervation of the muscles used to produce it.

Suggestions for a scientific study of psychology

In this section I shall indicate in a general manner how a scientific study of psychology can be carried out. The more precise formulation of problems requires the creativity of coming generations of psychologists in terms of the reference system developed.

The examinations undertaken in Part 1 of this book of problems met with in the study of psychology led to the conclusion that the point of departure for this study must be placed in use of language. In the second part of the book I have hitherto underlined that by use of language I mean use of language in the normal adult individual. In order to arrive at an identification of the events to be made the subject of the study, use of language was characterized by saying that it involved understanding of some sort. Understanding was further specified as understanding in an individual who is to understand that another individual is attempting to communicate something to him. A fundamental requirement of understanding as specified above was found to consist in the understanding that some definite category was represented. In accordance with this line of reasoning *an event may be said to have occurred when an individual has understood that some definite category is represented.* In what follows I shall outline how events of various types identified according to this procedure can be studied.

By taking as the point of departure use of language in the normal adult individual I am saying that man's conceptions of his environment as well as of himself must be determined by his use of language.

As has been emphasized, this position is not an idealistic one. However, it does emphasize the fact that unless the theorist is capable of relating his studies to use of language, he will not be in a position to understand what he is doing. In Chapter 13 it was noted that this point of departure does not restrict the research worker to studying events in the normal adult individual, although it does place the requirement on his studies that he shall be capable of conceiving of the events studied in terms of use of language. Therefore, when he studies what may be regarded as abnormal use of language in man (the study of which according to this line of reasoning represents the study of abnormality), he will have to determine this use by relating it to what can reasonably be conceived of as normal use of language. If it is objected that such a determination is difficult to make, I shall reply that the history of the study of abnormality in man may be said to reveal that it seems to be difficult to undertake this type of study precisely because it is so difficult to determine what may be meant by abnormality. Furthermore, when the research worker studies events taking place in individuals of species other than man, he will have to conceive of these events in terms of use of language. This requirement, it will be noted, only appears strange as long as one believes it possible to conceive of man and his environment in terms of consciousness or of behaviour. In connection with this point, attention should be called to the fact that the requirement discussed here does not imply that the comparative psychologist cannot make comparisons between activities in species other than man the subject of his investigation. It only means that the activities to be compared must be conceived of in terms of man's use of language.

Moreover, as was made clear in the introductory chapter to this part of the book, the placing of the point of departure in use of language does not imply that communication cannot take place in other ways than by verbal expression. Communication may take place by pointing, gestures, by the device of rituals, or by specifically developed training procedures. However, it must be required that in whatever way communication is undertaken, its relationship to use of language in the normal adult individual must be specified. In this connection I shall repeat that by use of language is meant language as spoken, and, therefore, that the research worker must take care that he does not overlook any characteristic of spoken language. (Cp. Chapter 12.) The point made here, of course, does not represent a denial of the fact that aspects of use of language may be characterized by comparing them to the functioning believed to take place analogically in accordance with the functioning of some artificially constructed system. The requirement is only that the research worker making this type of comparison must be capable of stating what particular aspect he is trying to characterize. As was made clear in Chapter 8 this is not as easy to do as research workers applying this technique often seem to believe.

A main problem in outlining the type of research with which we are concerned is arriving at criteria for determining when understanding may be said to have occurred in some individual. When account is taken of the fact that language is used in a seemingly endless variety of situations, it will be understood that no simple criteria can be stated which allow the research worker to arrive at this determination. At this point I should like to emphasize the fact that in any branch of science a determination of what is regarded as knowledge is made in terms of all cultural knowledge relevant to the problem studied. For this reason, a determination of this sort is never a simple one, nor can it be undertaken in a way which gives absolute certainty that the events studied have occurred as postulated in the scientific system.

In order to be able to characterize the events studied in a fruitful manner it is usually important to specify the occurrence of the events as accurately as possible in the temporal dimension. Consequently it is important to devise techniques for determining the moment in time when understanding according to the fundamental principle of communication can be said to take place. Here I shall have to restrict myself to calling attention to the fact that understanding, as conceived of here, may be said to occur when an individual understands what another individual has attempted to communicate to him. Understanding must therefore not be conceived of as continually being present in an individual, even if the individual repeatedly and in a variety of different situations might most probably be capable of understanding what was communicated to him by some specific procedure.

After having outlined in general terms the procedure to be followed in a study of psychology I shall proceed to discuss how in terms of the reference system developed the research worker may formulate problems of theoretical significance. It follows from what has been said about the procedure, that, unless statements of a general nature can be made concerning the conditions under which the events identified can be said to occur, the researcher will only have arrived at a description of a particular case, i.e. the way language is used in some particular situation by some particular individual or by some particular group of individuals. Statements of this type, it will be understood, can hardly be of much usefulness. Unfortunately, due to the fact that up to now reference systems for the study of psychology have been lacking, the overwhelming majority of theoretical statements made by research workers in psychology seem to be of this type. Evidently, in order to state a significant theoretical problem the research worker will have to arrive at general statements regarding the conditions under which various types of events identified by the reference system may be said to occur. Since the theorist cannot possibly be expected to anticipate all types of events to be identified, it is not reasonable to attempt to make statements which must apply to all types of events which the research worker might imagine as identifiable. It must be left for future research to decide on the extent of the generality of the theoretical statements to be made. Still, in line with what may be said to characterize scientific thinking, it is probably to be expected that the more general the statements regarding the conditions can be made, the more useful the statements will be.

Apparently, fruitful research problems would be those that — when adequately handled — allowed the theorist to characterize either properties in the organism or aspects of its environment relevant to some type of event involved in understanding. One way of characterizing the environment of man as well as that of a variety of other species has already been developed in the study of perceiving. This study, which originated, as mentioned in Chapter 2, around the middle of the nineteenth century, may be said to aim at characterizing various types of events in terms of physical descriptions. As was emphasized in Chapters 3 and 4, this study takes as its point of departure language as actually used, and subjects to a study various types of events identified by a procedure which is entirely in accordance with the procedure outlined here. In this study representations of categories referred to by words such as 'colour', 'hue', 'brightness', 'size', 'location', 'pitch', 'loudness', 'coldness', 'warmth', 'saltiness', 'sourness', etc. have been described in terms of physical dimensions such as wavelength, intensity of light, measurable areas and distances, frequencies and amplitudes of sound waves, temperatures, etc. As has been emphasized, this study has been a fruitful one, even if it has turned out to be difficult to extend the range of types of events which might be described in physical terms. As was pointed out in Chapters 3 and 4, the fact that the descriptions undertaken in physical terms have proved to be useful should not of course lead one to the conclusion that a physicalist description is possible for use of language. (A criticism of the physicalist position was given in Chapter 9.) It does, however, show that it is possible to make statements of a general nature about various types of events communicated about when language is used.

Another way of arriving at general statements concerning certain types of events would be to study understanding under specifiable abnormal conditions. Abnormal conditions of this type might, for example, be said to be present in individuals deprived of one or more sensory modalities, as, for example, in the case of the deaf and the blind. The presence of the various sensory modalities may reasonably be thought to constitute conditions of various sorts for the occurrence of understanding. Consequently a study of understanding under conditions where one sensory modality is lacking might allow one to arrive at statements of a general nature. In particular understanding in individuals who have developed without the aid of one definite modality should allow one to arrive at statements of a general type. Attention should be called to the fact that unless such a study contributes to the understanding of normal functioning it will not contribute to the understanding of abnormal functioning. This is so because, as has been emphasized, abnormal functioning can only be understood in terms of use of language in the normal adult individual.

Apparently all types of abnormal functioning which have a cause of a general nature may be able to contribute to our understanding of the conditions under which various types of events can occur.

Thus the study of understanding in states of abnormal functioning induced by drugs or caused in other ways might lead to contributions to the theory of psychology.

In Chapter 5 attention was called to the difficulties attaching to a comparison of activities in individuals of different species. However, there can be no reason to believe that these difficulties cannot be overcome. By comparing understanding in individuals of different species one might be able to characterize various types of events by reference to known differences in properties of the organisms and their environments.

Another important way of arriving at statements of a general nature with regard to the conditions under which various types of events might be said to occur, would be to study the development of understanding in children. In Chapters 2, 5 and 9 I have pointed out various difficulties attaching to the study of ontogenetic development. It will be clear that the procedure described above only allows the research worker to determine whether or not understanding has taken place. It should be noted that because determinations of understanding are made in terms of the use made of language in the normal adult individual, it is not possible to make valid inferences about understanding in the child on the basis of negative results alone. The fact that an individual at some definite stage of ontogenetic development has not understood what another individual has attempted to communicate, does not make it possible for the research worker to state what is understood. A more careful examination of theoretical statements made by theorists in the study of ontogenetic development would probably reveal that in a number of instances these statements have been made on the basis of this type of false inference.

In order to arrive at general statements concerning conditions under which understanding might take place in a child one could proceed in the following way. First one could determine a stage of ontogenetic development at which the child does not understand what one is attempting to communicate to it. Next one could try at a later stage to specify the conditions under which this attempt is successful. As has been emphasized, it is not possible to give a complete account of how some definite type of understanding originates, but it is reasonable to believe that one could find conditions which contribute to a better understanding of how this happens.

One type of information useful in attempts to arrive at statements of a general nature with regard to understanding can be gained from a registration of the temporal order in relation to the ontogenetic stage at which events of various types may be said to occur. A consideration of this temporal order can reasonably be expected to lead to an increased understanding of the interaction between the organism and its environment of which the events may be said to be a result. As was made clear by Hamlyn in his criticism of the work of Piaget (discussed in Chapter 2), priority determined by reference to ontogenetic development must not be confused with priority of a logical nature. By logical priority is meant the fact that certain types of understanding presuppose other types of understanding. As was made clear in Chapter 13, the understanding of the representation of categories such as 'over', 'under' and 'beside' presupposes the understanding of representations of categories of material objects. Clearly use of language is dependent upon a variety of logical relationships of this kind. Not until relationships of this sort have been made clear can empirical studies of the type mentioned above be made. Otherwise the result will be confusion.

In connection with a developmental study of understanding one ought to bear in mind the difficulty discussed in the previous chapter. As was mentioned there, when an individual does not understand what another individual attempts to communicate to him, the reason may be either that he does not understand that the category is represented or that he does not understand that the sign used to make reference to the category represented is actually being used for this particular reference. If the latter type of understanding is lacking it cannot be concluded that the former type of understanding has not taken place. As has been made clear, it is not easy to arrive at a determination of whether only the latter or both types of understanding are lacking, but there seems to be no reason to believe that this difficulty could not be overcome.

In the remarks made above I have indicated how by a study of abnormal functioning and by a study of ontogenetic and phylogenetic development one might arrive at statements regarding the conditions under which the events identified by the reference system might be said to occur. One may ask: Why not attempt to arrive at general statements by a study of functioning in normal adult individuals? While it cannot be precluded that such a study might contribute to our understanding of the various types of events, it will be realized that as long as so little is known about the development and origin of man's use of language, it is difficult to imagine how one might characterize this use of language in general ways. For example, it is difficult to find groups of such individuals which can be said to differ in respects which are clearly specifiable. In all probability this type of research will only allow conclusions of the nature that individuals of groups which differ in various respects use language in a different way. In Chapter 6 I pointed to difficulties stemming from the lack of reference systems in the study of concept formation, problem solving and intelligence. The difficulty of characterizing use of language in the normal adult individual may be said to represent a main barrier to progress in registering individual differences in understanding.

The examination undertaken in Chapter 10 made clear that use of language had to be conceived of as necessary. However, as was made clear in Chapter 11 — during discussion of the ideas presented by Saussure — use of language and thus also understanding would also have to be conceived of as being arbitrary in some way. Apparently in order to arrive at a better understanding of thinking, it is of central importance to specify conditions which lead to understanding of a necessary and an arbitrary nature respectively. A consideration of these two types of understanding would seem to lead us into the study of thinking. Evidently one way of characterizing the activity of thinking is to say that it is concerned with events involved when understanding can be said to be arbitrary. In some way the activity of thinking seems to be concerned with what may be said to represent choices between different means to reach an end. These choices may be said to involve an arbitrariness of some sort. In contrast, in the activity of perceiving this type of arbitrariness does not seem to be involved to the same degree. Admittedly it is difficult to state more clearly what is meant by this arbitrariness.

Attempts to characterize the activity of thinking by saying that it involves some shift of attention do not seem to lead to fruitful formulations of research problems. It does not seem possible to imagine conditions of a general type which might be responsible for these shifts, for example, for the fact that the understanding that the category 'stone' is represented changes to the understanding that the category 'tree' or 'colour' is represented. This seems to preclude the possibility of speaking meaningfully of thinking as a process, as research workers so often attempt to do. (The difficulty of using the term 'process' was discussed in Chapters 2 and 8.) In connection with the difficulty of characterizing the activity of thinking in a general manner, the reader is reminded of the fact that the previous attempts in this direction were undertaken in terms of beliefs expressed in the empiricist and phenomenological philosophical traditions. These beliefs were found to be highly dubious. (Cp. Chapters 2, 3, 6, 10 and 11.)

A general difficulty involved in the study of psychology is found in the fact which has already been mentioned that the understanding that some definite category is represented is dependent upon the understanding that other categories are also represented. When language is used by the normal adult individual, the understanding that a given category is represented is obviously often dependent in a complicated manner upon other categories represented. This makes it difficult to state what is learnt in tasks assigned to a normal adult individual. For this reason a study of learning as affecting the normal *adult* individual will probably not allow us to state conditions of a general nature for the occurrence of any type of event. A study of the activity of remembering in the normal adult individual would seem to involve the same difficulty. To account adequately for what is remembered, it seems essential that the research worker should be able to state what is involved when that which is to be remembered is understood. This apparently leads to the problem of stating how reference to some definite category represented is dependent upon the understanding that other categories are represented.

Bibliography and References

There is a very extensive literature on all of the main problems dealt with in Part 1 of this book. I have tried to refer to articles and books which cover in a systematic way each of the problems discussed. In these books and articles the reader will also find comprehensive lists of references relevant to each problem as well as information on the various editions of the principal works.

In order to give some perspective on these problems, I have tried to refer to or quote the thinkers who formulated them at an early stage. Where I have not used the first edition of these works, I have referred to the orginal year of publication in square brackets in the text. Page references in the text always refer to the edition of the work listed here below.

The Encyclopedia of Philosophy (Ed. by P. Edwards, New York: Macmillan, 1967) has been abbreviated to *Encyc. Philos.*

Abagnano, N. Positivism. *Encyc. Philos.*, *6*, 414-419.
Abelson, R. Definition. *Encyc. Philos.*, *2*, 314-324.
Ach, N. *Über die Begriffsbildung,* Bamberg: Büchner, 1921.
Acton, H. B. (a) Berkeley, George, *Encyc. Philos.*, *1*, 295-304.
Acton, H. B. (b) Dialectical materialism. *Encyc. Philos.*, *2*, 389-397.
Acton, H. B. (c) Hegel, Georg Wilhelm Friedrich. *Encyc. Philos.*, *3*, 435-451.
Alexander, P. (a) Mach, Ernst. *Encyc. Philos.*, *5*, 115-119.
Alexander, P. (b) Poincaré, Jules Henri. *Encyc. Philos.*, *6*, 360-363.
Alexander, P. (c) Sensationalism. *Encyc. Philos.*, *7*, 415-419.
Alston, W. P. *Philosophy of Language.* Englewood Cliffs, N. J.: Prentice-Hall, 1964.
Alston, W. P. (a) Meaning. *Encyc. Philos.*, *5*, 233-241.
Alston, W. P. (b) Sign and symbol. *Encyc. Philos.*, *7*, 437-441.
Alston, W. P. (c) Language. *Encyc. Philos.*, *4*, 384-386.
Anastasi, A. *Differential Psychology.* (3rd ed.) New York: Macmillan, 1958.
Anscombe, G. E. M. The subjectivity of sensation. *Ajatus,* 1976, *36*, 3-18.
Ashby, R. W. Verifiability principle. *Encyc. Philos.*, *8*, 240-247.
Aune, B. Thinking. *Encyc. Philos.*, *8*, 100-104.
Bartlett, F. C. *Remembering.* Cambridge: Cambridge Univ. Press, 1932.

Berkeley, G. *A Treatise Concerning the Principles of Human Knowledge.* (Ed. by C. M. Turbane), New York: Bobbs-Merrill, 1957. (1st. ed. 1710.)

Bertalanffy, L. von. *General System Theory.* London: Penguin Books, 1968.

Binet, A. and Simon, T. Méthodes nouvelles pour le diagnostic du niveau intellectuel des anormaux. *Année Psychol.,* 1905, *11,* 191-244.

Bloomfield, L. *Language.* New York: Holt, Rinehart & Winston, 1933.

Boring, E. G. *Sensation and Perception in the History of Experimental Psychology.* New York: Appleton-Century-Crofts, 1942.

Boring, E. G. *A History of Experimental Psychology.* (2nd ed.) New York: Appleton-Century-Crofts, 1950.

Bourne, L. E., Ekstrand, B. R. and Dominowski, R. L. *The Psychology of Thinking.* Englewood Cliffs, N. J.: Prentice-Hall, 1971.

Bradley, F. H. *Appearance and Reality. A Metaphysical Essay.* (2nd ed.) London: Sonnenschein, 1906.

Brentano, F. The distinction between mental and physical phenomena. Transl. by D. B. Terrell. In R. M. Chisholm (Ed.), *Realism and the Background of Phenomenology.* Illinois: Free Press of Glencoe, 1960. (The selections are taken from *Psychologie vom Empirischen Standpunkt.* Hamburg: Meiner, 1955, 1959. (1st ed. 1874.)

Bridgman, P. W. *The Logic of Modern Physics.* New York: Macmillan, 1927.

Brown, R. *Words and Things.* Glencoe, Ill.: Free Press, 1958.

Brown, R. *A First Language. The Early Stages.* London: Allen & Unwin, 1973.

Bruner, J. S., Goodnow, J. J. and Austin, G. A. *A Study of Thinking.* New York: Wiley, 1956.

Bruner, J. S., Olver, R. R. and Greenfield, P. M. *Studies in Cognitive Growth.* New York: Wiley, 1966.

Carnap, R. *Meaning and Necessity.* Chicago: Univ. Chicago Press, 1947.

Carnap, R. Psychology in physical language. Transl. by G. Schick. In A. J. Ayer (Ed.), *Logical Positivism.* New York: Free Press, 1959. (The article was first published in German in *Erkenntnis,* 1931, *2,* 432-454.)

Carroll, J. B. *Language and Thought.* Englewood Cliffs, N. J.: Prentice-Hall, 1964.

Castañeda, H. N. Private language. *Encyc. Philos., 6,* 458-464.

Caws, P., Scientific method. *Encyc. Philos., 7,* 339-343.

Chisholm, R. M. Editor's introduction. In R. M. Chisholm (Ed.), *Realism and the Background of Phenomenology.* Illinois: Free Press of Glencoe, 1960.

Chomsky, N. *Syntactic Structures.* The Hague: Mouton, 1957.

Chomsky, N. Verbal behavior. By B. F. Skinner. *Language,* 1959, *35,* 26-58.

Chomsky, N. *Aspects of the Theory of Syntax.* Cambridge, Mass.: M. I. T. Press, 1965.

Chomsky, N. *Cartesian Linguistics.* New York: Harper & Row, 1966.

Chomsky, N. *Language and Mind.* (Enlarged ed.) New York: Harcourt Brace Jovanovich, 1972.

Clapp, J. G. Locke, John. *Encyc. Philos., 4,* 487-503.

Clark, W. E. le Gros. *The Antecedents of Man.* New York: Harper & Row, 1959.

Cohen, L. and Salapatek, P. *Infant Perception.* New York: Academic Press, 1975.

Cronbach, L. J. *Essentials of Psychological Testing.* (2nd ed.) New York: Harper, 1960.

Deese, J. Association and memory. In T. R. Dixon and D. L. Horton (Eds.), *Verbal Behavior and General Behavior Theory.* Englewood Cliffs, N. J.: Prentice-Hall, 1968.

Descartes, R. *Meditations on First Philosophy.* Transl. by E. S. Haldane and

G. R. T. Ross. In *The Philosophical Works of Descartes*. Vol. I. Cambridge: Cambridge Univ. Press, 1967. (1st ed. 1641.)

Descartes, R. *The Principles of Philosophy*. Transl. by E. S. Haldane and G. R. T. Ross. In *The Philosophical Works of Descartes*. Vol. I. Cambridge: Cambridge Univ. Press, 1967. (1st ed. 1644.)

Dixon, T. R. and Horton, D. L. (Eds.), *Verbal Behavior and General Behavior Theory*. Englewood Cliffs, N. J.: Prentice Hall, 1968.

Dummett, M. Frege, Gottlob. *Encyc. Philos., 3*, 225-237.

Ebbinghaus, H. von. *Über das Gedächtnis*. Leipzig: Duncker & Humblot, 1885.

Edwards, P., Alston, W. P. and Prior, A.N. Russell, Bertrand Arthur William. *Encyc. Philos., 7*, 235-258.

Estes, W. K. Towards a statistical theory of learning. *Psychol. Rev.*, 1950, *57*, 94-107.

Estes, W. K. Kurt Lewin. In W. K. Estes et al.: *Modern Learning Theory*. New York: Appleton-Century-Crofts, 1954.

Fages, J. B. *Comprendre le structuralisme*. Paris: Privat, 1967.

Fechner, G. T. *Elemente der Psychophysik, 1, 2*, Leipzig: Breitkopf & Härtel, 1860.

Fieandt, K. von and Moustgaard, I. K. *The Perceptual World*. New York: Academic Press, 1977.

Findlay, J. N. Hegel. In D. J. O'Connor (Ed.), *A Critical History of Western Philosophy*. New York: Free Press, 1964.

Frank, P. *Modern Science and its Philosophy*. Cambridge, Mass.: Harvard Univ. Press, 1950.

Frege, G. On sense and nominatum. Transl. by H. Feigl. In H. Feigl and W. Sellars (Eds.), *Readings in Philosophical Analysis*. New York: Appleton-Century-Crofts, 1949. (The article was first published in *Zeitschr. Philos. und Philos. Kritik*, 1892, *100*, 25-50.)

Furth, H. G. *Thinking without Language. Psychological Implications of Deafness*. New York: Free Press, 1966.

Furth, H. G. *Piaget and Knowledge. Theoretical Foundations*. Englewood Cliffs, N.J.: Prentice-Hall, 1969.

Gagné, R. M. Human problem solving: internal and external events. In B. Kleinmuntz (Ed.) *Problem Solving: Research, Method and Theory*. New York: Wiley, 1966.

Gale, R. M. Propositions, judgements, sentences, and statements. *Encyc. Philos., 6*, 494-505.

Galton, F. *Inquiries into Human Faculty and its Development*. London: Mac-Millan, 1883.

Gardner, R. A. and Gardner, B. T. Teaching sign language to a chimpanzee. *Science*, 1969, *165*, 664-672.

Garner, W. R. *Uncertainty and Structure as Psychological Concepts*. New York: Wiley, 1962.

Gibson, J. J. *The Senses Considered as Perceptual Systems*. Boston: Houghton Mifflin, 1966.

Goodman, N. The epistemological argument. *Synthèse*, 1967, *17*, 2-28.

Granit, R. *Receptors and Sensory Perception*. New Haven: Yale Univ. Press, 1955.

Graumann, C. F. Denken und Denkpsychologie. In C. F. Graumann, (Ed.), *Denken*. Cologne: Kiepenheuer & Witsch, 1965.

Guilford, J. F. *The Nature of Human Intelligence*. New York: McGraw-Hill, 1967.

Guthrie, E. R. *The Psychology of Learning*. New York: Harper, 1935.

Guthrie, E. R. and Horton, G. P. *Cats in a Puzzle Box.* New York: Rinehart, 1946.

Haber, R. N. and Haber, R. B. Eidetic imagery: I. Frequency. *Perceptual and Motor Skills,* 1964, *19,* 131-138.

Habermas, J. *Erkenntnis und Interesse.* Frankfurt am Main: Suhrkamp, 1973.

Hamlyn, D. W. (a) Empiricism. *Encyc. Philos., 2,* 499-505.

Hamlyn, D. W. (b) Epistemology. *Encyc. Philos., 3,* 5-38.

Hamlyn, D. W. Epistemology and conceptual development. In T. Mishell (Ed.), *Cognitive Development and Epistemology.* New York: Academic Press, 1971.

Harré, R. Philosophy of science, history of. *Encyc. Philos., 5,* 289-296.

Heath, P. L. (a) Concept. *Encyc. Philos., 2,* 177-180.

Heath, P. L. (b) Experience. *Encyc. Philos., 3,* 156-159.

Hebb, D. O. *The Organization of Behavior.* New York: Wiley, 1949.

Hegel, G. W. F. *Phänomenologie des Geistes.* Darmstadt: Meiner, 1952. (1st ed. 1807.)

Hesse, M. Laws and theories. *Encyc. Philos., 4,* 404-410.

Hilgard, E. R. and Bower, G. *Theories of Learning.* (3rd ed.) New York: Appleton-Century-Crofts, 1966.

Hinde, R. A. *Biological Bases of Human Social Behaviour.* New York: McGraw-Hill, 1974.

Hirst, R. J. (a) Perception. *Encyc. Philos., 6,* 79-87.

Hirst, R. J. (b) Phenomenalism. *Encyc. Philos., 6,* 130-135.

Hirst, R. J. (c) Realism. *Encyc. Philos., 7,* 77-83.

Hirst, R. J. (d) Sensa. *Encyc. Philos., 7,* 407-415.

Hockett, C. F. The origin of speech. *Scientific American, 203,* 1960, 89-96.

Hockett, C. F. *The State of the Art.* The Hague: Mouton, 1968.

Horton, D. L. and Dixon, T. R. Traditions, trends and innovations. In T. R. Dixon and D. L. Horton (Eds.), *Verbal Behavior and General Behavior Theory.* Englewood Cliffs, N. J.: Prentice-Hall, 1968.

Huby, P. M. Socrates and Plato. In D. J. O'Connor (Ed.), *A Critical History of Western Philosophy.* New York: Free Press, 1964.

Hull, C. L. Quantitative aspects of the evolution of concepts, an experimental study. *Psychol. Monogr.,* 1920, *28.*

Hull, C. L. *Principles of Behavior.* New York: Appleton-Century-Crofts, 1943.

Hume, D. *A Treatise of Human Nature, 1-3.* (Ed. by L. A. Selby Bigge) Oxford Univ. Press, 1955. (1st ed. 1739.)

Humphrey, G. *Thinking. An Introduction to its Experimental Psychology.* New York: Wiley, 1963.

Hunt, J. McV. and Kirk, G. E. Social aspects of intelligence: evidence and issues. In R. Cancro (Ed.), *Intelligence. Genetic and Environmental Influences.* New York: Grune & Stratton, 1971.

Husserl, E. *Ideen zu einer reinen Phänomenologie und phänomenologischen Philosophie. Drittes Buch. Die Phänomenologie und die Fundamente der Wissenschaften.* Husserliana, V. The Hague: Nijhoff, 1952. (1st ed. 1913.)

Johnson, D. M. *A Systematic Introduction to the Psychology of Thinking.* New York: Harper & Row, 1972.

Judd, B. D. Basic correlates of the visual stimulus. In S. S. Stevens (Ed.), *Handbook of Experimental Psychology.* New York: Wiley, 1951.

Kalish, D. Semantics. *Encyc. Philos., 7,* 348-358.

Kant, I. *Kritik der Reinen Vernuft.* Würzburg: Meiner 1956. (1st ed. 1781.)

Katz, D. Der Aufbau der Farbwelt. *Zeitschr. Psychol., Ergb. 7,* 1930.

Kaufman, A. S. Behaviorism. *Encyc. Philos., 1,* 268-273.

Kaufmann, G. Visual imagery and its relation to problem solving: a theoretical and experimental inquiry. *Reports from the Institute of Psychology. University of Bergen,* 1975, No. *3.*

Kendler, H. H. and Kendler, T. S. Concept formation. In D. Sills (Ed.), *Internat. Encyc. Science 3,* New York: MacMillan, 1968.

Kendler, T. S. Concept formation. *An. Rev. Psychol.,* 1961, *12,* 447-472.

Kessel, F. S., Imagery: a dimension of mind rediscovered. *Brit. J. Psychol.,* 1972, *63,* 149-162.

Kim, J. Explanation in science. *Encyc. Philos., 3,* 159-163.

Klüver, H. *Behavior Mechanisms in Monkeys.* Chicago: Univ. Chicago Press, 1933.

Koch, S. Clark L. Hull. In W. K. Estes et al.: *Modern Learning Theory.* New York: Appleton-Century-Crofts, 1954.

Koch, S. Psychology and emerging conceptions of knowledge as unitary. In T. W. Wann (Ed.), *Behaviorism and Phenomenology.* Chicago: Univ. Chicago Press, 1964.

Köhler, W. *Intelligenzprüfungen an Anthropoiden.* I. Berlin: König. Akad. Wiss., 1917.

Köhler, W. *Gestalt Psychology.* New York: Liveright, 1929.

Koffka, K. *Principles of Gestalt Psychology.* New York: Harcourt, Brace, 1935.

Krechevsky, I. 'Hypotheses' in rats. *Psychol. Rev.,* 1932, *39,* 516-532.

Kretzmann, N. Semantics, history of. *Encyc. Philos., 7,* 358-406.

Kussmann, T. (Ed.), *Bewusstsein und Handlung. Probleme und Ergebnisse der sowjetischen Psychologie.* Bern: Huber, 1971.

Kussmann, T. and Kölling, H. (Eds.), *Biologie und Verhalten. Ein Reader sur sowjetischen Psychophysiologie.* Bern: Huber, 1971.

Landesman, C. Consciousness. *Encyc. Philos., 2,* 191-195.

Lashley, K. S. Basic neural mechanisms in behavior. *Psychol. Rev.,* 1930, *37,* 1-24. (The article is reprinted in F. A. Beach, D. O. Hebb, C. T. Morgan and H. W. Nissen (Eds.), *The Neuropsychology of Lashley. Selected Papers of K. S. Lashley.* New York: McGraw-Hill, 1960.)

Lashley, K. S. The problem of serial order in behavior. In L. A. Jeffress (Ed.), *Cerebral Mechanisms in Behavior.* New York: Wiley, 1951. (The article is reprinted in F. A. Beach, D. O. Hebb, C. T. Morgan and H. W. Nissen (Eds.), *The Neuropsychology of Lashley. Selected Papers of K. S. Lashley.* New York: McGraw-Hill, 1960.)

Lashley, K. S. and Wade, M. The Pavlovian theory of generalization. *Psychol. Rev.,* 1946, *53,* 72-87.

Lawick-Goodall, J. van. *In the Shadow of Man.* London: Fontana/Collins, 1973.

Leeper, R. Cognitive processes. In S. S. Stevens (Ed.), *Handbook of Experimental Psychology.* New York: Wiley, 1951.

Lenin, V. J. *Materialism and Empirio-Criticism. Critical Comments on a Reactionary Philosophy.* Transl. by A. Finneberg. Moscow: Foreign Languages Publishing House, 1947. (1st ed. 1909.)

Lenneberg, E. H. On explaining language. *Science.* 1964, *164,* 635-643.

Lenneberg, E. H. *Biological Foundations of Language.* New York: Wiley, 1967.

Leont'ev, A. N. Zeichen und Bedeutung. In T. Kussmann (Ed.), *Bewusstsein und Handlung. Probleme und Ergebnisse der sowjetischen Psychologie.* Bern: Huber, 1971. (Translated by C. Brückner from the article originally published in *Voprosy Psychologii,* 1967, *2,* 14-22. (Abbreviated.))

Leont'ev, A. N. Aktuelle Entwicklungen der sowjetischen Psychologie. In T. Kussmann (Ed.), *Bewusstsein und Handlung. Probleme und Ergebnisse der sowjetischen Psychologie.* Bern: Huber, 1971. (Translated by T. Kussmann from the article originally published in *Voprosy Psichologii*, 1967, *6*, 7-22.)

Lian, A. *Object and Perceptual Identity. Erroneous Presuppositions in Psychological Studies of Colour and Space Perception.* London: Academic Press. In press.

Lie, I. Achromatic colour constancy. A re-examination of its empirical basis and functional significance. *Scand. J. Psychol,* 1970, *11,* 146-152.

Linsky, L. (a) Referring. *Encyc. Philos.,* 7, 95-99.

Linsky, L. (b) Synonymity. *Encyc. Philos.,* 8, 54-57.

Locke, J. *An Essay Concerning Human Understanding. 1-2.* (Ed. by J. W. Yolton) London: Everyman's Library, 1961 (1st ed. 1690.)

Luria, A. R. *The Role of Speech in the Regulation of Normal and Abnormal Behavior.* New York: Liveright, 1961.

Luria, A. R. *The Working Brain.* Transl. by B. Haigh. London: Penguin, 1973.

Lyons, J. *Introduction to Theoretical Linguistics.* Cambridge: Cambridge Univ. Press, 1971.

Mach, E. *Die Analyse der Empdindungen,* 4. Aufl. Jena: Fischer, 1903. (1st ed. 1886.)

MacIntyre, A. Existentialism. *Encyc. Philos.,* 3, 147-154.

MacLeod, R. B. Phenomenology: a challenge to experimental psychology. In T. W. Wann (Ed.), *Behaviorism and Phenomenology.* Chicago: Univ. Chicago Press, 1964.

MacNabb, D. G. C. Hume, David. *Encyc. Philos.,* 4, 74-90.

Maier, N. R. F. Reasoning in humans. I. On direction. *J. Comp Psychol.,* 1930, *10,* 115-143.

Malcolm, N. Behaviorism as a philosophy of psychology. In T. W. Wann (Ed.), *Behaviorism and Phenomenology.* Chicago: Univ. Chicago Press, 1964.

Malcolm, N. Wittgenstein's Philosophical Investigations. In G. Pitcher (Ed.), *Wittgenstein. The Philosophical Investigations. A Collection of Critical Essays.* New York: Doubleday, 1966.

Malcolm, N. Wittgenstein, Ludwig Josef Johann. *Encyc. Philos.,* 8, 327-340.

Malcolm, N. The myth of cognitive processes and structures. In T. Mishell (Ed.), *Cognitive Development and Epistemology.* New York: Academic Press, 1971.

Mandler, G. Association and organization: facts, fancies and theories. In T. R. Dixon and D. L. Horton (Eds.), *Verbal Behavior and General Behavior Theory.* Englewood Cliffs, N. J.: Prentice Hall, 1968.

Mandler, C. and Kessen, W. *The Language of Psychology.* New York: Wiley, 1959.

Mandler, J. M. and Mandler, G. *Thinking: From Association to Gestalt.* New York: Wiley, 1964.

Martin, N. M. Carnap, Rudolf. *Encyc. Philos.,* 2, 25-33.

Marx, K. Theses on Feuerbach. In F. Engels: *Ludwig Feuerbach and the End of Classical German Philosophy.* Moscow: Progress, 1973. (Notes written 1845.)

Mazlish, B. Comte, Auguste. *Encyc. Philos.,* 2, 173-177.

Merlau-Ponty, M. *Phénoménologie de la perception.* Paris: Gallimard, 1945.

Mill, J. S. *A System of Logic.* London: Longmans, Green, 1956. (1st ed. 1843.)

Miller, G. A., Galanter, E. and Pribman, K. H. *Plans and the Structure of Behavior.* New York: Holt, 1960.

Miller, G. A. and McNeill, D. Psycholinguistics. In G. Lindsay and E. Aronson (Eds.), *Handbook of Social Psychology.* Reading, Mass: Addison-Wesley, 1968-1970.

Moore, G. E. The refutation of idealism. In G. E. Moore: *Philosophical Studies.*

London: Routledge & Kegan Paul, 1970. (The article was originally published in *Mind*, 1903, *12.)*

Morris, C. *Signs, Language and Behavior.* New York: Prentice-Hall, 1946.

Mounin, G. *Saussure ou le structuraliste sans le savoir.* Paris: Seghers, 1968.

Mowrer, O. H. *Learning Theory and Behavior.* New York: Wiley, 1960.

Mowrer, O. H. *Learning Theory and the Symbolic Processes,* New York: Wiley, 1966.

Murphey, M. G. Peirce, Charles Sanders. *Encyc. Philos.,* 5, 70-78.

Murray, H. A. et al. *Explorations in Personality.* New York: Oxford Univ. Press, 1938.

Nagel, E. *The Structure of Science. Problems in the Logic of Scientific Explanation.* London: Harcourt, Brace & World, 1961.

Needleman, J. Existential psychoanalysis. *Encyc. Philos.,* 3, 154-156.

Neisser, U. *Cognitive Psychology.* New York: Appleton-Century-Crofts, 1967.

Neisser, U. Changing conceptions of imagery. In P. W. Sheehan (Ed.), *The Function and Nature of Imagery. New* York: Academic Press, 1972.

Nelson, J. O. Moore, George Edward. *Encyc. Philos.,* 5, 372-381.

Newell, A. and Simon, H. A. *Human Problem Solving.* Englewood Cliffs: Prentice-Hall, 1972.

Norman, D. A. *Memory and Attention. An Introduction to Human Information Processing.* New York: Wiley, 1969.

Norman, D. A. Introduction: models of human memory. In D. A. Norman (Ed.), *Models of Human Memory.* New York: Academic Press, 1970.

O'Connor, D. J. Aristotle. In D. J. O'Connor (Ed.), *A Critical History of Western Philosophy.* New York: Free Press, 1964.

O'Connor, D. J. Substance and attribute. *Encyc. Philos.,* 8, 36-40.

Oléron, P. *Recherches sur le dévelopment mental des sourds-muets. Contribution a l'étude du problème langage et pensée.* Paris: Centre national de la recherche scientifique, 1957.

Osgood, C. E. *Method and Theory in Experimental Psychology.* New York: Oxford Univ. Press, 1953.

Paivio, A. *Imagery and Verbal Processes.* New York: Holt, Rinehart & Winston, 1971.

Palmer, R. E. *Hermeneutics. Interpretation Theory in Schleiermacher, Dilthey, Heidegger and Gadamer.* Evanston: Northwestern Univ. Press, 1969.

Passmore, J. (a). Logical positivism. *Encyc. Philos.,* 5, 52-57.

Passmore, J. (b). Philosophy. *Encyc. Philos.,* 6, 216-226.

Pawlow, J. P. Zwanzigjährige Erfahrungen mit dem objectiven Studium der höheren Nerventätigkeit (des Verhaltens) der Tiere. *Sämtliche Werke, B. IV.* (Ed. by L. Pickenhain) Berlin: Akademie-Verlag, 1953. (Pavlov's first report on his work on conditioned reflexes was published about 1903.)

Pears, D. *Wittgenstein.* London: Fontana/Collins, 1971.

Peirce, C. S. To Lady Welby. On signs and the categories. In A. Burks (Ed.), *The Collected Works of Charles Sanders Peirce,* Vol. VII. Cambridge, Mass.: Harvard Univ. Press, 1958. (This letter to Lady Welby was written in 1904.)

Peirce, C. S. Questions concerning certain faculties claimed for man. In C. Hartshorne and P. Weiss (Eds.), *The Collected Papers of Charles Sanders Peirce.* Vol. V. Cambridge, Mass.: Harvard Univ. Press, 1960. (This article was first published in 1868.)

Perky, C. W. An experimental study of imagination. *Amer. J. Psychol.,* 1910, 21, 422-452.

Peters, R. S. and Mace, C. A. Psychology. *Encyc. Philos.,* 7, 1-27.

Piaget, J. *The Psychology of Intelligence.* Transl. by M. Piercy. London: Routledge & Kegan Paul, 1950.

Piaget, J. *Biology and Knowledge.* Chicago: Univ. Chicago Press, 1971.

Piaget, J. *Psychology and Epistemology. Towards a Theory of Knowledge.* Transl. by P. A. Wells. London: Penguin Books, 1972.

Pitcher, (Ed.), *Wittgenstein. The Philosophical Investigations. A Collection of Critical Essays.* New York: Doubleday, 1966.

Ploog, D. and Melnechuk, T. (Eds.) Are apes capable of language? *Neurosciences Research Program Bulletin,* 1971, *9,* No. 5.

Poincaré, H. *La Science et l'hypothèse.* Paris: Flamarion, 1956. (1st ed. 1902.)

Pongratz, L. J. *Problemgeschichte der Psychologie.* Bern: Francke, 1967.

Prætorius, N. Det perceptionspsykologiske stimulusbegreb. *Nord. Psykol.,* 1969, *21,* 301-319.

Premack, D. Language in chimpanzee? *Science,* 1971, *172,* 808-822.

Price, H. H. *Thinking and Experience.* London: Hutchinson, 1953.

Pylyshyn, Z. W. What the mind's eye tells the mind's brain: a critique of mental imagery. *Psychol. Bul.,* 1973, *80,* 1-24.

Quine, W. V. *Word and Object.* Cambridge, Mass.: M. I. T. Press, 1960.

Quine, W. V. Two dogmas of empiricism. In *From a Logical Point of View.* New York: Harper & Row, 1961. (The article was first published in *Philos. Rev.* 1951.)

Quinton, A. M. Contemporary British philosophy. In D. J. O'Connor (Ed.), *A Critical History of Western Philosophy.* New York: Free Press, 1964.

Raaheim, K. Problem solving: a new approach. *Acta Univ. Bergensis. Ser. Hum. Litt.,* 1961, No. 5.

Raaheim, K. *Problem Solving and Intelligence.* Oslo: Universitetsforlaget, 1974.

Raaheim, K. and Kaufmann, G. Is there a general problem-solving ability? *J. Gener. Psychol.,* 1974, *90,* 231-236.

Ramsey, F. P. *The Foundations of Mathematics and Other Logical Essays.* (Ed. by R. B. Braithwaite) London: Routledge & Kegan Paul, 1954.

Ramsperger, A. G. Critical realism. *Encyc. Philos., 2,* 261-263.

Reitman, W. What does it take to remember? In D. A. Norman (Ed.), *Models of Human Memory.* New York: Academic Press, 1970.

Rickman, H. P. Dilthey, Wilhelm. *Encyc. Philos., 2,* 403-407.

Robischon, T. New realism. *Encyc. Philos., 5,* 485-489.

Rommetveit, R. *On Message Structure. A Framework for the Study of Language and Communication.* London: Wiley, 1974.

Rorschach, B. *Psychodiagnostics.* Bern: Huber, 1942.

Ross, S. *Logical Foundations of Psychological Measurement. A Study in the Philosophy of Science.* Copenhagen: Munksgaard, 1964.

Rossvær, V. *Kant og Wittgenstein.* Mineograph, Univ. Oslo, 1971.

Rubin, E. *Visuell wahrgenommene Figuren.* Cophenhagen: Gyldendal, 1921.

Rubin, E. Die Nichtexistenz der Aufmerksamkeit. *Bericht über den IX Kongress für Experimentelle Psychologie,* 1926, 211-212.

Rubin, E. Über Gestaltwahrnehmung. *VIIIth International Congress of Psychology,* 1927. (The article is also published in E. Rubin: *Experimenta Psychologica.* Copenhagen: Munksgaard, 1949.)

Rubinstejn, S. L. *Prinzipien und Wege der Entwicklung der Psychologie,* Transl. by P. G. Klemm. Berlin: Akademie, 1963.

Russell, B. *Logic and Knowledge. Essays 1901-1950.* (Ed. by R. C. Marsh) London: Allen & Unwin, 1956.

Russell, L. J. Leibniz, Gottfried Wilhelm. *Encyc. Philos., 4,* 422-434.

Ryle, G. The theory of meaning. In C. A. Mace (Ed.), *British Philosophy in the Mid-Century. A Cambridge Symposium.* London: Allan & Unwin, 1957.

Ryle, G. *The Concept of Mind.* London: Penguin Books, 1949.

Ryle, G. Thinking. *Acta Psychol.,* 1953, *9,* 189-196.

Saugstad, P. Problem-solving as dependent on availability of functions. *Brit. J. Psychol.,* 1955, *46,* 191-198.

Saugstad, P. An analysis of Maier's pendulum problem. *J. Exper. Psychol.* 1957, *54,* 168-179.

Saugstad, P. Availability of functions. A discussion of some theoretical aspects. *Acta Psychol.,* 1958, *13,* 384-400, and *Nord. Psychol.,* 1958, *10,* 216-232.

Saugstad, P. *An Inquiry into the Foundations of Psychology.* Oslo: Universitetsforlaget, 1965.

Saugstad, P. Effect of food deprivation on perception-cognition. *Psychol. Bul.,* 1966, *64,* 80-90.

Saugstad, P. and Raaheim, K. Problem solving and availability of functions. *Acta Psychol.,* 1957, *13,* 263-278, and *Nord. Psychol.,* 1957, *9,* 205-220.

Saussure, F. de. *Course in General Linguistics.* Transl. by W. Baskin. (Ed. by C. Bally and A. Sechehaye). London: Owen, 1960. (The course was given as lectures during the years 1906-1911.)

Schmitt, R. (a). Husserl, Edmund. *Encyc. Philos., 4,* 96-99.

Schmitt, R. (b). Phenomenology. *Encyc. Philos., 6,* 135-151.

Sclesinger, G. Operationalism. *Encyc. Philos., 5,* 543-547.

Schneewind, J. B. Mill, John Stuart. *Encyc. Philos., 5,* 314-323.

Searle, J. R. Proper names and descriptions. *Encyc. Philos., 6,* 487-491.

Segal, S. J. Assimilation of a stimulus in the construction of an image: the Perky effect revisited. In P. W. Sheehan (Ed.), *The Function and Nature of Imagery.* New York: Academic Press, 1972.

Shannon, C. E. and Weaver, W. *The Mathematical Theory of Communication.* Urbana: Univ. Illinois Press, 1949.

Sheehan, P. W. (Ed.), *The Function and Nature of Imagery.* New York: Academic Press, 1972.

Simpson, G. G. *The Meaning of Evolution.* New Haven: Yale Univ. Press, 1949.

Skinner, B. F. *The Behavior of Organisms.* New York: Appleton-Century-Crofts, 1938.

Skinner, B. F. *Verbal Behavior.* New York: Appleton-Century-Crofts, 1957.

Skinner, B. F. Behaviorism at fifty. In T. W. Wann (Ed.), *Behaviorism and Phenomenology.* Chicago: Univ. Chicago Press, 1964.

Skinner, B. F. *Contingencies of Reinforcement. A Theoretical Analysis.* New York: Appleton-Century-Crofts, 1969.

Skinner, B. F. *About Behaviorism.* New York: Knopf, 1974.

Smith, L. and Bjerke, T. *Utviklingspsykologi.* Oslo: Universitetsforlaget, 1974.

Spence, K. W. The emphasis on basic functions. In M. H. Marx (Ed.), *Psychological Theory. Contemporary Readings.* New York: Macmillan, 1951. (The article was first published in *Psychol. Rev.,* 1948, *55,* 67-78.)

Spence, K. W. Theoretical interpretations of learning. In S. S. Stevens (Ed.), *Handbook of Experimental Psychology.* New York: Wiley, 1954.

Staats, A. W. *Learning, Language, and Cognition.* New York: Holt, Rinehart & Winston, 1970.

Stevens, S. S. The operational definitions of psychological concepts. *Psychol. Rev.,* 1935, *42,* 517-525.

Stevens, S. S. Ratio scales and confusion scales. In H. Gulliksen and S. Messick (Eds.), *Psychological Scaling. Theory and Applications.* New York: Wiley, 1960.

Strawson, P. F. *Individuals. An Essay in Descriptive Metaphysics.* London: Methuen, 1959.

Stumpf, C. Zur Einteilung der Wissenschaften. *Abh. königl. Preuss. Akad. Wiss. zu Berlin, Phil.-Hist. Classe,* 1906, 1-94.

Taylor, C. Psychological behaviorism. *Encyc. Philos., 6,* 516-520.

Thayer, H. S. Pragmatism. In D. J. O'Connor (Ed.), *A Critical History of Western Philosophy.* New York: Free Press, 1964.

Titchener, E. B. *An Outline of Psychology.* New York: Macmillan, 1896.

Thorndike, E. L. *Animal Intelligence, Experimental Studies.* New York: Macmillan, 1911. (1st ed. 1898.)

Tolman, E. C. *Purposive Behavior in Animals and Men.* Berkeley: Univ. Calif. Press, 1932.

Tolman, E. C. Operational behaviorism and current trends in psychology. *Proc. 25th. Anniv. Celebr. Inaug. Grad. Stud.* Los Angeles: Univ. South Calif. Press, 1936. Also in M. H. Marx (Ed.), *Psychological Theory.* New York: Macmillan, 1954.

Tranekjær Rasmussen, E. *Bevidsthedsliv og Erkennelse.* Copenhagen: Munksgaard, 1956.

Ulich, R. Apperception. *Encyc. Philos., 1,* 138-140.

Vinacke, W. E. *The Psychology of Thinking.* (2nd ed.) New York: McGraw-Hill, 1974.

Vygotsky, L. S. *Thought and Language.* Ed. and transl. by E. Hanfmann and G. Vakar. Cambridge, Mass.: The M. I. T. Press, 1962.

Walsh, W. H. Kant, Immanuel. *Encyc. Philos., 4,* 305-324.

Walsh, W. H. *Metaphysics.* New York: Harcourt, Brace & World, 1963.

Walsh, W. H. F. H. Bradley. In D. J. O'Connor (Ed.), *A Critical History of Western Philosophy.* New York: Free Press, 1964.

Warnock, G. J., *English Philosophy since 1900.* New York: Oxford Univ. Press, 1966.

Warnock, G. J. Kant. In D. J. O'Connor (Ed.), *A Critical History of Western Philosophy.* New York: Free Press, 1964.

Watson, J. B. Psychology as the behaviorist views it. *Psychol. Rev.,* 1913, *20,* 158-177.

Watson, J. B. *Psychology from the Standpoint of a Behaviorist.* (3rd ed.) Philadelphia: Lippincott, 1929. (1st ed. 1919.)

Watzlawick, P., Beavin, J. H. and Jackson, D. D. *Pragmatics of Human Communication. A Stury of Interactional Patterns, Pathologies, and Paradoxes.* New York: Norton, 1967.

Weitz, M. Analysis, philosophical. *Encyc. Philos., 1,* 97-105.

Werner, H. and Kaplan B. *Symbol Formation. An Organismic-Developmental Approach to Language and the Expression of Thought.* New York: Wiley, 1967.

Wertheimer, M. Untersuchungen zur Lehre von der Gestalt. II. *Psychol. Forsch.,* 1923, *4,* 301-350.

Wertheimer, M. *Productive Thinking.* New York: Harper, 1945.

White, A. R. G. E. Moore. In D. J. O'Connor (Ed.), *A Critical History of Western Philosophy.* New York: Free Press, 1964.

Whorf, B. L. *Language, Thought, and Reality.* (Selected writings.) (Ed. by J. B. Carroll.) Cambridge, Mass.: M. I. T. Press, 1956.

Williams, B. Descartes, René. *Encyc. Philos., 2,* 344-354.

Wisdom, J. O. Unconscious, psychoanalytic theories of the. *Encyc. Philos., 8,* 189-194.

Wissler, C. Correlation of mental and physical tests. *Psychol. Monogr.,* 1901, No. *16.*

Wittgenstein, L. *Philosophical Investigations.* Transl. by G. E. M. Anscombe. Oxford: Blackwell, 1953.

Woodworth, R. S. *Experimental Psychology.* New York: Holt, 1938.

Woodworth, R. S. and Schlosberg, H. *Experimental Psychology.* (Rev. ed.) London: Methuen, 1961.

Woodworth, R. S. and Sheehan, M. R. *Contemporary Schools of Psychology.* (3rd ed.) New York: Ronald Press, 1964.

Woozley, E. D. Universals. *Encyc. Philos., 8,* 194-206.

Wright, G. H. von. *Explanation and Understanding.* London: Routledge & Kegan Paul, 1971.

Wundt, W. *Grundzüge der physiologischen Psychologie.* Leipzig: Engelmann, 1874.

Wundt, W. *Grundriss der Psychologie.* Leipzig: Engelmann, 1896.

Wundt, W. Über Ausfrageexperimente und über die Methoden zur Psychologie des Denkens. *Psychologische Studien.* 1907, *3,* 301-360.

Zaporozec, A. V. and Zincenko, V. P. Wahrnehmung als Handlung. In T. Kussmann (Ed.), *Bewusstsein und Handlung. Probleme und Ergebnisse der sowjetischen Psychologie.* Bern: Huber, 1971. (Transl. by U. Wilmer from the article published in A. Leontyev, A. Luriya, A. Smirnov (Eds.), *Psychological Research in the U.S.S.R.,* Vol. *1.* Moscow: Progress, 1966.)